Is World Order Evolving?
An Adventure into Human Potential

SYSTEMS SCIENCE AND WORLD ORDER LIBRARY

General Editor: Ervin Laszlo

Explorations of World Order

DE ROUGEMONT, D.
The Future is Within Us

GIARINI, O. & LOUBERGE, H.
The Diminishing Returns of Technology: an Essay on the Crisis in Economic Growth

LASZLO, E. & BIERMAN, J.
Goals in a Global Community
Vol. 1: Studies on the Conceptual Foundations
Vol. 2: The International Values and Goals Studies

LASZLO, E.
The Inner Limits of Mankind: Heretical Reflections on Today's Values, Cultures and Politics

LASZLO, E. & VITANYI, I.
European Culture and World Development: UNESCO Joint Studies for the European Cultural Forum

MARKLEY, O. & HARMAN, W.
Changing Images of Man

MASINI, E.
Visions of Desirable Societies

SAUVANT, K.
Changing Priorities on the International Agenda: The New International Economic Order

TEVOEDJRE, A.
Poverty: Wealth of Mankind

Innovations in Systems Science

AULIN, A.
The Cybernetic Laws of Social Progress

COOK, N.
Stability and Flexibility: An Analysis of Natural Systems

CURTIS, R. K.
Evolution or Extinction: The Choice Before Us

GEYER, R. F.
Alienation Theories: A General Systems Approach

GEYER, R. F. & VAN DER ZOUWEN, J.
Dependence & Inequality: A Systems Approach to the Problems of Mexico & Other Developing Countries

JANTSCH, E.
The Self Organizing Universe: Scientific and Human Implications of the Emerging Paradigm of Evolution

Is World Order Evolving?

An Adventure into Human Potential

by
JAMES DILLOWAY

PERGAMON PRESS
OXFORD · NEW YORK · BEIJING · FRANKFURT
SÃO PAULO · SYDNEY · TOKYO · TORONTO

U.K.	Pergamon Press, Headington Hill Hall, Oxford OX3 0BW, England
U.S.A.	Pergamon Press, Maxwell House, Fairview Park, Elmsford, New York 10523, U.S.A.
PEOPLE'S REPUBLIC OF CHINA	Pergamon Press, Qianmen Hotel, Beijing, People's Republic of China
FEDERAL REPUBLIC OF GERMANY	Pergamon Press, Hammerweg 6, D-6242 Kronberg, Federal Republic of Germany
BRAZIL	Pergamon Editora, Rua Eça de Queiros, 346, CEP 04011, São Paulo, Brazil
AUSTRALIA	Pergamon Press Australia, P.O. Box 544, Potts Point, N.S.W. 2011, Australia
JAPAN	Pergamon Press, 8th Floor, Matsuoka Central Building, 1-7-1 Nishishinjuku, Shinjuku-ku, Tokyo 160, Japan
CANADA	Pergamon Press Canada, Suite 104, 150 Consumers Road, Willowdale, Ontario M2J 1P9, Canada

Copyright © 1986 James Dilloway

All Rights Reserved. No part of this publication may be reproduced, stored in a retrieval system or transmitted in any form or by any means: electronic, electrostatic, magnetic tape, mechanical, photocopying, recording or otherwise, without permission in writing from the publishers.

First edition 1986

Library of Congress Cataloging in Publication data

Dilloway, James.
Is world order evolving?
(Systems science and world order library. Explorations of world order)
Bibliography: p.
Includes index.
1. International organization.   2. Civil rights (International law)
I. Title.   II. Series.
JX1954.D54   1986   341.2   86–734

British Library Cataloguing in Publication Data

Dilloway, James
Is world order evolving? : an adventure into human potential. —
(Systems science and world order library)
1. Sociology
I. Title   II. Series
303   HM51

ISBN 0-08-033378-8

Printed in Great Britain by A. Wheaton & Co. Ltd., Exeter, Devon

To the memory of my parents,
and to those who have helped
along the way.

The world was not able to unify before 1950 for a very simple reason: there was no comprehensive plan upon which it could unify; it was able to unify within another half-century because by that time the entire problem had been stated, the conditions of its solution were known, and a social class directly interested in the matter had differentiated out to achieve it. From a vague aspiration the Modern World-State became a definite and so a realizable plan.

H. G. Wells (1933)

Why has there been a retreat from internationalism and multilateralism at a time when actual developments both in relation to world peace and to the world economy would seem to demand their strengthening? We need to consider this question carefully if we are to make our institutions work better. I hope very much that political scientists and intellectuals the world over, as well as political leaders and diplomats, will ponder this essential problem on the occasion of the fortieth anniversary of the United Nations.

J. Perez de Cuellar, UN Secretary General (1984)

Preface

In paying tribute to the late Aurelio Peccei, founder of the Club of Rome, the Rector of the United Nations University, Soedjatmoko, has proposed the topic: "Is there a future for freedom?" as one meriting holistic examination. Although the association is fortuitous, that question could well serve as a title for this inquiry, which seeks to appraise the irreducible *conditions* of human freedom, both present and future, in a worldwide milieu. Specifically, what is looked at here is, first, a whole range of developmental issues raised by mankind's struggle to attain a loose frame of order within a global habitat; and, next, the significance for that struggle of a massive continuing effort by the UN to implement a basic world code of human rights and duties.

Even to venture into such ill-mapped terrain is to invite hazards, not the least being possible misunderstandings. It thus behoves the writer to make clear first of all his assumptions, something of his method and any special interests he may have in the questions discussed.

As to the first of these, the starting-point is scientific, and humanistic in the sense that humans are assumed to depend on their own unaided efforts. The quality of humanness being itself a social product, psycho-social evolution follows from present and emergent potentialities of *Homo sapiens*. Cumulating learning and workable discoveries thus produce not only technical advances but growing awareness too, both as to the widening consequences of human action and the relatedness of all phenomena, living and non-living alike. Human values not only can but *must* be derived from facts observed about the conditions of social life. It is held that a systematic extension of humanist thinking to cover both the practical and the normative conditions of development, including human rights and duties, can throw a new light on the whole development process. All this implies that while evolutionary forces are at work that go deeper than the conscious aims of individuals or governments, such forces are not necessarily benign and may lead to 'disaster' as well as to 'progress'. If present human potential embraces two conflicting clusters of propensities, plus an ability to learn, outmoded institutional remnants from the past can still distort today's behaviour and future aims alike.

As to method, an attempt has been made to deal with some essentials in their technical, economic, socio-political and normative aspects. Being an adventure for the writer as well as the reader, the work proceeds by successive steps or stages. This is true both of the analysis itself and of any conclusions or proposals, medium- or long-term, most of which emerge in the last three chapters. One advantage of this procedure is that it gives scope for some major 'taboo questions' — those which, being collectively 'repressed', cannot be aired officially — to be properly discussed. What I am saying here is that while most forward-looking studies, taking human make-up as constant, choose to rely mainly on technical extrapolations, this is not feasible where the strengths and frailties of humankind are seen as vital to the outcome.

What, then, of the author's own special interests? He has been directly involved with international questions for some 36 years, for 22 of them as a member of the UN Secretariat and currently as representative at the United Nations of an accredited non-governmental organization, the International Humanist and Ethical Union. In the present context it may be pertinent that he has lived through all but the first 10 years of this century without ever joining a political party.

It is both necessary and pleasing to acknowledge here a debt to a great body of research — by the UN Secretariat, outside organizations and individuals — that is bringing the technical, legal, economic and social evolution of an incipient world community more and more to public awareness. In notes and references I have tried to acknowledge a debt to many different studies, reports and statistics of the United Nations and its subsidiary bodies, the World Bank, the International Labour Office, the World Energy Conference and many other collective or individual sources. World data on Accessions to Human Rights International Instruments and on Multilateral Disarmament Agreements respectively that are incuded in Annexes 2 and 3 are those collated and periodically revised by the United Nations.

I must acknowledge the help received from non-official bodies or individuals. This includes permission to use material from the wealth of statistics and research issued under the auspices of the Overseas Development Council, Washington DC, in annual publications cited in the text; and also to use material from an important world modelling investigation carried out at the *Fundación Bariloche*, Buenos Aires under the auspices of the International Development Research Centre, Ottawa. Among the help given by individuals I am especially indebted to Professor Jean Blondel, of the University of Essex, who has very kindly prepared and made available new data, completely revised from those he drew up originally for an Appendix listing *Some Characteristics of the Countries of the Contemporary World*, which appeared in his book *Comparing Political Systems*, issued in 1972. The data have proved invaluable as a basis for some of the researches and tables appearing in the present volume. Work on humanistic ethics done by A. J. Bahm, Professor of Philosophy at the

University of New Mexico, and notably his ideas on Justice, have equally proved of value in part of the analysis. Elsewhere I have been much indebted also to an imaginative treatment of *Goals for Mankind* in a project for the Club of Rome by Ervin Laszlo, who is both a member of the UN Secretariat and Editor of the Systems Science and World Order Library. Another magnificent source of inspiration has been afforded by the annual reports on World Military and Social Expenditures, by Ruth Leger Sivard. It goes without saying, however, that for the use made of these and many other investigations I alone must be held responsible.

References to, or brief quotations from other relevant works, which are hereby gratefully acknowledged, have been identified throughout the text and in a list of references contained at the end of the volume. This is not to forget that any such wide-ranging enquiry is indebted to the work of innumerable other seekers after truth whose contribution can be acknowledged only in general terms. Quantitative data for different countries or regions have been selected to illustrate underlying features of the global situation rather than simply to present the latest national or international statistics.

A few more remarks are in order. First, many people involved in world order and human rights matters may not know that it was a pioneer Declaration of the Rights and Duties of the World Citizen, originally drafted by H. G. Wells in the London of 1940, that was the true forerunner of the Universal Declaration and of the two binding UN Covenants that now underpin it. That is why the text of that document is included here in Annex 1. It was in fact at the suggestion of the H. G. Wells Society of London that the present inquiry was originally undertaken.

My final remark is in effect a postscript. Only after the present text was completed did I become aware of certain further developments that may help to lend substance to one of the Conclusions reached in the final Chapter. These developments seem to suggest that an urge towards fundamental worldwide measures may still be gaining ground. I refer here to such recent innovations as the Brundtland Commission, comparable internationally to an independent Royal Commission on the United Kingdom model, which is headed by a former woman Prime Minister of Norway and is charged to investigate those *practical* obstacles which obstruct sound environmental policies, as well as to propose long-term strategies for sustainable action. Other similar steps being taken, also under UN auspices, include the creation of an Inter-Action Council, comprising 26 representative former heads of government and headed by a former UN Secretary General. Here the mandate is to assist solutions to priority issues ranging from peace and security to financial and trade problems.

JAMES DILLOWAY

Le Muy

Contents

Contents

List of Figures

List of Tables

Table

1

Introduction: The Shaping Forces of Concern

To catch the mood of our time this inquiry has to open with an over-simple statement of today's fundamental options. We seek to elucidate a looming human problem, and the chance of its solution, that has become ever more menacing and urgent for mankind over the past 40 years. For the problem confronts our own kind, the social animal *Homo sapiens*, which evolves through co-operative learning but is uniquely aggressive against its own species.

The solution to our problem is not difficult in itself. It lies mainly in the acceptance of an idea, and that idea is a very simple one. Since the human animal has acquired an incidental power to poison its habitat and to destroy its own and other living species, it has simply to absorb, and then to internalize into its political, social and economic arrrangements, the fact that the earth and all its beings have become a single unit of common concern, the sole support of living things as well as the basis of all man's life and hope.

Technically, all this presents no problem, for sufficient knowledge and productive power are now to hand to make such a change. What remains to seek is an overriding consensus on a common political interest in survival. But powerful inbuilt channels of momentum make such an outcome far from certain, since mankind's fatal within-species divisiveness remains strongly at war with the human genius for co-operative advance.

The origins of this critical state of the world are very recent. Those of us over 60, say, have lived through a new era of freshly accelerating change in means of transport and communication, in population growth and in knowledge and technique, both useful and destructive, that has reached a point where the representatives of some 4,400 million humans, grouped in 170 or so national states, are today seeking through the United Nations an international frame which will somehow provide for further advance together while preserving their independence of action and their diversity of aims and motives.*

*At 1 January 1982 there were 163 independent states with populations above 50,000, according to calculations supplied personally to the author by Professor Jean Blondel. Other smaller states also exist.

1

If this inquiry is to throw any light on the present predicament it will have to be supremely wide-ranging, covering the essence of what we know empirically about ourselves in a world setting, what are the realistic rights and duties of men and women as participants in group life and as political or economic agents. We shall have to survey some basic facts and trends of world economy and society as it now is as well as new codes, new institutions, new principles which seek to reduce imbalances and lessen areas of ignorance or conflict. Fresh ground will have to be broken in search of those unremarked but all-pervasive mechanisms which obstruct the rise of a loose frame of world order.

For it has to be assumed as a *point de départ* that the gulf between open-minded aspiration and actual political achievement is not yet finally unbridgeable. Despite conflicting motives and unsound beliefs a potentially unifying set of standards — that proclaimed under the banner of human rights — has been asserted throughout the world and is now fighting strongly for acceptance. Every new discovery illumines fresh and hitherto unsuspected relationships, consequences and obligations which eventually stir up countervailing ideals. We have to see how far this counter-acting dialectic of free discovery and incidental widening of vision might advance a more enlightened self-interest.

Opening a New Vista

It is a near-paradox that war, or the threat of war, can bring not only unity of purpose and an ordering of immediate priorities, but a broadening of vision about the desirable future. Such was the case in 1940, a year which saw a fairly sudden crystallizing in our awareness of a new stage in world affairs. It was virtually one man who singlehandedly brought this new phase into public view. In a long series of books and articles H. G. Wells had been spelling out the implications of a global spread of instant communications and productive power without any corresponding awareness of a new world milieu. The fact that the mass-production of a motor-car or an aeroplane already called for a bringing together of scarce materials from every corner of the globe had not yet impinged on the consciousness of economic man.

At the same time there was a new stirring-up of ideas about human rights and duties. Again it was H. G. Wells who put together, in the London of 1940, a fundamental new world code of rights and duties for the modern citizen aimed at instilling the idea that for the genus *Homo* the world was now one. An eminent Committee was set up to refine the world code, a great debate was organized in the national press, and the ensuing World Declaration of the Rights of Man was translated into ten languages and distributed to 300 editors in 48 countries. By 1942 Wells had produced a definitive version of this Declaration, which was in fact the true precursor, unequalled today in certain respects, of the Universal Declaration of Human Rights adopted by the United Nations in 1948 and followed 28 years later by binding Covenants on Civil and Political Rights and Economic, Social and Cultural Rights respectively.

This was one major strand in a revolution in thinking that sprang from two world wars and became finally crystallized in the second. But such is the learning capacity of man, the social animal, and such is the logical and dialectical process implicit in his penchant for material discovery, that many other strands in the opening-up of the idea of world order have emerged over the last four decades, building in turn on an interlinked series of major innovations that accompanied the technical revolution of the preceding two centuries.

Even this is only that part of the emancipating process known, more or less directly, to us. Over the last 10,000 years mankind has passed through a series of technical revolutions, and several transformations of self-awareness, that have enlarged the bonds of group-life and opened successive new vistas of understanding, common obligation and future choice. A hundred centuries is perhaps only one two-hundredth part, or even less, of the present life-span of man-like creatures on the earth but, in that brief development of near-human living, man's language codes have arisen and such means to common action as systems of measurement, science and mathematics; the wheel for transport, domestication of animals and planned food production; organized urban life with systems of government law, ethical principles and medical care; and finally such productivity-aiding techniques as metal smelting, use of inanimate energy, printing, methods of navigation and so onwards to powered transport, electricity, television, electronic computers and much else. Nearly everything we take for granted in the modern state has arisen from a social evolution that has occupied a mere one thousand decades or, say, four hundred successive generations. To be aware of this brief time-scale is an essential first step in understanding our present problems of world order.

It has also become commonplace to believe that the rise of technical mastery over the environment, produced by spectacular advances in the physical sciences, has not been matched by a similar knowledge-based power of collective self-control that would allow the fruits of science and ethical consensus to be translated into a viable social milieu. This is certainly true, and not unexpectedly so. But despite much evidence to the contrary we cannot claim lack of knowledge as the main source of present discontents. Once a few more unifying discoveries have been made about the springs of mental functioning in human-kind — when knowledge of self comparable to that of the genetic code has been gained — many strands in the understanding of man as a social animal may be woven together. This will not produce harmony but it could help to define more clearly the true limits of human potential.

A Modern Synthesis

To bring together and apply what we now know that is relevant to the quest for world order requires a use of several new ways of thinking that have begun to emerge only in the second half of this century, though some of them have been nascent in various trends of thought over the past 150 years. Why do discoveries arise in this way? To arrive at some preliminary hints towards an answer one has to realize that human development, like all development, is not haphazard but follows an internal logic of interacting processes in which everything is related to everything else.

One basic postulate in our analysis will be that there is a single process or logic of human development. This is not a teleological assumption and it does not imply any Victorian idea of progress or of its inevitability. Social evolution is not an inevitable process and each manifestation of it has been unique because it occurs in a unique environment and follows a unique sequence of historical events. Where it operates the process involves interlocking biological, social, psychological and environmental components of the man-centred system whose interaction so far has made for evolutionary progression. The criteria and parameters we can recognize are not, and should not be, anthropomorphic. Neither, I repeat, do they postulate any man-made conceptions of 'progress'. Given the biologically evolved human animal with his unique spine, jointed structure of arms, legs and hands and a hominid brain, plus a suitable environment and the social consequences which follow from a long period of nurture, a capacity for abstract thought and language, tool-making skills and a quality of seeking group life, 'other-regard' and approval, the world's societies have borne witness to unique flowerings of culture, personality-types and economy which may emerge in distinct habitats and sequences of circumstance. This is not to leave out genetic factors or the uniqueness of each individual. It does not ignore the rise of specialization or division of labour, a hierarchical organization administering a code of law, a unifying frame of explanatory beliefs which we know as ideology, and much else. Neither can the rise of anti-social behaviour under intense social and political pressures be forgotten. But comparative studies of the evidence synthesized from anthropology and other disciplines, when applied to the world's economic and political systems, amply confirm the nature of social evolution thus far.

Without anticipating our later analysis, this deep-seated need for a human community has the most profound, and even decisive, consequences. It is through group life that specialization multiplies the return from technique and increases both leisure and the means of subsistence. Group life has many other implications, however, both for the individual and for the stability of the group. It provides for nurture, protection, a transmission of knowledge from generation to generation, and for the internalizing by each participant of a set of ideas or beliefs that supplies an explanatory frame for the customs, laws and objectives of his community. But group life goes still further, since it also supports a reciprocal process — a mutual recognition of role, status and what I may call 'other-regard', creating for every individual a sense of self and a personality that are social acquirements in the fullest sense.

It has been argued by Hobhouse (L. T. Hobhouse, 1924) that a community develops as it advances in scale (or numbers), in efficiency, in freedom and in mutuality. All of these criteria except the first relate to the effectiveness with which a society fulfils the material, mental and community-serving needs of the humans who coexist within it. Certainly one objective indicator of how far social existence has been a positive factor in human survival is given by the growth in numbers, to which can be added rising longevity and the spread of conditions for effective existence *in human terms* — e.g. shelter, protection, learning and a material surplus to ensure these things. What we have to examine in this inquiry is how far mankind has now arrived at a crisis, a major turning-point in this socializing process at the stage where it has to accommodate to the conditions of a single world environment.

One element for understanding problems of world order is a valid time-perspective. To illustrate this very simply Figure 1 sums up the trend

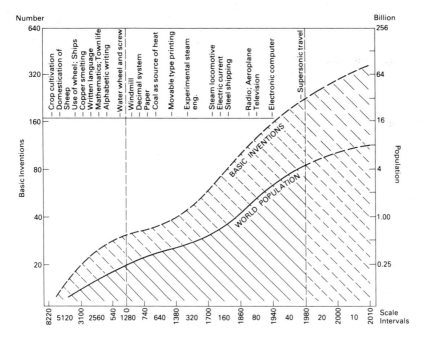

FIG. 1. Estimated Development Trends of World Population and Basic Inventions over the last 10,000 years. (Logarithmic Scales.)

of world population over the last 10,000 years and for the next thirty years ahead, and, related to it, a few of the major human inventions and the trend in the rising number of these over the same period. The curve of inventions is based mainly on the results of a careful analysis by Lilley (S. Lilley, 1948), in which mechanical inventions of fundamental importance were summed from the year 5500 BC until 1943 AD. Both axes of the diagram are drawn to logarithmic scales, so that equal intervals along the horizontal axis represent a successive *doubling* of time periods from the year 2010 backwards, while equal intervals on the vertical axis show a successive doubling in world population (right-hand scale) or in number of inventions (left-hand scale) respectively. This method of presentation thus produces an apparent 'foreshortening' in time towards the past since equal scale intervals backwards show periods of time increasing exponentially, i.e. at a common percentage rate, as do the vertical scales also when measured upwards.

For our purpose there are two main advantages in this mode of presentation. In the first place, if the same data were plotted on normal arithmetic scales the curves would appear as virtually coinciding horizontal lines near the foot of the diagram, until they suddenly shoot upwards almost vertically in the nineteenth century, close to the extreme right-hand edge. The important point is that by using logarithmic scales we can see clearly the essential similarity of the two curves. This brings out a fundamental point — that for human societies, on average, technical and intellectual development are both exponential processes. In other words, the growing interaction of more and more unique personalities, each with different experience, produces a cumulating body of stored knowledge which in turn, though at a slower pace, discloses a web of hitherto-unsuspected relations between phenomena, ever-new consequences of human acts and policies and an opening-up of new prospects and obligations for successful social living.

This is a fundamental aspect of development that I shall seek to elaborate in other connexions throughout these pages. Even at this preliminary stage we can see how this development potential, which is neither continuous nor certain, operates in our own time within the economic system. In most cases that economic 'growth' which is the outcome of discoveries in technique occurs through innovations which magnify human productivity per worker. This is augmented by discoveries in how to transport usable natural resources so that, *up to an optimum point*, productivity is enhanced and costs reduced by a growing scale of operation and output. This question of scale is equally fundamental to our inquiry. Many mammoth organizations today, and notably those that have proliferated from their countries of origin to spread over much of the earth, have come to exceed an optimum scale even when considered in terms of economic efficiency. If we go further and apply other criteria —

accountability, resource conservation and environmental hazard — such organizations can often be seen to be counter-productive too in human terms. This, however, is a complex subject which will be discussed further at a later stage.

Before leaving Figure 1, it is useful to recall how world population has grown overall. Thus at the beginning of the time period considered, at 8220 BC, or roughly at the dawn of civilization in pre-history, the total number of people on earth many have been of the order of 60 million, while the rate of increase was so slow that it took around 5000 years for world population to double itself (Llewellyn-Jones, 1975). Even by the time of the first vertical line of our diagram (the year 0 AD in Figure 1) this doubling time was still of the order of 1650 years according to Llewellyn-Jones. Using this same indicator of the growing supportive power of world economic society we find that the later doubling times for the total numbers of the world's people have decreased roughly as follows:

1650	200 years
1850	100 years
1925	75 years
1975	50 years

Since about 1980 world population, which currently totals about 4400 million, has probably reached a peak in its overall rate of annual increase at around 1.8 per cent per year, and is just beginning to show the effect of intensive population control policies, pursued in a growing number of developing countries in response to the efforts of the United Nations Population Commission. Even so, world population is still doubling about every 35 years. As we shall see later, it will go on increasing in the aggregate for a long time to come — a major obstacle to UN efforts to create elementary conditions of well-being in many countries of the developing world.

What other elements of our inquiry have to be broached in this introductory chapter? In getting to grips with today's salient world problems we shall have to distinguish those aspects of the *de facto* world system that form a continuum — a common web of interaction linking all people in a mesh of mutual relationship and dependence — from those that are distinctive to different nations or groups. These latter arise from unique combinations of circumstance — historical sequences, contacts with other peoples, differences of habitat, climate, natural resources and geographical position, all perhaps acting with or through genetic influences of long standing. There are, too, some near-paradoxes in human aims as proclaimed through political processes, when these are compared with a community's objective needs and true interests as assessed by the same group of people. There is yet a further distinction to be made. Although nations or organizations increasingly draw up plans and policies, much of human activity is still based on the exercise of free individual choice. That which arises from human wills in competition or conflict is interwoven with the results of national imperatives, and again with complex unseen chains of circumstance that flow from the dynamics of numbers in human communities, or from the even less understood phenomena of environment or human ecology.

First, however, we have to confront another question: How did the intellectual construction arise that brings humankind to grapple with the essential unity of the world? In looking into that question, within a time frame confined to the last three centuries or so, we can lay bare some subtle cumulating processes of awareness that make men self-conscious in relation to society, development and human habitat.

The Intellectual Underpinning of a Unified World

If humankind has built up that complex of language, knowledge, artefacts and institutions we are pleased to call civilization in a mere four hundred generations, it has erected our intellectual frame of modernity, or at any rate that part of it which sees all the phenomena of our world as interrelated in a dynamic process, in less than four per cent of that time — in a mere sixteen generations or so.

I have tried in Table 1 to bring together some discoveries which underlie our present system of knowlege about ourselves and our environment that will have to be applied in this book. The list is a personal selection and is by no means exhaustive. A few of the more recent items may well be thought controversial and some of the innovations have a complex origin. If by accident I am thought to have done less than justice to this or that discovery I apologize in advance. It should be noted that the list of 27 items concerns the origins of our system of thought about world economy and society and thus ignores recent advances in the biological sciences, in physics or in geology, for example. The items selected are those pertaining to a discipline or world view that is still emerging.

It is possible to rearrange the components of Table 1 in five major groups according as they pertain to the evolutionary process in living things, the natural and human environment, the economic system, the social system or the idea of human development as it relates to these. This rearrangement can be seen in Figure 2. I propose now to go through the main innovations in socio-economic thinking one by one. The reader can gain some idea from Figure 2 how each of these is interrelated with the rest of the field as a whole.

The first major change in man's socio-economic and political thinking and practice in modern times was the rise of a quite new philosophy of economic life inspired by an enormous enlargement of horizons wrought in the late eighteenth and early nineteenth centuries by new applications of

Some Formative Discoveries in the Rise of Modern Thinking about World Economy and Society
(Innovations listed in column 1 are arranged in chronological order of their introduction)

No.	Innovation[a]	Year or Period of Introduction[b]	Pioneers or Developers[b]	Forerunners[b]
1	2	3	4	
1	*Theory of a Self-Generating Economic System*	1776–1848	A. Smith, J. S. Mill	Sir W. Petty (1690)
2	Founding of a Geological Time-Scale	1815 on	W. Smith, C. Lyell	J. Hutton (1785)
3	*Principles of Liberal Democracy*	1820–70	J. Bentham, J. Mill	J. Locke (1689)
4	*Theory of Organic Evolution*	1859 on	C. Darwin, A. R. Wallace	A. de Candolle, etc. (1830)
5	*Primacy of Economy in Social Change*	1859–67	K. Marx	R. Owen, etc. (1813)
6	Theory of the Unconscious	1900	S. Freud	J. F. Herbart (1821)
7	Energy Basis of the Economic System	1922	F. Soddy	I. Fisher (1906)
8	Concept of Situational Analysis in Society	1927–48	W. I. Thomas, L. J. Carr	—
9	World Unity of Economy and Environment	1930–40	H. G. Wells	—
10	Concept of Social Character	1931 on	E. Fromm, etc.	W. McDougall (1920)
11	Analysis of Social Sources of Personality	1934	G. H. Mead, etc.	—
12	Nature of Ideology in Society	1936	K. Mannheim	D. de Tracy (1801)
13	*World Code of Human Rights*	1940–42	H. G. Wells	—
14	Analysis of Modern Unitary Thought	1948	L. L. Whyte, etc.	—
15	Role of Productivity in Level of Life	1949 on	J. Fourastié, etc.	—
16	Systems Theory	1950 on	L. von Bertalanffy, etc.	W. Koehler (1938)
17	*Modern Theory of Social Evolution*	1955	W. Goldschmidt, etc.	L. T. Hobhouse, V. G. Childe, etc. (1924)
18	Concept of Social Unconscious	1962	E. Fromm	C. Jung (1917)
19	Adverse Effects of Self-Generating Economy	1967 on	E. J. Mishan	—
20	*Steady-State Conservationist Economic System*	1968	H. E. Daly	K. Boulding, etc. (1966)
21	Commitment to World Environment Conservation	1968–72	Swedish Initiative	—
22	Projective Modelling of World Economic System	1972 on	J. Forrester, D. Meadows, etc.	—
23	Comparative Study of World's Political Systems	1972 on	J. Blondel, etc.	—
24	Comparative Study of World's Economic Systems	1973 on	R. L. Carson, P. J. D. Wiles, etc.	—
25	*Development as an International Normative Concept*	1975 on	K. M'Baye, etc.	—
26	Analysis of World Development Goals	1977 on	E. Laszlo, etc.	—
27	Comparative World Indicators of Quality of Life	1978 on	M. D. Morris, J. D. Grant, etc.	J. Tinbergen, etc. (1976)

[a]The theories and principles considered most basic to current ideas of world development are italicized.
[b]While an effort has been made to list pioneers and periods of introduction mainly associated with particular theories etc. there are a few cases where development has been complex.

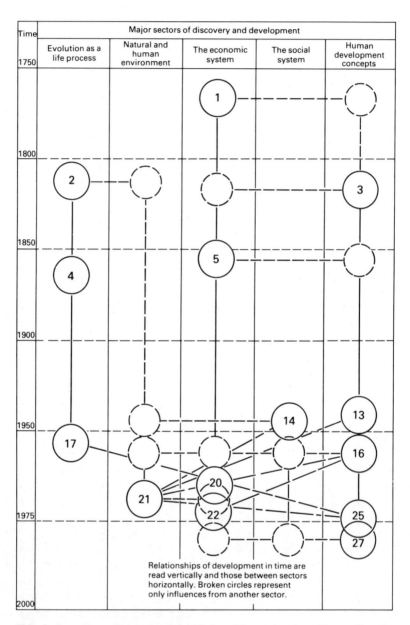

FIG. 2. Some Interrelations between Modern Discoveries about Human Development. (To be used in conjunction with Table 1. Main items are numbered as in Table 1.)

non-human energy and mechanical power, notably for forging, pumping, spinning and ship propulsion. This new economic doctrine coincided in time with the perfecting of Watt's steam engine and with the Declaration of Independence by thirteen American colonies but, unlike them, it has remained to this day a foundation of conventional wisdom, the unquestioned justification of all those market economies and mixed economic systems that have spread across the world since the early nineteenth century. In our day this economic philosophy is having momentous and critical consequences that are still unresolved. As first described by the philosopher Adam Smith in 1776, later refined by David Ricardo and put into a modern context by J. S. Mill, it simply drew together the threads of economic life as they were becoming visible in eighteenth-century Britain. The genius of Smith lay in the apparent logic of development he then saw to be at work and in particular in the seductive appeal to human nature of his logical deductions as to what seemed a happy paradox governing the mechanics of economic life — that out of the spontaneous self-interest of a newly mobile labour force and traditional owners of land and capital on the one side, and the entire body of consumers on the other, the desires of all could best be balanced and the good of society promoted and developed through an 'unseen hand' of competition.

The second revolution in social and political thinking — a buttress and a logical outcome of the first — came fully into view only 45 years later. Adam Smith's radical economic principles needed a quite new theory of a liberal democratic state to enshrine the new-found market freedoms of capitalist society and protect its individuals against what seemed the outworn constraints of established government institutions. This goal was duly attained through new doctrines of liberal democracy first clearly formulated between 1789 and 1820, in the first place by Jeremy Bentham and James Mill respectively (C. B. Macpherson, 1977).

Ideas of liberal democracy have evolved considerably since the early nineteenth century. For one thing the whole operative theory of representative government has moved from property and other restrictions on voting rights to full adult franchise, while much of the democratic philosophy has gradually been adapted to the ethos of a later age as the state has encroached on the market and economic inequality has been reduced. However, the main and critical role of western-style liberal democracy up to the present day is that it has remained in theory the unquestioned bastion of a free market society both in the economic and the political sense. Only in the newly developing world and in the centrally directed economies of this century has the term 'democracy' been re-adapted to embrace a different theory of government.

The origins of our geological time scale, and the subsequent founding of a theory of organic evolution by natural selection, were almost equally far-reaching for today's world. Modern ideas about the restless erosion and

renewal of the earth's outer shell had first to be brought to consciousness
by James Hutton in his *Theory of the Earth*, first communicated in 1785,
and by the engineer William Smith, who hit on the principles of
stratigraphy and the superposition of strata, with their distinct organic
relics, only 6 years later but published his ideas long after, at about the
time of his pioneer map of the geology of England (1815). Between this
time and Darwin's famous year of 1859 (item 4 of Table 1) a whole series of
specialists, from Baron Cuvier onwards, and notably including Sir Charles
Lyell with his epoch-making 'Principles of Geology', the Geneva botanist
Augustin de Candolle with his 'war of nature', and Thomas Malthus, all
paved the way for the Darwinian bombshell.* Since that era the bounds of
geological time have been pushed ever backwards, as well they might be to
allow for the full evolution of life forms on earth.

Today the ideas of evolutionary and dynamic change have become true
foundations of our thinking. Even before 1900 several early social thinkers,
from Tylor and Herbert Spencer to L. T. Hobhouse and beyond, had
seized on and developed the idea of the special social nature of evolution in
man (item 17 in Table 1). In our own day we are going beyond this to build
up a major socio-economic and ethical system of development thought to
replace the over-simple early work in this field — a fact of primary
importance for this study. A careful and consistent first synthesis of the
true nature of social evolution as such was that developed by the
anthropologist W. Goldschmidt in 1959 (Goldschmidt, 1959).

We are much indebted also to a series of individual social innovators and
researchers at work between the mid-nineteenth century and the early
years of the twentieth century. Among those who helped to complete a
breakdown of that illusory static rationalism emanating from the earlier
period of the eighteenth century Enlightenment were Marx and Freud.
Everyone is now aware of their influence in showing up much that remains
irrational in our economic practice on the one hand and our individual
thought processes on the other. In the case of Karl Marx however (and
perhaps to a lesser extent in that of Sigmund Freud) the final contribution
to today's world is certainly a two-sided one. On the one hand he
successfully turned our minds to the primacy of economic forces as the
engine of social change. He also forced men to perceive some of the flaws
in a self-generating economic philosophy when applied to a newly-dynamic
world. But by proclaiming a fallible hypothesis dressed up as a dogma of
religious certainty he has split the modern world and perhaps delayed the
advent of a world order based on common sense. Nevertheless, twentieth
century man has begun to question two economic dogmas, and not merely
one, and that at least must be a great step forward.

This latest tendency of today's economic thinking was perhpas begun by

*The full story is brought together in *Darwin's Century*, by L. Eiseley (Doubleday, New York, 1958).

Frederick Soddy, the discoverer of isotopes, who demonstrated how the real economy was in fact a process of energy conversion (item 7 in Table 1). Soddy influenced H. G. Wells to some extent but, beyond Wells and later empirical analysts like Jean Fourastié (item 15), who laid bare the economic logic of our rising concern with productivity in the post-war world, the true economic heritage which sprang from the nineteenth century critics of 'business as usual' is to be found, transmuted by way of humanist thinkers like J. S. Mill and J. A. Hobson, in the work of E. J. Mishan and still later proponents of a 'steady-state' economic system of which a systematic pioneering exposé is that of H. E. Daly (see items 19 and 20 in Table 1). It should be carefully noted here that this emergent 'non-growth' philosophy refers to selective and sustainable development rather than to a purely static economic system as such.

Let us now turn briefly to discoveries that are important in helping us to understand the social dimension of world economic society. Again this list is clearly a personal one. Some of the five items included under this head in Table 1 might strike the academic historian as less worthy of mention than certain concepts developed during the four decades 1880–1920 by such formative pioneers of social science as Emile Durkheim, Vilfredo Pareto or Max Weber. Other novelties — the far-reaching theory of opinion measurement for example, or the principle of least effort formulated by G. K. Zipf in 1949 (to say nothing of the bureaucratic law of C. Northcote Parkinson) are certainly formative elements in our thinking today — or should be. The items numbered 8, 10, 11, 12 and 18 in Table 1 certainly vary widely in importance but are included either because they offer useful, if untested, explanatory models; or, like items 8 and 11, offer practical means of understanding how society really functions. Thus situational analysis can, and in my view has to, underlie the valid theory of how social change works at an interpersonal and institutional level. G. H. Mead's analysis of selfness as emerging from all social interaction likewise underpins all attempts to explain what humanness consists of and how it is transmitted. The role of ideology too is fundamental in understanding national identity; while (particularly if you have had to work with many nationalities) the twin notions of social character and the social unconscious are useful tools in helping to explain how well-defined human groups are differentiated mentally from one another.

Having outlined some broad intellectual strands in the opening-up of the modern world, it is time to point out that a very remarkable convergence — even a synthesis — of basic thinking and technique has been taking place over the years 1940–1980 that has so far gone quite unremarked. This concerns man's awareness of the essential unity of his natural and human worlds and in particular the interrelatedness of all their phenomena. To draw out this seminal fact we must refer to the last eleven items included in Table 1 — that is, to items 9, 13, 14, 16 and 21–27 respectively.

As mentioned earlier in this chapter, this revolution was started off in 1940 when H. G. Wells, having hammered home the idea that the entire earth now formed a proper frame for the world's activity, went on to show that a world code of human rights was an essential unifying force in moving towards such a web of diversified interdependence. Though now practically forgotten, Wells's World Declaration was the true precursor of the Universal Declaration of Human Rights adopted in 1948, and of all that is now following in that domain. In particular, this incipient theory of rights and duties as a unifying global conception is becoming intertwined with modern ideas of social evolution and economic development. This amalgam in turn is producing an intense debate on the nature of a supposed 'right to development' following the introduction of the theme by K. M'baye of Senegal.

But these first hesitant steps in the direction of world order have been underlain by other necessary discoveries — technical, philosophical, and economic — that have been moving towards a parallel synthesis since 1948 or even before. First, many specialists have contributed to developing a body of systems theory that is now being applied, with varying success, to simulate the working of human beings, economic and other organizations, ecology and environment as well as the design of computers and much else. This in turn has for the first time made possible an investigatory and projective modelling, using mathematical models of the world economy — an important if tentative step forward.

There are two more pieces to fit into this jigsaw of theory. In 1968 serious attention began to be focused in Sweden on the natural environment and the need to conserve it. Interest in this subject was not new but it *was* new that the whole question be brought to the attention of the international community as posing a problem of world dimensions. I well remember the novelty this presented even to the Economic Commission for Europe of the UN, which was used to handling such matters. Since 1972 the World Environment Programme has of course been a major part of the United Nations' activity, though with variable success, as we shall later see.

The other jigsaw item is an all-embracing philosophical theory about how human beings have now to categorize the phenomena of the world, including human phenomena, and how they have to see all the inter-relations of change therein as a continuous process towards decreasing assymetry. Now this theory, that of unitary thought, analysed with great richness of detail and history by Lancelot Law Whyte in 1948, though it is by no means well known, has coincided with a number of trends in science that are moving in the same direction. That direction, broadly speaking, is towards abandoning dual concepts to categorize phenomena that are now well understood — e.g. 'body' and 'mind' — and equally to abandon a static rationalism in definition or explanation in favour of a view of entities as existing in a state of continuous change. Without elaborating here, both these tendencies are exemplifed today in some changing conceptions of research in psychology, among other disciplines. For our inquiry the new theory is important in stressing the interrelatedness of the human world and its natural environment in a single system, as well as the relatedness of the process of change in both.

To complete our survey of a mental frame for studying problems of world order we arrive at items 23, 24, 26 and 27 of Table 1. These, too, comprise important tools for understanding. Personally I have always found comparative international analysis extremely enlightening, as when data for different countries can be arranged in a developmental sequence which accords with other common data for the same states. Systematic comparisons of national economic and political systems, and of the diversity of development goals, are now being pursued with sufficient rigour to allow highly suggestive insights as to their relative efficiency in human terms. Certainly the last item on our list contributes to this aim since it offers direct measurement of the physical quality of life by objective indicators, as given by suitably combining rates for infant mortality, adult literacy and expectation of life at age one. Comparable disparity reduction rates can also be obtained over a given period. These data having been worked out for most of the countries of the world they offer a particularly good illustration of what is possible. However, much other work can be done on economic, political and social indicators of different kinds and a good deal of this has gone forward within the United Nations system.

Many of the developments summed up in Table 1 will be applied to world problems in the course of this inquiry.* Some of the interrelations are already displayed in Figure 2. Because certain of the more recent innovations — mainly twelve of those developed since 1940 — have converged to offer some promise of an integrated approach, I have tried to show how they are related to one another in a further diagram, which is included as Figure 3.

Is World Development on Course?

On this point, consider first two propositions. Because our system 'man' evolved from a wider natural order the human species has to stay in harmony with its total environment if it is to survive and prosper. But the modern characteristics of *Homo sapiens* emerge in a social frame, an economic system and now a political world milieu. These in turn *reflect* an inherent balance of human potentials and also *produce* ever-changing emergent qualities of social man within physical and social limits set by nature.

*Some new types of analysis will also be developed and applied.

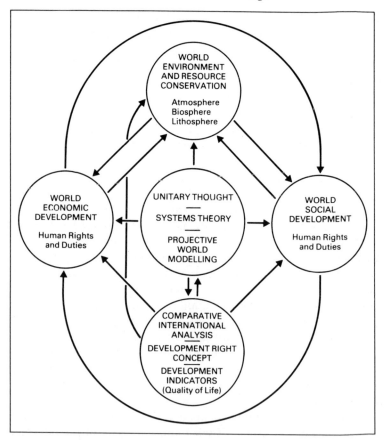

FIG. 3. Outline Conspectus of Emerging Theory and Practice for World
Development.

We thus arrive at the following questions: How 'good' a society does
human nature permit? And how 'good' a human nature does society
permit? By 'good' I here understand 'self-actualizing' (A. Maslow, 1971).
We must clarify this problem of interaction between the system 'man', with
its wide range in intrinsic components of character, aptitude and
personality, and two other systems: first, that of the total natural
environment, and next (at the level of a self-governing community), the
economic system, which produces its own controls over working population and consumer, its own conditioning to norms of behaviour and its own
dualism of true and false motives. How far it promotes 'self-actualization'
depends on the nature of the task performed and the scarcity (and thus the
status) of the aptitude in question. Our social and political systems within
the national state likewise satisfy or deny, in widely varying degree, those
human needs for group living, sharing and contributing to common aims

and goals that are affected by official or 'mass' culture and ideology. Erich Fromm has summed up this dynamic relationship of processes between man and the component systems of society in two sentences:

My main thesis is simply that the analysis of the system 'man' must become an integral part of the analysis of the system 'enterprise' or the system 'society'. . . . If you ask, "What is the optimal functioning of the system 'man'?" you might answer, "It means the optimal development of all his faculties, minimal friction and waste of energy within man, between man and man, and between man and his environment." (E. Fromm, 1970).

In practice the world's nation-states are managing in very varying degree to satisfy man's more basic needs, not only those needs for nurture, food, shelter and education, but also needs to express, or channel, those opposite and too-often conflicting bundles of propensities and values we call 'masculine' or 'feminine' respectively — on the one hand the urges to compete, to seize and to assert; and on the other to care, to share and to support. Anti-social reactions too can be stimulated by inappropriate societies. One stance adopted throughout this inquiry is that human society thus far is the net resultant of the relative survival-value of those essential qualities that make up mankind. Growing understanding is part of the development process and thus there may still be scope for building a viable world society. But the conditions of that society today impose new and unfamiliar constraints.

What, then, are those constraints? One facet of development to date has been the ever-growing *scale* of successful communities, starting with small bands of families and expanding slowly through trade and conquest to the early empires, thence to the nation-state and on to the great regional groupings of today.

This growing unification of the world is now manifested by a series of *de facto* networks of organized interdependence, which include those covering:

— Scientific and technical knowledge;
— Information and news;
— Finance, including currency and investment needs;
— International division of labour;
— Environmental repair and resource conservation;
— The overseeing of peaceful development;
— Protection of observance of human rights and duties.

At our present stage these webs are maintained through the United Nations organization, a series of UN specialized agencies (e.g. for world health, weather, postal services, etc.) and five UN regional economic commissions, plus various research institutes and innumerable inter-

IWOE-C

national professional bodies, all backed up by some 800 accredited international non-governmental organizations covering mainly ethical or professional fields of interest. These last seek to maintain a two-way exchange between the world's governments in the UN and the world's people.

As is well known, these efforts are too often frustrated at the apex simply because there is as yet no clear move towards international control over national sovereignty in the overseeing of peaceful development. The United Nations can sometimes exercise a considerable moral force. It is increasingly active in setting standards in many fields and also in spotlighting the more glaring abuses of human rights throughout the world. It is showing the way to limit population growth with some success. Collective action on environmental abuse is under way. It is focusing new light on the world's weather and climate; working effectively to control epidemic diseases and to promote elementary health care; working also to ameliorate the plight of refugees and the effects of natural disasters. In trying to set up an International Sea-Bed Authority to oversee the exploitation of under-sea natural resources it has in 1982 taken a first hesitant step towards an exercise of collective world control in the interest of all. This step has so far been largely thwarted by a single government, working on behalf of its private commercial interests, so that the final outcome is not yet clear.

We may conclude this introductory review of the world order problem by pointing to the nature of the main opposing forces which confront each other. On the negative side we have first the political–ideological cum military–commercial spectrum of incipient conflict that is in part deliberate but to a greater degree is simply self-perpetuating. At its centres in the main arms-construction states the process at work is a unique kind of self-generating *economic* phenomenon. That process is unique because it embraces a preferential contract by state customers to develop techniques which have no commercial constraints of consumer saturation. Moreover it is self-perpetuating because the creating of a specified demand immediately arouses emulating demands from competing states. The mushrooming process is kept moving too by an international competition for exports, often to pairs of fancied combatants or to 'friendly' dictatorships concerned with repressing opposition.

A second major threat to mankind is also largely commercial in origin, arising from concealed or unaccounted diseconomies of economic activity that proliferate through over-free exploitation of the technical advances following from new scientific knowledge. One such possibly mounting threat to future life on earth arises from excessive man-made dissemination of carbon dioxide, particulates or dust, sulphur and nitrogen oxides and perhaps aerosols in the atmosphere, disturbing in the process the protective balance of its upper layers. There are many such pollutant problems, often all too visible, but I will simply refer to an overall conclusion of Mostafa Tolba, Executive Director of the UN Environment Programme, speaking at the tenth anniversary review of UNEP's work. Reporting a marked deterioration of our shared environment on almost every front since 1972, he foresaw that lack of effective action would bring ". . . by the turn of the century an environmental catastrophe which will witness devastation as complete, as irreversible as any nuclear holocaust."

A third major component of the human dilemma is also well-known in general terms. It lies first in a combination of extreme poverty, malnutrition, disease, illiteracy and ignorance that in varying degree affects some 30 per cent of the world's population and up to 60 per cent of the world's sovereign states. Some 35 per cent of all states are governed either by military or highly personal rule and well over half by no-party or single-party systems. In the typical developing country affluent, well-educated élites, large-scale poverty and the most massive institutionalized corruption, if not torture and repression, go hand in hand. All this poses a major problem area that shrieks unheard at the interdependence of the real world. But many-sided international efforts are gaining some success. If population growth, with its excessive urbanism, can be brought under control, this is not the most unyielding of our human dilemmas.

What common attitude, or positive philosophy, can we set against this depressing chronicle? Later in this book we shall be detailing the recent spread, through the United Nations, of an evolving world code of human rights and duties that transcends the diversity of humankind with all its divisive faiths and loyalties. Starting from a developing country (Senegal) a new synthesis of these rights and duties is being worked out internationally that seeks to define a single but many-faceted 'right to development' marking the growing-together of human beings in a global milieu. The idea that is emerging is that rights and duties of development apply both collectively, to peoples and states, and to individuals, as citizens, both being embraced by international law.

The first emphasis, as in Article 7 of the UN Charter of the Economic Rights and Duties of States of 1974, was on state responsibility in the economic field:

> Every State has the primary responsibility to promote the economic, social and cultural development of its people. To this end, each State has the right and the responsibility to choose its means and goals of development, fully to mobilize and use its resources, to implement progressive economic and social reforms and to ensure the full participation of its people in the process and benefits of development. All States have the duty, individually and collectively, to co-operate in eliminating obstacles that hinder such mobilization and use.

Over the years these ideas have evolved somewhat, so that the UN

International Development Strategy for the Third United Nations Development Decade (1980) contains the following idea:

> The development process must promote human dignity. The ultimate aim of development is the constant improvement of the well-being of the entire population on the basis of its full participation in the process of development and a fair distribution of the benefits therefrom . . .

The emerging concept of a development right in individual terms has as its object the integral development of the individual in the sense of his 'multidimensional fulfilment'. This properly requires an observance within each state of all basic civil, political, economic, social and cultural rights enshrined in the two binding Covenants on human rights already mentioned, and a principle from the Universal Declaration of Human Rights (Article 29) which states that ". . . everyone has duties to the community in which alone the free and full development of his personality is possible." In this new 'moral imperative' of development all countries are to be seen as still in course of development. Of the many obstacles to the full exercise of human rights and duties, grossly inefficient economic systems and the absence of a viable political democracy are among those which produce extremes of ignorance, disease and poverty — the all-too-common antithesis of human rights.

So we see that free international debate, despite the present anti-social climate, is now arriving at the very point where its conclusions are confirmed by objective research in the human sciences. This, I believe, is a momentous first conclusion at which we can arrive. But the question remains to ask: Is it enough?

PART I

Some Dimensions of World Order

2

The Discovery of One World

Despite the prescience of a few individuals seemingly far ahead of their time — like Roger Bacon in the thirteenth century, Leonardo da Vinci in the fifteenth, John Stuart Mill in the nineteenth century and a name often mentioned in these pages in the twentieth — it follows from what has been said earlier that human development thus far has followed an internal logic marked by interlinked advances[1] in science, technique, self-awareness, ethical understanding, social invention and government that are all compounded of a power to learn, to experiment, deduce, refute, adapt, anticipate and even, perhaps, to plan. In the form of a historical sequence this process unfolds through an ever-evolving logic in the situations created by individuals, institutions, events and the forces their interplay evokes. If all this is indeed true then perhaps there is some point in starting an overview of the present human predicament by looking first at the historical dimension of its rise from around the year 1200, and then going on to see whether such a course can offer any clues about the choices that lie ahead.

The First Awakening

Why begin at the year 1200? First of all it was from this time on that European civilization began to absorb a number of fundamental technical advances — notably inventions to improve transport, agriculture and fixed rotating motive power — and was also on the verge of wood block printing. During this century the effectiveness of domestic animal power was to be greatly increased by the perfecting of a modern type of harness and a newer form of the plough (S. Lilley, 1948). The ship's rudder came to supersede the primitive oar for steering and the magnetic compass was introduced. These were among a number of innovations which replaced what had been the main source of work-power in antiquity — slave labour applied on a massive scale. However, not all these inventions were indigenous. Although the known world remained only a shadowy frame, several basic devices were introduced by way of trade routes with the Far East, including the use of paper itself.

Technical progress of the kind experienced in medieval Europe would seem to have had many unseen consequences in changing the entire mental climate. Gains from useful discoveries could help to dispel belief in magical, divine or mystical causation and strengthen the view, new in a medieval context, that change, including purposive, man-made change, is possible, that man can harness nature unaided for the common material betterment. Even by 1300 such an idea remained far from open acceptance. Government and economic activity was still mainly a static, localized affair resting on traditional role, status and religion. The prevailing 'social character' of the individual was 'tradition-directed'[2] — defined within a narrow circle of relatives and citizens of like craft or position — and was to remain so for another two centuries until the imperatives of wider travel, rising technology, a growing scale and variety of output and the advance of new empirical knowledge finally broke down the belief that life was demarcated, determined and guided by divine providence.

Despite this mental climate, the first small steps towards acceptance of basic rights were taken at the beginning of our period. Charters or petitions presented to the King by the barons of the day were aimed at limiting his absolute powers and forging a frame of impartial justice. The famous example was the signing of Magna Carta by King John in 1215, thereby creating a Common Law recognizing a "community of the realm" and, for his more exalted subjects, "trial by the law of the realm and the judgement of their peers" (A. Harding, 1966). Virtual non-recognition of the ordinary citizen, which persists to this day in international law, is a relic of the medieval practice of seeing only a sovereign as 'free from the overlordship of any other mortal' — a circumstance which today is posing awkward questions for the concept of individual rights in an international context.

This long struggle of the civil order to circumscribe royal prerogatives was to endure for nearly five centuries. Not until 1628 was there a Petition of Right of Parliament again invoking Magna Carta and other feudal law against royal property rights and the so-called divine right of kings. This, however, was quickly followed by the Habeas Corpus Amendment Act of 1679 and in 1689, under William and Mary, a Bill of Rights which laid down a 'constitutional contract', sealed the English Revolution and finally asserted the supremacy of Parliament as the source of the law. From 1718 the House of Commons, which at this time represented mainly landed interests, was re-elected periodically — initially every seven years.

The years between 1600 and 1750 were an active prelude to the true Industrial Revolution. They saw a growing development of trade, the first stages of experimental science and the improvement of many basic inventions, from timepieces and more accurate sea navigation to textile machinery and mine drainage. The spread of city building equally called for much-improved pumping for water supply and the whole period, from 1560 until Newcomen's engine of 1712, saw the first efforts to harness steam power. Improvements in large-scale machinery and goods transport encouraged some concentration of industry where the necessary capital could be raised, thereby leading to a slowly growing scale of operation that could produce far greater output per man employed. In this way the old guild system of industrial craft workers was slowly split apart. By 1700 these early signs of industrial capitalist enterprise were coming into view, with groups of employees working for undertakings in the emergent industries of mining, blast furnaces, printing and weaving. This new trend came to be imposed on a community that was still mainly locally oriented and agrarian, the last vestiges of the medieval guild system lingering on until 1813, when the Statute of Artificers was finally repealed.

Rights of Man Emergent

The century that followed the English Revolution and the Bill of Rights of 1689 witnessed the first stirrings of many revolutionary and libertarian ideas in a wider setting. This opening-up process included the *de facto* inception of a financial and commercial trading system in Britain itself, thereby setting the scene for the main Industrial Revolution that was to arise in that country and spread throughout the world. Behind it too was a new climate of unfettering rationalism that sprang from such writers as John Locke, Jean-Jacques Rousseau, Voltaire and others. This period even threw up a first Project for Perpetual Peace, a scheme for a Confederation of European Heads of State who would come together to prevent war.

Up to this point we have been chronicling two distinct and slowly emerging trends — the one towards an awareness of individual rights and the other leading to an ever-expanding range and scale of human aims and activity. The year 1776 was momentous in witnessing major advances in both these fields. On the one hand men first heard the ringing libertarian sentiments of the rights of mankind proclaimed in the Declaration of Independence by thirteen north American colonies — a clarion call that preceded the adoption of constitutions by each of them. In the same year the new conditions of economic life were brought clearly into view by the publication of Adam Smith's *Enquiry into the Nature and Causes of the Wealth of Nations* — a work completed in the very city (Glasgow) where James Watt was simultaneously perfecting his steam engine.

The pace of change was speeded up by both these events. Only thirteen years later an historic and quite explicit Declaration of the Rights of Man was proclaimed in Paris, to become the even fuller Declaration of the Rights and Duties of Man and the Citizen some five years later as a Preamble to the Constitution of Year III of the French Revolution. This whole statement of rights, though it remained the most complete expression of social foundations up to the time of the USSR Constitution of 1936, did not and could not yet proclaim what we know as democracy or representative government. It was enough to feel that all are born with equal rights, including liberty of the person, freedom of thought, of speech, of the press, of work and of ownership. Public office must be accessible to all, social distinctions being founded only on usefulness to the community. Recalling Rousseau's *Contrat social*, law was to be the expression of the general will and the nation the seat of sovereignty. Following Baron Montesquieu's observations on the British system in *L'Esprit des lois* (1748), the executive, legislative and judiciary powers were to be kept separate. Unlike the conceptions of Jefferson and Rousseau, however, the Constitution provided for two classes of citizens — active and passive — and voting qualifications depended on property or on armed service in the field.[3]

In the years immediately preceding these momentous happenings a private system of credit and finance was being created in Britain that could operate worldwide. As early as 1666 it had been stated in a British court that ". . . the law of merchants is the law of the land" (Harding, *op cit.*) and by the mid-eighteenth century this had become largely true, even though restraint of trade was still a crime and cornering the market for profit remained an offence until 1772, and even beyond. London was becoming the world's centre of exchange, yet, as Harding (*op. cit.*) has pointed out ". . . commerce, capitalism and industry of necessity grew up in a society of landlords and peasants". The Crowley Iron Works, that eighteenth-century forerunner of the modern conglomerate, ". . . represents the moment of transition from medieval communalism to modern management, from the domestic to the factory system, from . . . paternalism . . . to rabid exploitation." Yet it should not be thought that such developments were eagerly welcomed. On the contrary, the pressures of world trade and home-produced technology were forcing a major adaptation of a tradition-oriented society — one in which monopolies had a protected legal status — against active resistance from many quarters.

By this time eighteenth-century society was reaching the point where it required a body of philosophy to justify convincingly the ruthless exploitation that came, by the logic of an evolving situation, to represent the enlightened entrepreneurial virtues as then conceived. A theory of democracy had been growing up from the time of Rousseau and Jefferson and, indeed, from the days of Sir Thomas More's *Utopia* (1516). But this was essentially pre-industrial and pre-capitalist, opting for relative equality between citizens and thus for limited rights in private property for each. The mainstream of liberal thinking, from John Locke onwards, recognized for the first time the full freedom of market forces and thus accepted great inequality between traditional owners and employees.

With the Market to Modernity

The great catalyst that set a seal of authority on the new socio-economic system of market society was the appearance of *The Wealth of Nations* in 1776. In the light of the times this seemed to show that the collective welfare of all was best served when each man laboured to further his own interests, the anonymous 'invisible hand' of market forces securing an objective balance in the use of labour, capital and resources and a distribution of the products that — ignoring the fact that citizens had to compete on very unequal terms — was non-arbitrary and non-discriminatory. The whole theory seemed so providential because it accorded absolutely with the motivated reasoning of those with the power to decide. This blend of ethics and self-reliance soon brought forth a matching theory of liberal democracy based on utilitarian principles to complete a body of myth that has purported to serve most of the world to this day — a world so different from 1776 that it takes an obscurantist miracle to keep our eyes averted from the truth.

We see therefore that the nineteenth-century climate of fevered industrial expansion emerged slowly and in the face of some resistance. But its appeal to the underlying human potential for greed and acquisitiveness was so strong, and the convergence of many strands of technical and intellectual change so irresistible, that the seal of rationality could not be long withheld. Even thus, the new economic doctrine was so far out of line with emerging human ideals that it soon produced some reasoned reactions, including the remarkable stream of now-resurgent thought stemming from J. S. Mill, Ruskin and Kropotkin to J. A. Hobson, E. F. Schumacher and beyond. The one counter-doctrine that has survived politically to motivate a large part of the modern world — that of Karl Marx — has proved in practice to be little less fallacious than the original, depending as it did on a mechanistic myth of historical determinism. Yet the reaction of Marx to classical market theory, from 1848 on, did disclose one valid and shining truth to all: the continuing primacy of economic forces in marking out the range and direction of human life both material and mental.

The rest of the social and economic story up to the end of the Second World War is both sensational and familiar. Its details can therefore be filled in by reference to many excellent sources, beginning with an early contemporary account in G. R. Porter's *Progress of the Nation* of 1847. (G. Porter, 1847).

The nineteenth century saw the rise of a worldwide struggle for territory and resources that followed an expansion of geographical discovery, colonization, population and markets. Their interweaving forms a rich tapestry of material progress, bigger and better wars and a European awakening to the notions of a long geological past, a seemingly assured future and the painful coming to awareness of many unsuspected social obligations. Among other things, Henri Dunant's view of the battle of Solferino (1860) led to his founding of the Red Cross in 1862 and to that organization's subsequent humanizing of the conditions of war through the Geneva Conventions of 1949 and their later up-dating as recently as 1977. The history of public education, too, is a very recent story, at least in Britain. While the first attempt to link government with the provision of elementary education by such agencies as church schools was made in the Education Act of 1856, it was only in 1870 that the Forster Act provided for publicly-maintained schooling, forty-eight years later before the school-leaving age was raised to fourteen, and not until 1944 that a Minister of Education came to watch over a three-tier system of primary, secondary and further education, with secondary schooling included for all.

The accelerating pace of near-total change is summed up by the spate of familiar basic inventions that led the way, starting with railways (1830), the telegraph (1837), the transatlantic cable (1866), the gas engine (1860), typewriters on sale (1874), the telephone (1876), electricity supply and hydro-electric generation (1881), the steam turbine (1884), the petrol engine (1885), transatlantic radio and turbine merchant shipping (1901), powered aircraft (1903), transatlantic flight (1919), regular air services (1920) and television (1929).

Neither economic practice nor modes of government have kept pace with these liberating and productivity-promoting trends. Business cycles continued to punctuate the gradual rise per head in average wealth and income up to the great depression of 1929–32. Only for two decades following the Second World War did western market economics find a temporary success formula in the full employment prescriptions of John Maynard Keynes. Soon the combined effects of Dr Spock's permissive child-rearing advice, wider consumer credit, trade unionism, mass advertising and a rapid rise in transnational corporations over the years 1950–1970 were to induce an inflationary fever of unrealizable mass expectation that has mushroomed into the 1970s just as the end of an era of irresponsible growth-at-any-cost has come fully into view. In eastern Europe, on the other side of the ideological divide, sustained growth has also slackened, though in a more orderly manner, in the face of world recession.

The Birth of Internationalism

While the first assertions of human rights in 1776 and 1789 were not notably extended in their content until the approach of the Second World War, the dim outlines of one world first came into common view about 70 years earlier. The International Red Cross dates essentially from 1864 and it was very nearly the first of a spate of functional world organizations that came into existence from 1860 onwards. Europeans were colonizing the globe and between 1800 and 1920 their numbers, in all areas of settlement, rose from 24 to 39 per cent of total world population — a trend that has been strongly reversed ever since 1930. Following the spread of empire and the railways a world trade pattern of raw material imports and manufactured exports grew up in the second half of the nineteenth century to replace an earlier self-sufficiency in the infant centres of Europe's industry.

Seen in this perspective, both the idea and the technology of one world are very new inventions. It is hardly surprising that when this incipient world community took its first hesitant steps towards a world government, with the founding of the League of Nations after the First World War, the political structures and procedures it set up were tentative and on the whole doomed to failure. What the League *did* accomplish, generally unknown to the world at large, was the creation of some elements of a world civil service dedicated to analysis and publication on a common basis — the first vital steps towards a world research unit to provide pooled information and uniform statistics.

On the verge of the Second World War some attempts were made, quite independently of one another, to re-define or update earlier statements of the rights of man. While a new Soviet Constitution appeared in 1936 a non-official *Complément* to the French Declaration of 1789/93 was drafted at Dijon in the same year. In 1940 a correspondence on war aims developed in *The Times* newspaper and, reacting to this, H. G. Wells contributed a letter containing a draft for a completely new Declaration of Rights intended to become "the common fundamental law of all communities and collectivities assembled under the World Pax". This text was later refined through much discussion by an eminent Drafting Committee set up for the purpose, and after a long public debate in the press. Through the efforts of Lord Ritchie Calder and the Editor of the then *Daily Herald*, later to become Lord Francis Williams, a digest of the issues and arguments was translated into ten languages and distributed to editors in forty-eight countries.[4]

The final Preamble and Declaration as published by H. G. Wells from 1940 on had a major impact in the western world. It was followed by a series of political pronouncements, beginning with a Declaration of United Nations issued by 26 countries in January 1942 and with a pledge to continue the fight against the Axis Powers. What we now know as the United Nations Charter, based on proposals agreed in 1944 by China, the United Kingdom, United States and USSR, was finalized and adopted by 50 countries meeting at San Francisco in 1945 at a United Nations Conference on International Organization. The United Nations Organization finally came into being when the Charter had been ratified by the above-mentioned four countries and France, plus a majority of other signatories, on 24 October, 1945.

Broadly the UN exists to maintain international peace and security, to provide the means for states to co-operate ". . . in solving international

economic, social, cultural and humanitarian problems . . ." and to promote
". . . respect for human rights and fundamental freedoms". Apart from the
General Assembly, where decisions may carry considerable moral weight,
and its six major committees (of which the first three concern our subject
more directly since they concern, respectively, political and security
matters, economic and financial matters, and social, humanitarian and
cultural matters), the major functional organs of the UN system for our
purpose are the Security Council and the Economic and Social Council.
Only the Security Council has the power to take collective decisions that
are obligatory on member states and it is the fact that most decisions
reached are in the nature of recommendations only that can make some of
the more publicized UN action ineffectual in the face of international
terrorism or of the many national regimes that are not accountable in any
real sense to the citizens they supposedly represent.

   The real continuing work of the UN family of organizations, most of it
virtually unknown to the general public, consists of co-operation and
exchange of experience through expert technical working groups functioning in the five regional economic commissions and elsewhere; and thus in
the innumerable economic, scientific, technical and legal analyses, surveys,
projections, statistics, agreed standards, etc., prepared by specialist
members of the Secretariat and by national rapporteurs working in
collaboration. The richness, volume and variety of essential effort covered
in this way produces an enormous (and available) literature on matters
varying from cartography, energy, environment and water resources to
housing, industry, agriculture and transport. Since 1948 a central part has
been played by the five regional economic commissions — those for
Europe (Geneva), Africa (Addis Ababa), Asia and the Pacific (Bangkok),
Latin America (Santiago) and Western Asia (Beirut), as well as by the
specialized agencies and other bodies considered later. By 1978 this
embryonic essay in world government had already grown to a scale calling
for 8711 international meetings annually in Geneva alone — a 50 per cent
rise in five years.

   Reverting to the origins of the UN system, it was in January 1946 (7
months before the death of H. G. Wells), that the first part of the session
of the United Nations General Assembly held in London had before it a
draft for a Declaration of Fundamental Human Rights and Freedoms. In
the same year the Economic and Social Council, as one of its first acts, set
up a UN Commission on Human Rights, which at once went to work to
complete a Universal Declaration (adopted by 50 countries on 10
December 1948) and the two basic Covenants that make up today's
International Bill of Human Rights. It is salutary to remember that these
two latter, together with an Optional Protocol also discussed in a later
chapter, took 18 years to reach their final form and did not enter into force
until 3 January and 23 March 1976 respectively, 28 years after the

Universal Declaration of Human Rights had proclaimed Wells's theme of a fundamental code of law for every citizen of the world.

An Emerging Structure of World Government?

In this outline of the slow march towards a conscious world order we have almost reached today's point of vantage — but not quite. It is hardly a secret that our over-complex global civil service, with its fragmented bureaucracy and lack of effective backing or decision making, is ill equipped to bring either order or progress to a world still largely unable to recognize its essential interdependence and unity. Unless backed by powerful external forces imposed by war, natural disaster or technology, reason permeates very slowly in penetrating ignorance, traditional enmity, ideology and — above all — those institutional channels of a state which preserve the main activating roles of vested interest.

During the 60s and early 70s it became clear that successive Development Decades of effort by the United Nations family were proving ineffectual in redressing a fundamental imbalance in the world economy. At the same time an increase in the numbers of newly independent but have-not states was reversing the voting power of the developed world to produce a majority of 'non-aligned' countries with a primary stake in development. Our sketch of mankind as slowly moving in the direction of an organized one-world will not be complete without a final word on how, in the face of these trends, the entire United Nations system has come to be completely re-ordered to confront a Third Development Decade for the 1980s.

A first attempt to improve the lot of developing countries was made in 1970, with the adoption of an International Development Strategy. On average third world countries were to aim to step up their Gross National Product by 6 per cent per year (3.5 per cent per inhabitant). To help achieve this, developed countries were to contribute aid equal to 1 per cent of their GNP annually, 70 per cent of it as grants or long-term loans. Poor countries were to increase annual domestic saving to 20 per cent of GNP by 1980 and speed up various reforms.

By 1973 it had become evident that this mutual aid approach was over-simple and would not work. In the following year the General Assembly called for the inception of a New International Economic Order, by which was meant a sustained improvement in the unsatisfactory terms of trade of the developing world, an expanding world economy and reform of the international monetary system to ensure a better flow of real resources to developing countries. In December 1974 a Charter of the Economic Rights and Duties of States was adopted which, for the first time, set out some principles to govern the economic behaviour of independent states. Again, and not surprisingly in the climate that prevails, the response was very limited, developed countries seeing little incentive to help others commercially without some prospect of gain while the 'third world states', through their non-aligned 'Group of 77', attributed their plight to the selfishness of the rich.

And so we arrive at the latest phase of UN evolution — a scheme, adopted on 20 December 1977, to Restructure the Economic and Social Sectors of the UN System, so as to form a comprehensive global framework for all activities. To see this step in perspective one has to realize that the United Nations organization has grown from a membership of 51 states in 1945 to 159 in 1984; that it has acquired or created a long list of agencies that in the main are only loosely linked, since they possess separate governing bodies, separate financing and separate work programmes; and that the entire UN family now comprises some 45,000 staff dispersed throughout the world.

The *ad hoc* growth of these different functional bodies can be seen from Table 2 and Figure 4. With the reordering begun in December 1979 these and many other organs are intended to form a more cohesive structure. Under the authority of the General Assembly, the Economic and Social Council (ECOSOC) acts as the UN principal organ for policy-making and co-ordination in the socio-economic field, formulating policy recommendations addressed both to member states and to the system of organizations as a whole, with the regional commissions playing a two-way role at the regional level.

To anyone familiar with the real situation at first hand, this will prove an awesome task. ECOSOC, which comprises 54 members, has itself amassed over 160 subsidiary bodies in the course of its work. Apart from five regional economic commissions, several standing committees and commissions dealing with such questions as Natural Resources, Transnational Corporations, Human Settlements and other expert bodies on matters like Crime Prevention, Geographical Names and Transport of Dangerous Goods, the list includes six functional Commissions — on Statistics, Population, Social Development, Human Rights, Status of Women and Narcotic Drugs. The mere enumeration forms a conspectus of the task of worldwide economic integration that now confronts mankind, as can be seen from Figure 5.

Let us now stand back and take a long view over these eight centuries of evolution in government and society towards an administered world consensus. We may conclude that today's crude international framework, which has been forced on the world by the logic of events, is becoming reasonably strong in those fields where basic common standards are required, as in mapping or agreed statistics. Understanding of the dynamic causal patterns of world phenomena, e.g. climate and weather, diseases, various resource distributions or aspects of the ecological balance, is coming within our grasp. Worldwide surveillance or control of some basic

TABLE 2
Principal Members of the United Nations Economic and Social System
(arranged by decades in order of establishment)

Title	Acronym	Headquarters	Year of establishment
Universal Postal Union	UPU	Berne	1875
International Labour Organization	ILO	Geneva	1919/46
International Telecommunication Union	ITU	Geneva	1934/47
United Nations	UN	New York	1945
Food & Agriculture Organization of the UN	FAO	Rome	1945
World Bank	World Bank	Washington	1945
UN Educational, Scientific and Cultural Organization	UNESCO	Paris	1946
UN Children's Fund	UNICEF	New York	1946
International Civil Aviation Organization	ICAO	Montreal	1947
World Health Organization	WHO	Geneva	1948
International Monetary Fund	IMF	Washington	1948
General Agreement on Tariffs and Trade	GATT	Geneva	1948
UN Relief and Works Agency (Palestine Refugees)	UNRWA	Beirut	1949
World Meteorological Organization	WMO	Geneva	1950
UN High Commissioner for Refugees	UNHCR	Geneva	1951
International Atomic Energy Agency	IAEA	Vienna	1957
Inter-Governmental Maritime Consultative Organization*	IMCO	London	1958
UN Development Programme	UNDP	New York	1959
UN Conference on Trade and Development	UNCTAD	Geneva	1964
UN Institute for Training and Research	UNITAR	New York	1965
UN Fund for Population Activities	UNFPA	New York	1967
UN Industrial Development Organization	UNIDO	Vienna	1967
World Intellectual Property Organization	WIPO	Geneva	1967
UN Environment Programme	UNEP	Nairobi	1972
UN University	UNU	Tokyo	1973
International Fund for Agricultural Development	IFAD	Rome	1974
World Food Programme	WFP	Rome	1975
World Food Council	WFC	Rome	1976
UN Centre for Human Settlements (Habitat)	UNCHS	Nairobi	1978

*Now the International Maritime Organization (IMO).

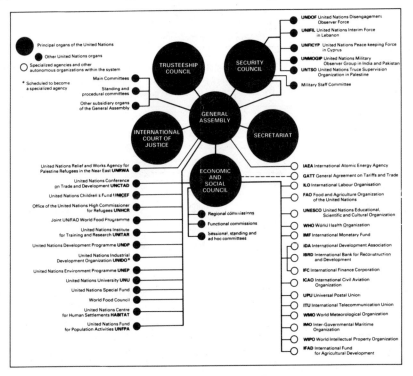

FIG. 4. Structure of the United Nations System.

sources of regional imbalance, such as epidemics, natural disasters or refugee problems, is steadily gaining ground. Diffusion of basic common social standards in areas like education, human rights and population control is no longer an insuperable problem. What *does* continue to elude mankind is an active political consciousness of interdependence in areas open to the play of power, fear and envy through aggressiveness and greed, i.e. the fields of military posturing and economics. Institutions in this domain, and notably those concerned with arrangements for a rational output and distribution of basic goods and services, remain unnecessarily primitive and non-viable at the world level because they are still primitive and non-viable within the nation-state itself.

The UN as a Stage in World Organization

As we have outlined it above, the United Nations organization at its present stage is a body seeking to define achievable standards and to work towards their realization mainly through consensus and voluntary co-operation between sovereign governments. In general this co-operation works through such means as:

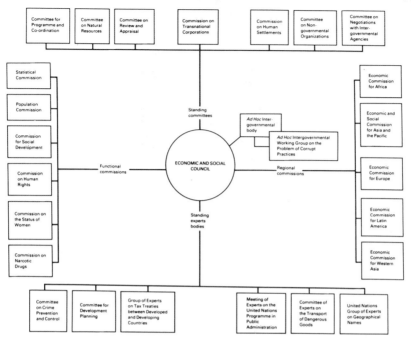

FIG. 5. Main Subsidiary Bodies of the Economic and Social Council (not including 16 Specialized Agencies and other Autonomous Bodies and 13 United Nations Organs which Report to ECOSOC).

— common standard-setting;
— security decision-making and peace-keeping by consensus;
— common statistics;
— financial, technical and humanitarian assistance;
— conduct of international research and planning;
— exchange of information;
— custodianship of scarce resources, and training.

For the purposes of this investigation it is essential that we be aware that this present stage of world co-operation is, on the one hand, the outcome of a long evolution in knowledge, communication and technique, acting with an ever-diminishing time-lag; and, on the other, that it has to be in transition towards a more effective frame, better geared to free self-realization in a state of peace. Far from our first impressions of the UN as a vast machine betraying a weary sameness as it goes through its endless bureaucratic motions, the organization is in fact now to be seen as in a state of rapid evolution.

This time-dimension can be seen more clearly when the beginnings of international standard-setting are brought into view.* In the earliest stages

*Some of the early documentary sources can be seen at a permanent exhibition housed in the United Nations Library at the Palais des Nations, Geneva.

it was ideals of universal peace, rather than economic questions, that most stirred men's minds. Credit for the first draft covenant providing for a 'Universal Peace Organization' is generally accorded to King Georg Podiebrad of Bohemia, whose scheme dates from 1462. Just over half a century later, in 1517, Erasmus, the Dutch humanist thinker, set out in Rotterdam his *Complaint of Peace*, in which European rulers were entreated to settle their disputes by arbitration and thereby create the conditions for a lasting peace. Only eight years later Hugo Grotius produced his seminal work *De iure belli ac pacis*, which defined the principles of international law as resting on the doctrine of Justice and thus on the obligation of rulers to submit grievances to peaceful arbitration. A few years earlier the Duc de Sully had given in France a full account of a 'Great Design' for a European confederation of states, anticipating by nearly a century a detailed *Project de paix perpétuelle* published by the Abbé Saint Pierre, which has been mentioned earlier. This last scheme provided for a 'European Union' with a general assembly, a permanent international secretariat and standing armed forces.

If the seventeenth and eighteenth centuries saw the rise of the idea of international organizations, the nineteenth was marked first by the setting-up of Peace Societies in London and New York, followed in 1830 by a similar body created by J. J. Sellon in Geneva. Universal Peace Congresses continued to be organized, at which general disarmament and a permanent court for international arbitration were among the main issues. In 1867 an "International League for Peace and Liberty" was created and sited, also in Geneva, by Charles Lemonier, Victor Hugo and Garibaldi, followed twenty-five years later by the founding of an International Peace Bureau at Berne. In the words of the UN Secretary-General, J. Perez de Cuellar, the International Peace Conferences held at The Hague in 1899 and 1907 ". . . marked the first recognition of a multilateral responsibility for global peace". The President of the Second Conference was able to state that for the first time State representatives had gathered ". . . to discuss interests which they have in common and which contemplate the good of mankind".

We thus see that, unlike today's stress on problems raised by a technical and economic integration of the world, the early history of international comity was largely, if unsuccessfully, concentrated on creating conditions of peace. To some extent the entry into force of the Covenant of the League of Nations on 10 January 1920, with Sir Eric Drummond of Britain as the League's first Secretary-General and Geneva as its seat, widened the field of international concern to include some of the present types of co-operation, although neither the organization's coverage (some 44 states in 1920, rising to 57 by 1937) nor its scope for action, were ever on a scale to match the present UN. Some border disputes, e.g. between Bulgaria and Greece and Colombia and Peru, were resolved under its auspices and many large-scale initiatives were embarked upon, though most ended in failure. The organization proved to be ahead of its time and ahead of the prevailing world climate. It sought to fill some wide gaps in available means of international co-operation and in that respect has afforded a precedent on which the more experienced international machinery of today has been able to build. To this end the League had already set up many bodies, including Commissions for Economics and Finance, Health, Communications, Opium and Intellectual Co-operation, among others.

We can thus see how the United Nations has been able to shape up to a later, ensuing stage in the evolution of fundamental international machinery, where it is now poised for a further radical step forward that is already presaged by new conditions of rapid change. Yet it has reached this point without resolving the perennial threat of armed conflict, even under the decisive conditions of a nuclear age. The first resolution adopted at the first session of the UN General Assembly was already concerned with nuclear disarmament. All that has so far been achieved by agreement is to restrain the horizontal proliferation of nuclear weapons, to prohibit their use on the sea-bed, in outer space and in Antarctica, and to outlaw certain excessively injurious or indiscriminate conventional arms, as well as all bacteriological weapons and military environment-modification techniques. The increasing complexities of a world community of sovereign-state systems is calling forth new norms and new thinking, but it equally demands new steps towards a loose frame for maintaining order.

Notes

1. From slow improvement in means of transport and communication, in cumulating knowledge and recorded experience, as well as in the productivity of labour, the interaction of persons and ideas has come to follow a compound-interest law so that the advance of science, technique, economic and social change have all become exponential in kind.

2. This is a reference to a three-stage typology of the prevailing social character of individuals which represents an adaptation to underlying demographic, institutional and economic evolution witnessed in what is now the developed world. The theory recognizes major stages of demographic and economic growth as calling forth, first a 'tradition-directed' social character, changing to an 'inner-directed' type in the Renaissance and Reformation periods and on through an economy of scarcity, and finally to the more 'other-directed' personality of mature population and advanced capitalistic development. The theory is that of David Riesman, together with N. Glazer and R. Denney (*The Lonely Crowd* — Yale University Press, 1950).

3. Two chambers were provided for, the lower body to initiate proposed legislation having a minimum age of thirty, and the ultimate decision-making Council comprising married members over forty.

4. The full story is told by Lord Ritchie Calder in *On Human Rights* — a digest of the inaugural H. G. Wells Memorial Lecture given on 7 December 1967 at Conway Hall, London (The Wellsian, vol. 11 no. 3 1968, published by the H. G. Wells Society).

3

Global Society Now: The Facts

In one very real sense the problems of man's global habitat are problems of distribution — either today's uneven spread of population and political power, of currently vital natural resources and their trading or geopolitical relationships; or else the persisting effects of past patterns of the same sort that confuse the present and make workable solutions harder to come by. The world now comprises some 170 rival concentrations of people, culture, climate and history, all guarding scarce resources and seeking either to extend — if population and home market permit — or merely to protect their habitual spheres of influence. This vast geo-political pattern becomes ever more unstable as knowledge and technique advance while traditional codes and mechanisms falter and draw nearer to collapse.

So much for the uncertain but tangible world of human motives. Underlying its logic of ever-evolving situations created by interacting minds and institutions a deeper and ill-understood 'natural logic' is at work — economic, social and ecological in kind — that exerts a long-term influence on the future outcome irrespective of conscious aims. This is the domain where resources, habitats and climate interact with demographic and economic trends to produce consequences still largely unknown. This deeper logic of social evolution in a natural environment has replaced the more instinctive adaptive process of the animal kingdom.

There is no room here to discuss in detail the dynamics of human environment, much less to get involved in geo-political interpretation. What can be done at the outset is to survey in outline the present range of human development throughout the world, using some key indicators of material and intellectual well-being as a starting point. Here then is where we shall begin.

Some Dimensions of World Development*

We have to begin with population, for it is grossly excessive rates of population increase in some under-developed regions that is the first major cause of extreme and persistent poverty over large areas of the earth,

*See a remark in the Preface on choice of statistical data.

particularly in some 35 countries of Africa and Asia where very low average incomes show little chance of improvement.

It is for this reason that Table 3 is arranged in decreasing order of population growth-rates (column 5).[1] Because the figures shown are broad regional averages, they do not bring out the extremes to be found in different countries. They do show, however, that for half the world's people population is rising by 2.6 per cent or more per year (actually between 2.6 and 3.4 per cent in individual countries) as compared with rates between zero and nearly 1.0 per cent in the developed countries.

As we shall see, the consequences of this situation are momentous. First, the pressure on major cities and urban areas is growing rapidly in all regions so that in twenty years half the world's people will live under urban conditions.

For the developing world this trend is having economic and social consequences of major import. Cities have never been able to expand at the rates now imposed. All that is happening is that great shanty towns lacking any elementary amenities are proliferating around the fringes of cities of the developing world, *bidonvilles* built of old cans by people who are drawn to the metropolis in search of work and emancipation. Column 8 of Table 3 shows that it is precisely in the regions where this rash of poverty is most pronounced that the largest proportions of young people are to be found. What we call 'the problem of youth' is in reality the problem of unoccupied young men and women, with neither inspiration nor enterprise to engage their excess of energy. In most of Africa, Southern Asia and Latin America — just those regions where hope is mostly at a discount — we see that 42–44 per cent of the entire population is under 15.

Table 4 concentrates not on a geographical breakdown but on a division of the world's people in terms of income per inhabitant, as expressed by average Gross Domestic Product (GDP) per head in 1970. In fact each of the entries is based on conditions in as large a sample as possible of countries for which the requisite details can be obtained, the conditions illustrated referring in general to 1975 or the rate of development from 1970 up to that year.[2]

In the upper part of the table we see that the poorest group (column 2), with a national product per head of only 114 dollars per year, is also the one where output per head rises very slowly and where a high proportion of the population is engaged in low-productivity agriculture.

The middle section discloses some characteristics of the urban revolution now in full swing — notably the extreme contrast between urban and rural population growth rates throughout the developing countries and how this affects basic amenities of urban living as reflected by access to public water supply. This present urban growth at around 4.5 per cent is historically unique. In the nineteenth century, when Europe's demographic growth and migration to new countries was at its height, cities were being

TABLE 3

World Population — Its Distribution and Main Trends

(Regions arranged in decreasing order of annual population increase — col. 5)

Region	Population (mid-1978)		Density (inhabitants per km²)	Annual rate of population increase (%) (1970–1976)	Urban population as percentage of total		Percentage of total population under 15 (1975)
	Millions	Percentage of total			1970	2000	
1	2	3	4	5	6	7	8
Latin America	343	8	17	2.8	57	75	42
Africa	435	10	15	2.7	21	38	44
South Asia	1340	32	85	2.6	21	35	43
Oceania	22	1	3	1.8	70	83	31
East Asia[a]	1050	25	93	1.6	23	44	34
USSR[b]	261	6	11	1.0	56	75	26
North America	242	6	11	0.9	74	86	25
Europe	523	12	98	0.6	64	78	24
World	4216	100	32	1.9	36	50	36

[a] Of which China, with estimated population of 930 million.
[b] Also includes countries of Eastern Europe.

TABLE 4
The Worldwide Range in Living Conditions at Different Levels of Economic Development (c. 1975)

Category	Countries with Average GDP Per Inhabitant in 1970:[a]			
	Below $200	$200–$399	$400–$999	$1000 and over
No. of countries included	40 (20 below $100)	35	21	27
1	2	3	4	5
A. *ECONOMIC DATA*				
GDP per head (1975 average)[b]	114	348	757	3269
Annual increase 1970–75 (%)	1.1	3.5	5.1	1.9
Agriculture (% share in GDP)	40	24	10	4
Annual increase 1970–75 (%)	1.4	4.2	3.5	1.7
Manufacturing (% share in GDP)	13	18	20	26
Annual increase 1970–75 (%)	5.2	10.1	6.8	1.2
B. *DEMOGRAPHIC DATA*				
Urban population (% of total)	20	42	56	75
Annual increase 1970–75 (%)	4.4	4.7	4.2	1.6
Access to public water supply (%)	69	88	91	98(est.)
Rural population (% of total)	80	58	44	25
Annual increase 1970–75 (%)	2.1	1.4	1.1	−1.1
Access to public water supply (%)	15	18	55	70(est.)
C. *SOCIAL DATA*				
Infant mortality per 1000 live births	119	76	51	19
Average life expectancy at birth (years)	44	52	61	71
Calorie Intake below critical limit (% of population)	35	20	15	—
Population per physician (000s)	19.00	3.70	2.00	0.67
Adult literacy — 15 and over (%)	19	50	84	99
Expenditure on social services (% of GDP)	4	5	7	15

[a]Refers, so far as possible, to 123 countries with market or mixed economies for which some comparable UN data are available. These comprised some 66 per cent of world population in 1970. Fourteen countries with centrally directed economies (including 7 developing countries) are omitted owing to a partial lack of comparable data.
[b]Gross domestic product (GDP) refers to Gross National Product less any net income from abroad.

expanded at about 3.8 per cent annually in North America and 3.5 per cent only in Australia — all with the aid of large sums borrowed from Britain and other west European countries — a situation that does not obtain today.

The outcome of these extreme contrasts in development between the very poor and the comparatively rich countries is not properly measured by differences in average income. This income range is in fact about 50:1, although the mean values in Table 4 show a difference of 29:1 only. To get any real idea of the true contrasts one must turn to social indicators like the six shown at the bottom of Table 4. All are sensitive measures of real well-being which will later merit more attention. Here the figures show how smooth is the transition from intolerable general misery in the 30 or so least developed countries to those in Europe and North America that are the most highly developed and among the richest. It is difficult to envisage a modern society where 8 out of 10 adults are illiterate and cannot expect to live much beyond 40, or where one medical man must suffice for 19,000 people. In fact, however, the infant mortality rate in England and Wales was far higher in 1890–1895 (150) than the figure of 119 shown in Table 4 for the least-developed world today, and much higher still in France and the Netherlands in the same period. In Sweden it was still around 100 at the beginning of this century. Even for literacy, progress in nineteenth-century Europe was patchy. The literacy rate for the USSR in 1897 (admittedly with a different age-range of 9 to 49 years) was only 26, though it advanced rapidly (to 98.5 by 1959) under successive five-year plans of the new regime. The real difference between European development in the nineteenth century and that of the developing countries today is that the former was constrained by the advance of new knowledge whereas today's poverty persists in an already enlightened world.

Today's new effect of population policy on conditions of life is summed up in Figure 6.

Causes of World Backwardness

Why, then, is the 'developed world' confined to one quarter of the world's people concentrated in some 28 developed countries (euphemistically so called) while most of the rest languish in varying degrees of material misery?

We can consider at least five types of partial or possible explanation. The first — favourite answer of the third-world politician — is that nineteenth-century colonization was a systematic policy of oppressive exploitation by those who have become today's rich. While this *was* true of some parts of Africa, in particular, and while commercial exploitation does continue today in a more subtle and insidious form, it cannot serve to explain sufficiently why the world's economy is so ill balanced.

Again, we have to note that the world's authoritarian religions hold sway in most of those regions where today's population explosion proves so intractable. From Table 3 it can be seen that Latin America, with an overall annual rise of 2.8 per cent, offers a good case in point. Not only resistance to birth control, but resistance to emancipating ideas in general, is a strong feature of all tradition-bound cultures. Here we certainly have a major aggravating factor, albeit not a sufficient explanation, since family size is also bound up closely with the work-load of rural agrarian societies.

Crude Birth Rates: World, More Developed and Less Developed Regions, 1950–1975, and 'Medium' Projections 1975–2000

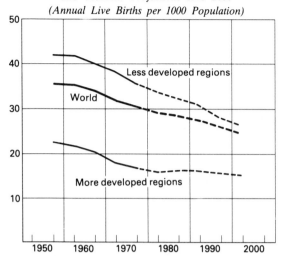

(Annual Live Births per 1000 Population)

Expectation of Life at Birth: World, More Developed and Less Developed Regions, 1950–1975, and 'Medium' Projections, 1975–2000

(Average Expectations for Males and Females at Birth)

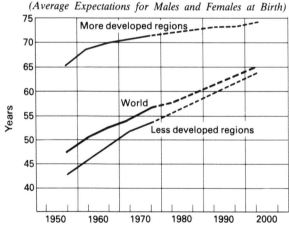

Source: World Population Trends and Prospects by Country, 1950–2000: Summary Report of the 1978 Assessment (United Nations Publication, ST ESA/SER.R.33).

FIG. 6. World Trends of Crude Birth Rates and of Expectation of Life at Birth, Actual and Projected (1950–2000).

Then, again, the long-term influence of climate must not be forgotten. The story of civilization thus far has entailed a 'poleward course of progress', from its early flowering in river basins of the 'fertile crescent' and thence northward towards the cold, grey but highly stimulating climates of Britain, in particular, and north-west Europe. Our whole 'protestant work ethic' is a product of high latitudes, and if indigenous high development is equally possible in any well-endowed region, the handicap of an economically remote or climatically variable tropical environment must prove substantial in the earliest stages of economic 'take-off'.

What, then, of the very variable distribution of essential natural resources as a factor in high civilization? Essential minerals, suitable plant habitats, abundant water, forests and energy reserves have gone far to create advantageous locations for the rise of agriculture and industry, as with the juxtaposition of coal, iron ore and labour during Europe's industrial revolution. Like the factors of population and climate already touched on, we have to give more time to natural resources in our summing up, as well as to the special poverty situations in regions like Africa.

Finally, there is a man-made component: the effect on the whole world pattern of development of a reliance on market-economy principles. If pure market theory, and free trade, actually prevailed in the real world, the factors of production would everywhere be drawn to their optimum use and a true world division of labour would exist in the sense that essentials would be produced where costs of output and transfer were at a minimum. For various reasons (and neglecting all non-economic criteria) this market theory cannot work effectively today, even within national frontiers.[3] If we look at Britain, where it all began, we find that two-thirds of the country is now a relatively deprived area and only in the small region of London and the home counties does average income and well-being approach the Common Market average, which is determined by a central core area stretching between London, Paris, Brussels and the Ruhr. In all these countries wealth and income too are very lopsided in their distribution — almost as much so, in fact, as in the income shares of the world's least-developed areas.[4] To cite once again the example of Britain, it emerges that 10 per cent of the population owns 67 per cent of the wealth (1973) and receives 27 per cent of all income. In 1968 the poorest tenth of the population received 2 per cent of total income — a proportion that has been estimated to be common to the Fed. Rep. of Germany at one extreme and India and Malawi at the other! Classical market theory assumes that all units of capital and labour have to compete on roughly equal terms, equal that is in the sense that each is too small to influence the market price. In fact, however, a tiny but influential number of transnational giants has now come to dominate the supply of basic goods and services world-wide, planning their prices, sales, transfers and location to satisfy private internal goals of long-term expansion. As with their domination of world trade, the international manipulations of private transnational concerns must tend to lessen any chance of re-creating a stable world monetary system. A similar situation of near-monopoly has come to characterize very large labour unions, also changing the entire nature of wage determination and economic management. Finally, it is largely the outcome of these two main trends over the last fifteen years that has produced an endemic trend of price inflation throughout the world. Inflation, which is the enemy of all rational behaviour and stability of purpose, was in this way the special and unique creation of market-economy systems, although it now tends to spread by export to nearly all countries of the world.

This whole situation — intrinsic inequality of regions, of producers, of labour and consumers, plus rabid instability of prices and of the entire monetary system, is a progressive, not a temporary phenomenon, and an unintended one at that, because it has evolved naturally in a system common to 90 per cent of the countries of the world. It is something quite separate from the national *policies* of governments, which today are tending to produce a confrontation between the privileged and the under-privileged. This confrontation, a denial of the real interdependence between countries, is certainly a short-term cause hampering development of poor regions, but it is only a complication as we shall see. Under present conditions, it would seem that, special drought conditions apart, two major *short-term* causes of slow development may lie within many of the poorer countries themselves — the ineffective role of unproductive agriculture in their poverty cycle and lack of needed land reform, plus a certain lack of self-reliant exchange of products within the Third World itself.

Prospects for Development

This is a subject deserving a book in itself. Keeping to bare essentials, one may perhaps start from today's energy situation and the world pattern of available energy resources.

To this end Table 5 first shows the post-oil-crisis world output and use of primary energy reduced to its simplest form.[5] By primary energy is meant all main solid fuels — hard and brown coal and some peat, plus crude petroleum, natural gas and hydro-electric power, with the small quantities of electricity from nuclear plants treated also as primary energy. This is the gross output and consumption balance before any conversion to refined fuels, all forms of energy being expressed in thousand million tonnes of coal equivalent.

We see first that the market or mixed economies, comprising some 69 per cent of world population, include 13 net oil-exporting developing countries — mostly among the members of OPEC* — who supply petroleum amounting to 28 per cent of the world's total energy content (mostly to industrialized countries of the market-economy world) but who themselves consume very little. The other 31 per cent of world population falls within centrally planned states which are, or could be, largely self-sufficient in energy.

Everyone now knows that, since October 1973, this hold of the OPEC

*Organization of Petroleum Exporting Countries.

TABLE 5

World Production and Consumption Balance of Total Primary Energy from Commercial Sources

Group	% of world population (1976)	Production (10⁹ tonnes)	% of Total	Consumption (10⁹ tonnes)	% of Total	Consumption per inhabitant (tonnes) 1960	1976
1	2	3	4	5	6	7	8
Market or Mixed Economies							
Developing Countries	52.2	2.12	20.9	1.34	13.8	0.28	0.61
(of which Net Oil Exporting Countries)	(7.3)	(1.60)	(15.8)	(0.34)	(3.3)	(0.23)	(0.40)
Developed Countries	16.2	3.72	36.6	5.58	57.3	4.46	7.08
Capital Surplus Oil Exporters	0.3	1.29	12.7	0.05	0.7	1.21	2.52
Centrally Planned Economies	31.3[b]	3.03	29.8	2.75	28.2	1.38	2.05
World Total	100.0	10.16	100.0	10.17[c]	100.0	1.40	2.41

Total Primary Energy[a] (coal equivalent)

[a]Primary energy here includes solid fuels (coal and lignite), crude petroleum, natural gas, hydro and nuclear electricity. Data refer to 1976.
[b]Which include 7 developing countries.
[c]Total includes consumption for bunkers, etc.

Note: Between 1973, the year of the OPEC oil crisis, and the end of 1984, total world energy consumption showed little change, rising by only 1.5 per cent in all the market-economy states and by 13.5 per cent in the centrally planned states. Composition of the total changed somewhat, with coal, petroleum and renewable sources playing a larger part in the total by 1984.

countries on the main energy consumers of the market-economy world has produced a major balance-of-payments and debt crisis that has reduced economic activity to a trickle. The entire situation is a response of developing oil-possessors to the stranglehold gained by some transnational companies (with the acquiescence of their home governments) over the world oil economy, mainly through excessive dependence of industrialized states on cheap oil. In the present context its main injurious effect is that a slowdown in the developed world has impeded any expansion of poor countries by holding back demand for their exportable products.

This, in brief, is the short-term energy situation. For a more long-term perspective Table 6 sums up the world pattern of available energy resources as at present known.[6] Units employed for this purpose are millions of Terajoules and Terajoules per head (columns 2–8) and millions of kilowatt-hours (columns 9–11).

The figures shown refer to reasonably assured, or proved and probable deposits, rather than to geological fuel reserves. Not only is knowledge gradually improved by new discoveries but the limits to exploitation may be further advanced. In recent years estimates of usable coal resources have been extended on average from about 5 to 6.2 per cent of geological reserves. For petroleum only some 30 per cent of the oil *in situ* can so far be recovered, though new techniques to 'mine' petroleum more systematically might greatly extend this figure in future.

With these reservations, established fuel, uranium and hydro-electric resources can be seen to be widely distributed over the earth, with coal four times as plentiful as petroleum in calorific content if the nearly unused oil shales and tar sands are excluded, but roughly equal otherwise. Although two-thirds of all hydro-electric potential, and most of the petroleum, is located in developing countries, the main solid fuels, including at present uranium, are held by the developed world. These contrasts are accentuated by differences in population as between the two groups of countries. Because Third World resources of energy are greater, in relation to present demand, than those of industrialized countries, plenty of scope remains for further development in the years to come. In particular, two thousand kWh per head of renewable hydro-electric resources, most of it undeveloped either in large or in micro-plants, could offer a major aid to economic take-off.

It has to be remembered, too, that differences in climate and social usage in many of the poorer countries militate against over-simple comparisons with consumerism. Thus, energy demand under near-tropical conditions is often met very largely from non-commercial sources — fuel wood, crop residues, animal waste and perhaps biogas digesters — often, it must be said, with harmful effects also in terms of land impoverishment and erosion. Some three-quarters of total energy needs in central and southern Africa, and half in south-east Asia, are met simply from fuel

TABLE 6

The World's Known Commercial Fuel and Hydro-electric Resources, and Relation to Present Demand

1	Exploitable fossil fuel reserves (total) 10⁶ Tj^a	Tj per head 1978	Of which (as % of col. 2) Solid fuels	Crude oil	Natural gas	Oil shales and tar sands	Fossil fuel reserves (col. 2) as multiple of total energy demand^b (years)	Uranium (low cost reserves,^c with production in non-breeders) 10⁶ Tj	Exploitable hydro-electric resources at average flow GWh/year	kWh per inhabitant	Per cent harnessed
	2		3	4	5	6	7	8	9	10	11
Africa	1236	3	31	45	17	7	352	209	2020	4640	1.5
Asia^d	6460	3	43	36	7	14	201	3	2643	1110	7.5
Latin America	536	2	13	67	15	5	100	15	1852	5430	6.0
Oceania	531	24	91	2	5	2	229	105	202	10,900	14.3
Europe^e	2927	6	88	2	6	4	54	49	722	1380	52.9
USSR	4617	18	76	8	13	3	144	—	1095	4220	11.2
North America	15,615	65	34	2	2	62	214	445	1273	5300	34.2
World	31,922	8	48	12	6	34	156	825	9807	2060	13.3
Developing Countries	8425	3	57	31	9	3	229	236	6358	2020	4.0
Developed Countries^f	23,497	22	42	2	3	53	141	589	3449	3270	30.5

Notes:

[a] 1 Tj (Terajoule) = 35 tonnes of coal equivalent (in round figures).

[b] Figures show the number of years fossil fuels could support total primary commercial energy demand at the 1971 level.

[c] Exploitable at up to $26 per kg (1974). If used for output in breeder reactors, figures would be multiplied by 60.

[d] The People's Republic of China contains half Asia's fuel and hydro resources.

[e] Excluding USSR.

[f] Refers to 28 countries in Europe, North America, Japan and Oceania.

wood, as compared with under one per cent in developed countries.

If energy resources, by themselves, are not a major cause of underdevelopment, this is at least partly true also of the dozen or so non-fuel mineral raw materials found essential to a modern economy, which are distributed between developed and developing countries in a ratio of something like 60:40, with centrally planned economies accounting for nearly half the first figure. For details see also Figure 23.

Bearing in mind all these various constraints on development, how then can we sum up purely material prospects for the developing world? Again ignoring a lack of space, it is possible to reduce a complex picture to the scope of a simple Table (Table 7) with the help of a new technique, a classificatory system and data developed by the Overseas Development Council (Washington).[7]

One salient feature of worldwide prospects today, and the most urgent, is the quite intolerable position of the group of very deprived countries. Table 7 (in columns 5 and 6) shows that for some 28 per cent of world population an inevitably slow improvement in the 60s (slow because of excessive population growth) has later fallen to near zero. If we take 30 mainly small territories of Africa and Asia with 260 million people, often landlocked and characterized by the UN as 'least developed', we find that average annual income has risen by only four dollars per head in the 70s (T. G. Weiss, 1979). Agricultural production in these countries, constant in the 60s, fell by 0.5 per cent per year between 1970 and 1977. Investment, which was rising by 5 per cent per year in the previous decade, declined by 2.4 per cent in an average year between 1970 and 1976. The point is that these trends are in strong contrast with the position in developing countries as a whole, a fact brought out also in Table 7. What has been happening is that a general slowdown in the high-income countries (accentuated since 1975) has aggravated a deepening poverty in those states — the lowest group — where simple manufacturing has not yet got under way.

We have seen that there are many causes of human underachievement at work. One of these is a weakness of governments for the wares of the arms manufacturer (columns 8 and 9 of Table 7). The indicator I have used to illustrate this is an index obtained by dividing military expenditure (1976 and 1980) by public education expenditure in the same years. Less poor states, in particular, come out as giving more weight to military posturing than to public education. In fact, however, this is a good deal less true of the poorest states, and since 1974 at least all groups have greatly increased relative spending on education.

More progressive economists are well aware that monetary measures like National Income or Gross Domestic Product are poor indicators of well-being. Not only does GDP exclude much useful household and voluntary effort but it also includes much that is harmful or useless. It is for these reasons that thought is being given, in the UN and elsewhere, to

TABLE 7

The Worldwide Range in Development Prospects at Different Levels of Average Income

Income group[a] or Region	No. of States	Population ('000 millions) (1984)	Average GNP per inhabitant				Military spending index[c]	
			US dollars (1982)	Mean % growth rate (1960–82)	Physical quality of life index (%) (1981)[b]	Literacy (%)	1976	1980
1	2	3	4	5	6	7	8	9
Low-Income[d]	39	1.331	250	1.2	46	37	1.25	1.00
(China-People's Rep.)	1	1.034	310	5.0	75	69	2.92	1.64
Lower-Middle	40	0.549	714	3.3	57	55	2.32	1.00
Upper-Middle	39	0.620	2058	3.6	74	73	1.27	0.70
High-Income	52	1.184	9364	3.4	95	97	1.06	0.93
All Developing Countries	141	3.603	787	3.1	61	56	1.61	1.06
All Developed Countries	30	1.115	9477	3.4	96	99	1.05	0.90
World	171	4.718	2842	3.2	69	66	1.13	0.93
Of which:								
Africa	53	0.531	801	1.8	46	39	0.54	0.71
Asia	40	2.692	959	3.5	63	57	0.98	0.86
Latin America	36	0.394	2062	3.3	77	79	0.43	0.34
Oceania	10	0.024	8618	2.2	88	88	0.43	0.41
Europe (inc. USSR)	30	0.816	7343	3.4	93	96	1.46	1.03
N. America	2	0.261	12,983	2.3	97	99	0.84	1.00

[a] Low income = under 420 US dollars per head.
Lower-Middle = 420–1069 US dollars per head.
Upper-Middle = 1070–3699 US dollars per head.
High income = over 3699 US dollars per head.

[b] As developed and used on a world scale by Overseas Development Council (Washington) (see item 7 in the Technical Notes), the Index is an average of three separate indicators — life expectancy at age one, infant mortality, and adult literacy — the first two being converted to index form by reference to the worst performance in 1950 as 0 and the best expected value in year 2000 as 100.

[c] Public education expenditure = 1.00 (see explanation in text).

[d] Excluding China, which falls within Low-Income group.

devising international non-monetary measures more sensitive to social and economic well-being.

One such indicator, shown in Table 7 (column 6), is that developed at the Overseas Development Council, Washington.[8] First a Physical Quality of Life Index sums up elementary physical well-being at a given time as defined by three key measures — infant mortality, life expectancy and adult literacy. All these rates are reduced to index form, the first two by taking the worst performance in 1950 and the expected best in year 2000 as defining a scale from 0 to 100 — i.e. 229 per 1000 (in Gabon) and 7 per 1000; and 38 years (in Guinea-Bissau) and 77 years respectively. The Table shows that large group averages for a PQL Index vary from 46 to 97, though individual countries show a much wider range than this. A second indicator — a Disparity Reduction Rate (DRR) also developed at ODC — measures the mean annual rate, since 1960, at which a country's level of achievement in the PQL Index has been rising towards 100.

Over the last ten years the lowest income group's DRR has probably fallen to a low level. The second lowest group, whose military spending has often been in excess of its education budget, also showed a low rate of improvement in DRR, even in the 60s. A good deal of evidence suggests that developing countries generally have for some time been advancing rather more slowly than those ranked as highly developed, although several exceptions do exist.

We have always to remember, however, that many statistical data in this entire field are provisional and fraught with problems. Nevertheless, one general conclusion from the evidence is that overall economic growth is necessary up to a certain level of well-being but that in practice there is often rather little correspondence between a rising production of goods and an advance in physical welfare.

This conclusion can best be summed up by setting out some social and economic data for individual countries. In Table 8 four groups of countries are arranged in order of column 4 — average income as reflected by GNP per head in 1982. Some figures are provisional and many are subject to possible revision.[9]

For comparison, the corresponding long-term Disparity Reduction Rates among these countries have varied between 0.6 (Mali), 1.4 (India), 2.3 (Colombia), 2.7 (Sri Lanka) and 4.0 (United States). Some have probably tended to slacken from the late 70s on.

A World of Interdependence

The creation of the UN organization implied at last a recognition of world interdependence. But its charter was founded on an interdependence between sovereign entities — nation-states — which are not effectively constrained by any code of law or duty. To the ministers of such

TABLE 8

Variations in Physical Well-being in Selected Countries at Different Levels of GNP per Head[a]

(Countries arranged in increasing order of col. 4)

Country	Population in millions (1984)	Growth rate of population (% per year)	GNP ($ per head) (1982)	Military spending index (1980)	Infant mortality (per '000 live births)	Life expectancy at birth	Adult literacy (%)	Physical Quality of Life Index
1	2	3	4	5	6	7	8	9
Mali	8	2.4	180	0.67	152	45	10	27
India	746	2.0	260	0.86	121	52	36	46
China (P.R.)	1034	1.3	310	1.64	71	67	69	75
Sri Lanka	16	1.4	320	0.37	43	69	86	85
Nigeria	88	3.2	860	0.77	133	49	34	41
Colombia	28	2.1	1460	0.50	56	63	81	77
Brazil	134	2.3	2240	0.21	75	64	76	74
S. Africa	32	2.5	2670	0.79	94	63	65	68
Iraq	15	3.4	3020[b]	2.31	76	57	26	51
USSR	274	1.0	6350	2.12	28	72	100	94
UK	57	0.1	9660	0.97	11	74	99	96
USA	236	0.7	13,160	1.11	11	75	99	97
Sweden	8	0.0	14,040	0.34	7	77	100	99

[a]For sources see items 7 and 9 in the Technical Notes to this Chapter.
[b]Refers to 1980.

states interdependence remains an academic concept. To them the world is
a ruthless competitive system, an economic market-place or a political
arena. Such restraint as does occur is inspired by fear of destruction and
anarchy rather than by any sensing of gains from interdependence. Only
within the UN system does co-operative planning sometimes offer a basis
for common action and even then it must be confined mainly within the
conventional limits of existing economic assumptions.

Under the pressure of events this situation is gradually changing. If we
accept an analogy between the interacting citizens of a nation-state,
co-operating for the common good in a division of labour under a code of
rights and duties, and the competing states of a *de facto* world community,
we see clearly what is implied by world environment, by interdependence,
by a loosely framed common code of law for mutual advantage.

These ideas are slowly being forced on the international community by
way of new computer modelling investigations, covering the main world
parameters of input, output and need, that have only now become
possible. Most of these have been carried out between 1972 and 1980,
sponsored either within the United Nations family or through the efforts of
uncommitted groups.[10]

Although founded on many different methods and aims, these global
studies strongly reinforce various new UN programmes discussed in later
chapters since they grapple with interrelations of such key questions as:

— stabilizing population growth;
— international monetary order;
— development financing through a world taxation system;
— an international division of labour;
— food production and distribution;
— rational use of energy and mineral resources;
— control of transnational enterprises;
— arms reduction;
— the human environment;
— management of ocean resources.

Since one can discern at least two main stages still to be gone through
before a unifying code of basic rights and duties for the world citizen can
become effective, let us look at these in turn. First a 'minimum floor' of
elementary well-being must be allowed to spread throughout the world.
Secondly, the existing world framework must be modified so as to secure a
reasonably stable monetary system, a loose international division of labour
and a confining of economic growth in a pattern compatible with the
world's external environment and its assets of common interest.

Anyone who has been close to these problems for many years will know
that 'development' is a long-range objective. Just as Leonardo da Vinci
could conceive a flying machine in the sixteenth century without there

being the slightest chance of building one for centuries to come, so development remains a slow process of interaction that cannot easily be short-circuited. Moreover, development is not necessarily synonymous everywhere with western ideas of consumerist gadgetry. In the RIO report on Reshaping the International Order (1976) it has been concluded that a development aim for the poorest countries of Africa and Asia in the twenty years to the end of this century would be a life-expectancy of 65 years, an infant mortality rate of 50 per thousand and a literacy rate of 75 per cent. From the work of the Overseas Development Council it can be shown that this implies a Physical Quality of Life Index of 77 by the year 2000 for all the countries involved — an objective needing a Disparity Reduction Rate for a country such as Mali of no less than 6.4 per cent per year!

Achieving primary development, we have seen, is first of all a question of reducing excessive population growth. Empirical research by II. Brown (1976) shows that it is precisely when a country's PQL Index reaches 70 or just above that birth rates in the developing world begin to fall rapidly with higher income, so that the real process of human development is then coming within reach.

The second major shift in attitudes — that towards a modified world framework — is perhaps just becoming visible on the horizon. It is largely a response to prospects opened by new simulation studies carried out through worldwide computer modelling.

Table 9 and also Figure 7 show a rough breakdown of world trade by value.[11]

This pattern of trade, totalling some 1309 billion US dollars in all in 1978, is supplemented by aid and credits from developed to developing countries, but even so it is nowhere near an optimal world interchange, as can be seen from Figure 7. A very large part of it simply represents transfers between subsidiaries of multinational corporations. Transfers between developing countries in particular ought to be far greater, and moving ahead more swiftly, if their economies are to become self-reliant.

Two concepts of truly Wellsian proportions — a world taxation system and an optimal international division of labour — are part of the radical re-thinking now under way. The first would work through a low tax on every country, levied proportionately as a percentage of national GDP, arms spending, trade or some other criterion. One of the constraints holding back useful development is lack of capital and such a tax could serve to even up any imbalance in the harnessing of resources, environmental protection, food production in developing areas, and so on.

Study of a world optimum in the division of labour also embraces this idea of capital transfers. It investigates, among other things, what transfers of capital would ideally be needed between regions to equalize their labour efficiency in producing goods with low transport costs. A recent study under the auspices of the International Labour Office[12] has shown that this

TABLE 9
Approximate Composition of World Trade by Value — 1970–78 (Percentages)[a]

From: \ To:	Developed market economies	All developing market economies	Centrally planned economies	World
Developed market economies				
1970	77	19	4	72
1978[b]	71	24	5	67
OPEC				
1970	80	18	2	6
1978[b]	76	22	2	11
Non-OPEC developing market economies				
1970	71	21	8	12
1978[b]	68	25	7	12
Centrally planned economies				
1970	24	16	60	11
1978[b]	27	17	56	10
World				
1970	69	18	10	100
1978[b]	67	23	10	100

[a]Percentages do not always total precisely 100 owing to small residual differences, and rounding off.
[b]Figures for 1978 rounded off and reprinted from John W. Sewell and the staff of the Overseas Development Council, *The United States and World Development: Agenda 1980* (New York: Praeger Publishers, 1980).

would in theory imply transfers totalling some 400 billion US dollars (1975 prices). That figure is probably an under-statement, but is certainly enormous. It amounts to about 46 per cent of the total value of world trade in 1975. But what is perhaps more pertinent is that the figure is about 6.5 per cent of world GNP in the same year — near the amount now set aside annually for arms production and military spending!

Notes

1. This Table is based on data in the Report on the World Social Situation 1978 (United Nations, New York, 1979) and other United Nations information.
2. The data have been collated from various Tables in *The World Social Situation 1978* (United Nations, New York, 1979).
3. The main reasons why market theory cannot work today are, first, that free competition now produces only indiscriminate growth with adverse side effects, and also leads to the triumph of a few giants, thus changing the rules of the game in their favour. In the process of stimulating ever-new markets to avoid saturation, an unappeasable fever of mass-expectation is created which leads to endemic price inflation.
4. In other words, percentage shares of income accruing to the poorest 20 per cent of the population in the poorest countries are fairly similar to those of the same group in high-income countries. It is the top 20 per cent of population who receive rather more in

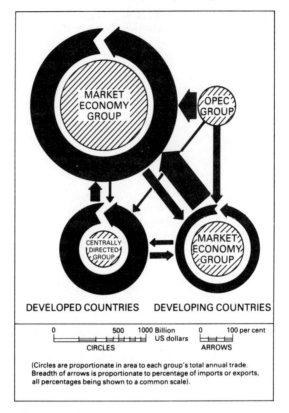

FIG. 7. Trade Flows within and between Major World Economic Groups (1978). (See
also Table 9.)

the poor countries. Income inequality appears to be most marked of all in the
middle-income developing countries.

5. Production and consumption data have been re-arranged and re-calculated in terms of
    coal equivalent from information contained in the World Development Report 1979
    (The World Bank; Washington DC, August 1979).

6. The data on exploitable fuel reserves and hydro-electric resources contained in this
    Table have been re-arranged and partially re-calculated from information for the
    countries of the world compiled in common form for the World Energy Conference
    Survey of Energy Resources 1974 (published by the US National Committee of the
    World Energy Conference, New York and available from the WEC Central Office,
    London).

7. The Overseas Development Council, Washington DC, in its annual publication *The
    United States and World Development* (issued by Praeger Publishers, New York,
    London, etc.) has gathered together a wide range of basic demographic and economic
    data and estimates, based on various United Nations and other reputable sources, for
    nearly all independent entities of the world. Data in Table 7 are based on selected group
    totals from Table E1, as re-arranged from the 1985 issue (Agenda 1985–86). A new
    indicator originally developed at ODC by M. D. Morris and J. D. Grant is shown in
    column 6 of Table 7 and a second is referred to in the text.

8. As described in *The United States and World Development: Agenda 1979* (*op. cit.*, see
    Note 7) and developed under the direction of M. D. Morris and J. P. Grant.

9. Sources and methods are as for Table 7, and are detailed in Note 7 above except for column 5, which is calculated, as described for Table 7 in text, from data on arms and public education expenditure in R. L. Sivard, 1983 (Tables II and III).

10. Examples are *Mankind at the Turning Point: The Second Report to the Club of Rome* by M. Mesarovic and E. Pestel (Dutton, New York, 1974); *RIO: Reshaping the International Order. A Report to the Club of Rome* (Co-ordinator J. Tinbergen and published by Dutton, 1976); *The Future of the World Economy*, by W. Leontief and others (United Nations publication, New York, 1976); and *Catastrophe or New Society? A Latin American World Model*, by A. O. Herrera and others (International Development Research Centre, Ottawa, 1976). The methods and assumptions of all these analyses are different and they are quite distinct also from studies like the first Brandt Commission report, issued in February 1980.

11. This Table presents a much-simplified outline, in percentage terms, of data on the world destination of exports compiled mainly from the UN Monthly Bulletin of Statistics and set out in the ODC publication referred to in Notes 7 and 8 above.

12. *The Optimal International Division of Labour*, by Bohuslav Hermann, a computer modelling investigation on a world scale which assumes that employment is to be maximized for the world at large (International Labour Office, Geneva, 1975).

4

The Human Dimension

If we wish to look at prospects for a world united by a self-interest in peaceful development then the qualities of the human animal, realized or realizable, must be central to our quest. It is in this sense that the present chapter sets out to probe the human dimension. In that dimension we include neither the global habitat of mankind nor its natural resources; nor yet man's social, economic or political systems, as such. What is in question is the combined human and animal propensities of *Homo sapiens* and their further potential for development in a world frame. In practice, however, socio-economic and political arrangements *cannot* be excluded from any human balance-sheet; for today they influence what beliefs men hold in common and the form of a society's perceived reality at a given time. They also shape the channels through which everyday motives are directed, as well as going far to define what is felt to be normal or abnormal behaviour in a given setting. All this, and a good deal more, gives to a community a special tone that is virtually unconscious to its individual citizens, since it may bear little relation to any professed ideology of the day.

In whatever mix human nature is genetically transmitted or socially moulded, those manifestations of humanness we find around us may be extended or inhibited also as they confront new life-situations or new possibilities. Because any such changes may in turn affect the social milieu and its development conditions, our total habitat is forever making social man anew, while creating fresh horizons for new citizens to confront.

It is common knowledge that human beings are too often frustrated in their efforts to move towards desired goals. From what has been said it would seem that we could begin this chapter by looking first at some confusing differences of view in trying to account for the sources of humanness itself, and then go on to investigate how or why modern societies are so often obstructed in giving effect to their desires. It may be salutary too to reflect on what all this might mean for the longer-term human perspective. Roughly, then, these remarks bring us back to the many facets of a two-sided question posed at the end of Chapter 1: How self-actualizing a human being can a society support? and, How self-actualizing a society can human nature support?

Contrasting Views about Man's Nature

It is remarkable that sound principles of the good life were already worked out by Iron Age man some 2500 years ago.* Ideas as to man's nature and the way to good living have been reformulated several times since then; but at the dawn of the Industrial Revolution, some two centuries ago, what were thought to be the conditions for social progress were finally laid down with much assurance by Adam Smith, Jeremy Bentham, Thomas Jefferson and others. So certain were those eighteenth-century views of man and society and so reinforcing the later apparent support received from Darwin and Spencer — backing as it did the experience of landowners and capitalists in an expansionary age — that those same eighteenth-century rules for man, society and economy have remained an unconscious bastion of Western theory and practice in our own grotesquely changed world of today. It is true that since Darwin's time a flowering of new sciences like genetics, neurology and anthropology have broadened the scientific vision, but not with sufficient force to oust a dual view of mind and nature that stems from the seventeenth-century concepts of René Descartes and the static rationalism of the Enlightenment. It is thus that we retain to this day, both in science and in much popular thinking, some widely contrasting views about the nature of man and the conditions in which his social ideals are best expressed. The fact that we still lack any full understanding of mental processes compounds this confusion, so that for the present purpose it will not come amiss if we try to sort out some of the contrasting positions now extant.

Aided by several extensions, such as systems theory, twentieth-century psychology has produced many models of man, most of them incomplete. The fact is that we cannot yet bridge the cardinal gaps in self-knowledge. What we can do is frame a working hypothesis that tries to remove at least some of the incongruities from surviving strata of thinking that do not go easily together — such as those which spring from cartesian dualism, strict behaviourism or Freudian theory, concepts of economic man or an over-simple deterministic view.

Martin Hollis, a philosopher, has reduced some contrasts underlying different views about man to two extreme models, which he names Plastic Man and Autonomous Man respectively (M. Hollis, 1977). Reduced to the simplest system form, these models are portrayed in Figure 8 (A and B). Here we see individuals as examples of open systems reacting to their total environment and subject to feedback from the interplay of character and personal experience. Plastic Man is in this sense a programmed feedback system. With many different emphases he tends to emerge from present-day studies of group behaviour, while Autonomous Man (B) has a

*i.e. beginning in China, Ancient Greece and the Near East and involving a succession of prescient individuals ranging from Confucius to Jesus.

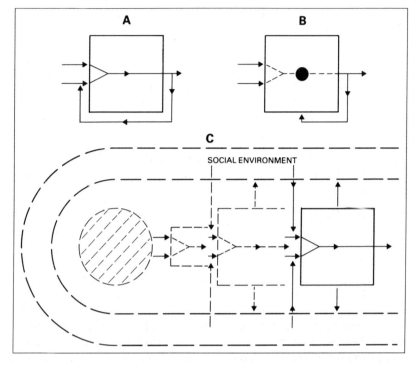

FIG. 8. Three Models of Man (Models A and B based on M. Hollis, 1977).

substantial self within, is more the creator of his social world, and most easily springs to mind when regarding a particular individual. The one is formed largely by adaptive response to the interplay of nature and nurture, while the other has an identity forged by personal choice as to what kind of person to become. While Plastic Man is a product of natural processes who can be steered by internalized law and science towards a humanly desired future, Autonomous Man bases the understanding of human society on "constant universal principles of human nature", so that man-made progress is to be furthered mainly by creating an environment which serves his true needs. On these two models, then, men and women can advance human potential mainly by family conditioning and education, or else mainly by creating a habitat congenial to man's propensities. A further model, which is shown in Figure 8 (C), sums up the standpoint about man's nature adopted in this present inquiry. It will be analysed a little later.

The two models discussed clearly encapsulate extreme but simplistic versions, if not caricatures, of the reality in our make-up. There is much more to be said about both, as well as intermediate positions to explore. Rooted in his day and his situation, Sigmund Freud's conception of man, for instance, seems near to that of Autonomous Man. To quote a perceptive reviewer in the *Spectator* of Freud's *Civilization and its Discontents* who is cited anonymously on the cover of the 1962 edition, this means that for Freud:

> Civilization is only made possible by individual renouncement. The instinctive life of man is one of aggression and egoistic self-satisfaction. The whole structure of culture has been designed to put prohibitions and curbs on him. The sense of guilt has become the maker of civilized humanity.

At the other pole strict behaviourism, because it denies that science can be pursued by any kind of introspection, equates the expression of personality with observable behaviour:

> The free inner man who is held responsible for the behaviour of the external biological organism is only a pre-scientific substitute for the kinds of causes which are discovered in the course of a scientific analysis. All these alternative causes lie outside the individual . . . These are the things which make the individual behave as he does. (B. F. Skinner, 1953.)

Looking more closely at the different views of man's nature that underlie some of the classics of social science, we find that they range quite clearly between the extremes of Autonomous and Plastic Man, as well as being associated with a similar range in the role accorded to culture and society as a determinant of personality. In Figure 9 I set out a few examples, taken from different disciplines, which suggest how far assumptions may vary.

It is high time to outline the particular model of man adopted here, as already summed up in Figure 8 (C). It follows unitary principles embracing such facts as that human emotions are linked to biochemistry through glandular action. The individual, however, is viewed not as a static specimen, but as an entity in a constant state of becoming. He or she comprises a unique assembly of transmitted propensities, moulded and modified by a unique sequence of developmental experiences.* Individual character, with its loves, hates and cruelty, is, in the words of Erich Fromm, ". . . the specific form in which human energy is shaped by the

---

*Central to this whole conception is a measurable and concretely established notion of personality that is also socially meaningful. To my knowledge the only theory that seems to fit this requirement is that stated by H. J. Eysenck in *The Biological Basis of Personality*, who outlines it as follows: "Anatomico-physiologico-neurological structures like the visceral brain and the reticular formation, the strength of whose functioning in responding to environmental stimulation is largely determined by heredity, give rise to stronger or weaker autonomic reactions, and to greater or less arousal; these emotional and arousal reactions, according to their strength, determine the habitual behaviour pattern of the individual — and this habitual behaviour pattern is what we call 'personality' — and measure in detail as extraversion–introversion, or neuroticism–stability." (H. J. Eysenck, 1972). Much has been built on this formulation to bridge the gap between experimental and social psychology.

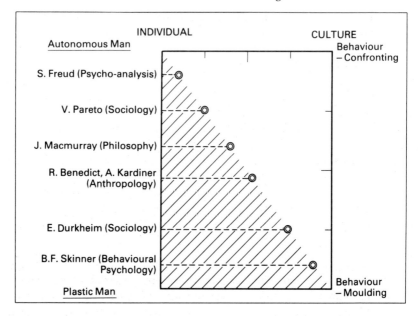

FIG. 9. Different Conceptions of the Nature of Personality.

dynamic adaptation of human needs to the particular mode of existence of a given society." (E. Fromm, 1942). *Homo sapiens* is thus self-defining, but he is always a social animal not just from choice, but of necessity. Human uniqueness, and its further development as embodied in language, knowledge, reasoning, culture and ethical ideas plus a sense of personal identity, all rely on membership of an organized social order. That social order, in turn, responds to the composite effect of the interacting inputs of its members.

Society as a Human Problem

Of all the myths that bedevil modern man one of the most beguiling is the myth that he now has the power to create a social order that matches his ideals. Probing more deeply into this proposition should lead us into a major facet of our inquiry.

A first point to note is that human beings are ambiguous in several important respects. This ambiguity arises from the fact that *Homo sapiens* is a somewhat vulnerable but self-aggressing member of the animal kingdom as well as a reasoning and sometimes a reasonable being, conscious of past and future and so of his own objectives. In the first role he has traditionally been in conflict with ignorance and the forces of nature but now increasingly he struggles with other men and women, and with himself. In both roles man is a social animal but as a self-conscious being another sort of ambiguity arises. For in society men seek togetherness and crave the love, esteem and recognition of others. But this craving for other-regard is only one side of the coin since the individual is also conscious that to the end of his life he is fearfully alone in a void of meaning. In the industrial world this aloneness has been much accentuated over the last hundred years by the atomistic philosophy and practice of market society, with its theory of individual competition and its roles of seller of labour and performer of specialized tasks in a complex but haphazard system of production and sale. Since 1950 there has, too, been a rapid disintegration of the old extended family group, accompanied by a falling away of some accepted consensual bonds of social control. But it is still true that part of the turbulent inner being of man chafes at the growing constraints of a social order, a fact much stressed earlier on by Sigmund Freud:

> . . . every individual is virtually an enemy of civilization, though civilization is supposed to be an object of universal human interest. It is remarkable that, little as men are able to exist in isolation, they should nevertheless feel as a heavy burden the sacrifices which civilization expects of them in order to make a communal life possible. Thus civilization has to be defended against the individual, and its regulations, institutions and commands are directed to that task. (S. Freud, 1928, rev. ed. 1962).

How wide-ranging in practice is the ambiguous side of man's nature can be seen from the reflection that modern *Homo sapiens* as an individual is at once:

Socially realized	yet	forever alone;
a libertarian	yet	authority-accepting;
freedom-loving	yet	certainty-craving;
science-creating	yet	prey to irrationality;
locality-rooted	yet	impelling constant change;
ideal-seeking	yet	greedy and grasping;
caring and nurturing	yet	humanly aggressive and cruel;
an internalizer of shared values	yet	self-assertive;
self-actualizing	yet	the slave of convention and tradition;
moved by conscience	yet	selfishly deceitful.

Looking down either side of this list one gets some idea of the range of human character in our species. Yet it would be too simple to believe that this variance, with all its consequences, is simply due to a chafing of natural man and woman against irksome social constraints. Today the truth appears to be somewhat more subtle: namely that certain mechanisms, within our social systems set up to encompass the vagaries of human nature, have acquired a momentum of their own. In the absence of any effective brakes or steering, some of these mechanisms are impelling the frames of our national communities, and thus our emergent world community also, in a direction opposed to that signalled by the all-too-weak call of human reason or conscience, and perhaps towards a cataclysmic resolution of present trends. What we have to examine here, probably for the first time, is how these mechanisms work.

Moving towards this aim, one should first try to understand what is involved for human beings when they seek either a consensus or a collective goal. Vilfredo Pareto, an economist and engineer but himself quite evidently the slave of some arbitrary preconceptions, has tried, in one of the less-read classics of social science, to unravel what is meant by logical and non-logical action in human affairs (V. Pareto, 1935). He sees aims as logical only if human conceptions of the consequences of actions — that is, of the causal links between means and ends — correspond to reality. Because man is fallible and his science still very incomplete, this can rarely be the case. But the necessarily non-logical (not illogical) character of most human thinking and behaviour can disclose an order, a kind of natural logic, in the structure of what is largely non-rational action in politics and social life. That order is marked by the existence of various contrasting sentiments or propensities (the 'residues' and 'derivations' of Pareto) including those which make for innovative combination and persistent conservatism.

Let us consider something more concrete — the difficulties or limitations human beings face, even today, that arise out of themselves and their nature, if they wish to give effect to economically or socially desired acts or policies (Table 10). These are hazards that may remain *after* agreement has been reached or at least substantial opposition avoided.

By simply listing these familiar sources of failing shown in Table 10, it is easy to see how vulnerable are the judgements and decisions we make, even in normal circumstances and when acting from the highest motives, leaving aside the fact that a large proportion of our ideas are not, as we assume, original, but are absorbed ready-made from our community. In framing the above list no account is taken of states of emergency which, in many unstable developing countries in particular, represent normality. Neither do we include the effects of a milder equivalent found in some advanced market democracies such as Britain — legitimized blackmail of public services and their users.

There are some further points. Note first that errors made by individuals may affect not merely themselves, but others with whom they interact. Equally, some sources of error have a cumulative effect, undermining confidence or lowering the threshold of slackness or dishonesty. If a good deal of invalid decision-making arises from ignorance of one kind or

TABLE 10
Some Common Sources of Error or Limitation
Affecting Thought or Action

Individual Influences
- Lack of knowledge or resources
- Rationalisation of true reasons
- Unconscious distortion of motive
- Effect of 'social unconscious' in inhibiting awareness of dubious practices

Collective Influences (Planners or Policy-makers)
- Lack of knowledge or technique
- Lack of essential data
- Ignorance of significant interrelations of phenomena
- Excessive effect of current situation
- Need for deflecting compromises

Institutional Influences (Individual or Collective)
(a) *Market Economy Influences*
- Legalized commercial deceit
- Legalized concealment of relevant facts
- Lack of knowledge of alternatives
- Manipulation of opinion or desire

(b) *Political or Administrative Influences*
- Deception
- Nepotism
- Other forms of partiality
- Corruption
- Suppression of information
- Bureaucratic self-interest

Overt Criminal Behaviour
(Not here distinguished)

---

another, a great deal stems from the pursuit of individual greed, from a lust for power or its retention, from adherence to beliefs for which there is no evidence, or from aggressiveness against out-groups. All in all, it is no surprise that states find such difficulty in moving in any discernible direction, much less in one which bears any resemblance to their professed collective aims.

National Systems and Their Channels of Motivation

Study of communities at different stages of development suggests that even at its simplest level a state, or in fact any self-governing entity, must embody at least five kinds of system each with an essential function, whether that function be to socialize and educate each generation; to contain and regulate the behaviour of citizens within acceptable limits; to meet common needs and individual wants for goods and services; to provide a hierarchy of government, administration and law; or to furnish a common tissue of beliefs and intercourse. In any modern state there must be other networks or systems, e.g. for sifting new knowledge, pursuing original research and communicating information throughout the organs of society. Adapting a grouping proposed by Barbu (Z. Barbu, 1971) the most elemental systems in a society must comprise the following types:

Communication — including language and other modes of inter-action.
Power and authority — including government, administration and law.
Economic system — including production and distribution of needs and
    wants.
Socialization — including indoctrination and education of young in
    accepted modes of life.
Consensual system — maintenance of common beliefs and ritual.

Although we have come to classify the world's national states as developed, developing or among the least developed, there is in fact no such thing as a developed state so far. Anyone familiar with international problems at first hand will know that, even by normal criteria, some states considered pre-eminent in the development stakes may have sectors that are less advanced than the corresponding services in a developing country. To take one simple example that was certainly true up to a few years ago, stream-flow records and research covering the river systems of Yugoslavia have been far more detailed and complete than the corresponding hydrological data for the United Kingdom. If the advanced states are *relatively* ahead of the field on some criteria, their overall levels of life remain far from offering models for the rest to copy.

In the light of such considerations one may try to devise a realistic outline framework for comparing the world's nation-states in human terms, such a frame being illustrated in Table 11. What emerges, when the details are filled in, is a simple profile that may help to distinguish areas of stress and others marked by continuing improvement. When the respective profiles for, say, El Salvador, Pakistan and Switzerland are compared, contrasts in any of the seven sectors of the Table will go a good way towards illustrating how nations differ in their development prospects. The extent to which these major sectors are related to or influence one another is brought out in Figure 10.

Table 11 and Figure 10 can be interpreted in different ways. For our immediate purpose they help to pin-point where and how human motivations are or can be either stirred up and expressed, or remain dormant in a social setting, so that it is worthwhile to pursue the question as it impinges on the individual citizen.

We are on fairly safe ground in starting off from the latter or negative side with the *Principle of Least Effort* (G. K. Zipf, 1949), even though some deductions from Zipf's evidence have been disputed. To explain the principle I prefer to use a metaphor and liken much human behaviour, when not otherwise strongly motivated, to that of water precipitated on a sloping land surface of varying porosity and hardness (resistance). We see

TABLE 11
Profile of a State System in Terms of Its Human Variables

A. *Physical Environment*
Geographical Position (latitude and longitude)
Climate (average temperature, Jan. and July)
Possessing access to sea or landlocked?
Is government environment-conscious?

B. *Demographic Position*
Population: (50,000 and under 5 million; 5–500 million; over 500 million)
Annual rate of increase (%)
Age composition; population under 15; or 65 and over (%s)
Population density (inhabitants per km²)
Urban population (%)
Infant mortality (per '000)
Average life expectancy (years)

C. *Governmental and Political System*
Type of government (highly personal or military; multi-party; centrally directed system)?
Political situation (stable or turbulent?)
Information system (free or controlled)?

D. *International Position*
Government policy (dominated by foreign government, independent or neutral)?
Economy (dominated by transnational corporations or independent)?
Foreign indebtedness (% of GNP)
Arms expenditure (% of GNP)
Is there a strong nationalist feeling (against one or more foreign states)?
Is the country occupied, in any sense, by foreign troops?

E. *Economic System*
Gross national product per inhabitant (£)
Annual rate of increase of GNP (%)
Imports and exports as % of GNP (per year)
Gross income received by top 20%; and by bottom 40% (%s)
Unemployed (as % of labour force)
Natural resources adequate or negligible (for energy; agricultural land; minerals)?

F. *Social Situation*
Is there a social security system for all?
Is there an old age pension for all?
Adult literacy (%)
Secondary school enrolment (%)
Crime rates (murder and robbery) (per '000)
Is there an established authoritarian religion? (75% membership or more)

G. *Human Rights Situation*
How many of the two basic UN Covenants and other UN Conventions have been acceded to?
Have large-scale violations (e.g. torture) been alleged or examined recently?
Is there a refugee problem (emigrants or immigrants)?

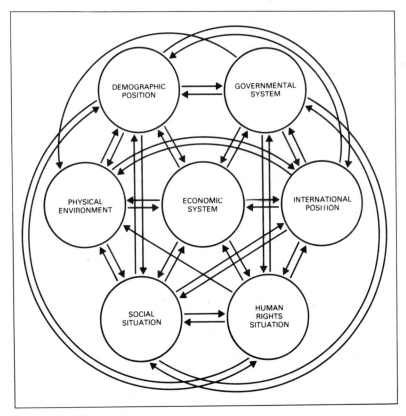

FIG. 10. Some Interrelations between Elements of a State System.

the results of such activity all around us in the eroded landscapes and river valleys sculpted in recent geological time. Aided by other eroding agents the water has taken a line of least effort, cutting its valley networks and creating an undulating terrain that is the precise outcome of following a line of least resistance. That the same course is characteristic of modern man can be noted by observing all sorts of everyday behaviour in the street — how, for example, a deviation from a constructed footpath will quickly appear if it does not accord with the short cut sanctioned by experience. The sinuosity of developed road systems in a lowland clay landscape likewise records the history of collective experience in overcoming obstacles to easy progress. There are many other observable signs of the same principle at work throughout society. One of the easiest to watch is that afforded by the behaviour of many motorists in crossing the central line at a corner so as to ease their passage, despite the all-too-evident risk in so doing.

A law of least effort operates most clearly in the short term and where other extreme motivation is at rest. But much of the time human beings *are* significantly motivated, particularly in the longer term and in the mass, especially in industrialized states. They are forced by the uncertainties of daily life to seek personal security and they are constantly egged on to pursue commercial self-interest and to acquire wealth, status and far more possessions than a prudent use of income would prescribe. To stimulate this process goods are not only intensively advertised but are made to wear out quickly and packed for sale in multiples, while artificial credit is provided to inflame still further the whipped-up competitive urge. For the dynamic and the privileged such motivations to power and wealth through competition are everywhere very strong. It is not surprising that the results achieved fully confirm the hierarchical nature of mankind in all forms of society. Another deep-seated motivation is suspicion or hatred of alien or distinctive out-groups. Unlike most other animals men fight or distrust other men as forcefully as they fight the forces of nature — a characteristic that has been much extended by technological progress. Finally, social beings are easily swayed by irrational creeds and arguments to follow courses of action that are not only against the best interests of their community but equally against their own common sense. Rationality ever faces an uphill fight.

The Human Factor in Change or Inertia

Such manifestations of humanness are all too familiar in today's industrial societies. What is not so obvious is the way in which overall change and development take place through the interplay of these impulsions in daily life. This question justifies our giving some attention to a familiar but little-analysed phenomenon — the logic of the situation (Figure 11).

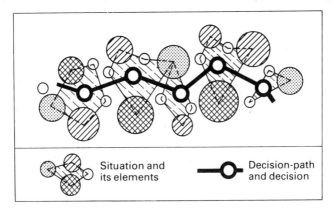

FIG. 11. Decision-path Determined by the Logic of the Situation.

Consider how individuals become aware of important facts and interact with neighbours, relatives, colleagues at work, fellow-members of organizations and so on in a constant sequence of situations, face-to-face or 'invisible'. Apart from personal conflicts, a new law may be enacted, the economic climate may change, new chances of advancement or new needs for retrenchment may present themselves. The life-path of every citizen is worked out from the interplay of informed judgements and choices of direction suggested or imposed by the logic of an ever-evolving situation. This, in fact, is the immediate source or determinant of socio-economic change at the grass-roots level of an industrial society. In simpler communities these life-paths will at most be much less fluid and determinable by choice and they may largely be bound up with survival or fatalistic acceptance. In simpler environments changes in family composition will loom larger than, say, career prospects; while the information available for making a choice may be minimal and grotesquely slanted by corruption, tradition or censorship.

If at this personal level the outcome of configurations of events and judgements in innumerable situations is the immediate source of economic and social change, it is clear that in its entirety the whole process has also to be seen as operating at higher levels of abstraction. At the level of government, for example, changes which affect the individual — such as those in laws or prices — may be introduced in response to opportunities stemming from new knowledge or techniques, international pressures or a need to placate voters. At both levels, it should be noted, people are not free to act spontaneously or even to watch every nuance of change. Individuals have largely to take the line of least resistance as determined by performance in a given role such as a job or career. In large measure the same applies to governments if they are not guided by any overall plan or scheme of priorities.

This brings us to the third and most dynamic level in man-made determinants of change, and one which overlies and largely determines the other two, at any rate in the richer economies. This is a constant search for gain from the exploitation of new discoveries in science and technology. Overall there is commonly one main outcome from this search — a fairly constant rise in productivity per unit of labour input. From time to time humanly beneficial discoveries are also made — new materials, products and techniques being developed which, although they may later produce unexpected upheavals in social arrangements, are free from deleterious side-effects. Rather more likely, however, are applications which attract irreversible capital investment before their health risks or other hazards come to light. While free science will get most popular blame for any such outcome, there are at least two reasons why this view is misplaced. First, commercial exploitation has no aim and no need to justify itself other than in terms of return on capital outlay. For this reason the outcome of technical advance can as easily be malignant as benign. Possibly as much as one-quarter of an economy's total output has no useful or even rational reason to exist. Already in 1975 the world's leading spokesmen for science, meeting in Geneva, issued a call to review all fundamentally new science and technology on human rights grounds, with a view to considering possible control of exploitation where dangers exist. Not surprisingly, this call went unheeded.

A second reason for not blaming free science is that much of it is no longer free. Today, the eccentric lone researcher of the last century is increasingly teamed up to serve goals of commercial or military advantage. This is why something approaching half the world's scientific and engineering manpower is now harnessed to arms-related industries. On both the above grounds we can thus reach a doleful if tentative conclusion. In a modern market economy, above all, any spontaneous contest between humane values and anti-human pressures is weighted rather heavily in favour of the latter. Ultimately this is because for governments freedom — which really means business freedom — spells employment, full pay and happy voters.

We have not yet exhausted this discussion of change in human affairs. But first let us hasten to correct any misapprehensions about the *ease* of change by looking at a human factor that has had little if any attention, but which acts to *prevent* socio-economic change (i.e. reform), often where it is most needed. I here refer to the very basic and widespread existence of what I shall call *channels of inertial motivation* in advanced economic societies. What are these channels? In essence they are closely circumscribed roles occupied by individuals whose functions are mainly representative or executive and whose success in pursuing the official and personal incentives of their careers depends on an uncritical acceptance of the *status quo*.

These channels of inertial motivation are perhaps especially visible among individuals filling such functions as the following, and particularly those free from any periodic check (e.g. groups three and five):

— National Government (cabinet minister, etc.).
— Local Government (councillor, etc.).
— Trade Unions (general secretary, etc.).
— Business (senior executive, etc.).
— Military Establishment (arms planner, etc.).

Among occupations of this type the 'logic of the situation' is dominated above all by two main factors: a strong vested interest in the values of the role, and their survival; and a constant flow of decision-making pressures which ensure whole-hearted performance. If each role determines both its primary aim and its secondary intrinsic interest, the various pressures of performance reinforce both. The machine is thus an inbuilt system of

interlocking momentum which is now so complex as to defy any but
long-term and forceful dismantling. Behind this self-perpetuating structure
lie two more basic facts. First comes the natural inertia of habit-forming
humans in a work-situation; and second the virtual irreversibility of most
decisions which posit an ever-growing time-scale of capital construction.
Note that any motivations *against* the public interest are as surely built into
this system as are its legitimate public aims. In either case radical change in
socio-economic institutions proves to be as difficult as technological
innovation is easy.

From this brief look at the question of change it is clear that the qualities
of human beings are closely involved with the processes behind change. In
contrast with the triumphs of scientific understanding we find that it is
extremely difficult in practice either to modify economic arrangements
within the state or to guide the application of new techniques in a way that
accords with humane values. This does not mean that changes do not
occur, but that both their origins and their effects are far more obscure
than we would like to believe. Although it is possible to probe the
constitution of distant galaxies or the ultimate nature of life with ever-
increasing confidence, a normal persona seems to lack enough self-
discipline to allow the freedom conferred by human powers to be realized
or even approached. Even as a biological urge, competitive self-assertion
seems likely to become obsolescent in under 50 years; but today this
impulsion remains so deeply ingrained by history as to pose a grave hazard
to man's future.

Looking at prospects for a future world order it thus behoves us to be
clear about how changes in institutions and socio-economic arrangements
do occur, and when we attempt this we arrive at the following main or
possible sources of such change;

1. Those brought about by alterations in the natural environment.
2. Those consequent on the unforeseen interaction of social or
   demographic trends.
3. Those arising from the incidental interplay of economic trends.
4. Those due to the intended consequences of scientific or technical
   discovery.
5. Those due to deliberate socio-economic policy or planning.
6. Those arising from unforeseen interactions between any of the
   foregoing.

We can illustrate these categories of change by noting first that those due
to natural environment can be wide-ranging or even decisive. They may
include such effects as encroachment of the sea, land erosion or
impoverishment, deforestation, climatic change, extinction of key species
— the last two due respectively to natural or artificial changes in the upper
atmosphere or to an upsetting of biotic systems. As a simple example of the

second group we may cite the effects of changes in child-rearing practices, as propounded in the early 1950s. Unplanned economic consequences may be illustrated by the policy of trying to sell more cars or to push cigarette smoking to boost revenue and employment, while simultaneously struggling to cope with rising medical and accident costs. By contrast we can count a so-called 'micro-chip revolution' and organ transplants as among the group of *intended* technical innovations, even though the former was also mainly a commercial promotion. Under the head of deliberate socio-economic policy or planning we have to distinguish between decisions imposed by a dictator or a small all-powerful clique; and true plans or projections — for instance those relating energy needs to output and population growth — that may be worked out by a continuing planning organ through co-operative discussion.

It has to be stressed that the sixth or last category of change — which is caused by an interaction between any of these different sorts of influence — is one that underlies all efforts at human understanding. This is because one overriding difficulty in implementing acceptable change in social arrangements is simply that the full complexities of human development are now too great to be encompassed properly within the planning process.

Human Qualities and Human Systems — The Two-way Interaction

Despite much scattered idealism and much utopian thinking it has to be recognized that human affairs will continue to be marked by tension, conflict, muddle and inadequacy. Mixed motives, too, cannot be eliminated from human conduct — a fact that all planning should seek to allow for. We have to assume that the statistical spread of key human traits, as well as abilities, follows a normal or bell-shaped curve of distribution. But how far do our basic systems themselves *reinforce* or inflame this fact of ambiguity? It is this question that has next to be explored.

Which of our modern systems should we then study? Many would argue that the patent incredibility of the present nuclear arms race, based as it would seem to be on a provocative mass of hysterical nonsense produced by one side or the other in a welter of competitive self-aggrandizement, offers a suitable case for treatment. But these perilous excesses, although largely economic in origin, are not quite common to all states, whereas the economic system is. We shall therefore start by looking at the foundations of the latter and then go on to consider how our political-economy set-up has evolved to its present stage, a main purpose being to see how far it is working to modify the balance between acquisitive and ideal-seeking qualities among its participating members.

Foundations of Economic Life

Any national economy has within its borders three sorts of resource from which to generate all its wealth and all its income: first, the natural resources of climate, geographical position, soil, forests, mineral ores, energy reserves, etc., known to the economist as *Land*: next, those other man-made resources built up by an application of inanimate energy and human skill — houses, factories, hospitals, power plants, libraries, schools, water and sewage systems, roads, airports, etc., all grouped together as *Capital*; and, finally, a body of human aptitudes, effort and experience in producing, organizing and manipulating these things known as *Labour*.

Rising for the moment above special interests and ideology, this land and this capital have to be used as effectively as possible to support the total work-force, plus all its dependents, the retired and others who do not work, so as to provide a livelihood for each while meeting all needs for capital equipment and an acceptable level of common services. In addition to certain needs which must be satisfied, every individual has variable wants, the range of which will depend on a current field of expectation. This latter is defined by the community's knowledge (or belief) as to what are its achievable economic horizons at a given time. However, whatever the level of aspiration, overall want-satisfaction cannot for long exceed the sum of the effort that is successfully expended.

The economic and social basis of such a community is thus a division of labour which allows the totality of talents and resources to achieve a result that is cumulative, ongoing and far greater in combined utility and satisfaction than would be the sum of its parts. In other words, livelihood, learning, leisure to create and transmit are enjoyed by those who are at once the originators of the activity and the recipients of its bounties.

Such a thorough-going division of effort does not function by itself. At the level of modern society it requires first of all a highly complex web of signals, directives and information to guide and co-ordinate behaviour. The different sectors of productive activity must somehow obtain their required raw materials, equipment and the labour to produce. Their output must equally be geared to achieve the want-satisfaction sought by consumers, whether these be final consumers or other producers of a finished product. Government revenue must be raised and various public restraints or incentives secured.

Looked at in another way, the whole complex division of labour is an interlocking pattern of exchange: not merely the cross-frontier trade which turns to national advantage the diverse expertise, climate or resources of another country, but exchanges of labour by consumers in return for the right to purchase consumer goods; transfers between specialist producers; and exchanges between users of services and those who provide them. Not only do various institutions of economic life reflect the particular pattern of signals and exchanges that regulate every facet of economic behaviour, but the fabric of society itself is imprinted with that design. Money transactions afford the medium by which the whole exchange system of labour, goods and services is able to function. They also allow the right to consume wealth to be stored or postponed, allowing diversity of needs in time, and capital investment, to be accommodated into the system.

This modern economic machine has to be steered, or at least kept moving within socially acceptable bounds, by some means linked to the political apparatus of government and the law. The two extremes, in a wide range of solutions to this problem of the ordering of the socio-economic system, are, on the one hand, a completely decentralized pure market economy; and on the other a planned economy that is entirely directed from the centre. We recognize the first as the system outlined in the textbooks. It is self-generating in that it relies on the motive power of pure competition working supposedly in a *perfect market* — competition between single households as final consumers; between individuals in a free market for labour; and between many producers, to secure the factors of production and therewith to satisfy the demands of the consumer. This is an exchange system in which equilibrium is maintained between aggregate supply and aggregate demand by self-regulating signals given to the different categories of producer and consumer in the various markets for goods, labour and services by an impartial price mechanism. Prices and price changes are the signals in the market place which serve to keep supply and demand in a self-regulating state of balance. Resources, at least in theory, are automatically applied to their most effective use.

The opposite extreme is that of the centrally directed economy. A central planning organ of government works out the change of output required for each sector of activity to meet a co-ordinated series of plans and balances covering resources, labour and requirements. Inputs of materials, energy and labour per unit of output required are calculated in detail for each product from the previous performance level, with due allowance for advances in technique and productivity. Overall objectives and priorities are kept fully in mind so that the total supply of consumer goods, housing and services are adjusted to per capita needs as judged by central government in the light of capital investment needs, overall output priorities, rising standards of living and the accompanying social pressures of expectation. Within these limits a consumer market and a producer market for materials will serve as a means of allocation through choice, on the one hand by households and on the other by some managers of productive enterprises. Activating signals consist in the main of legally binding directives from a central planning organ to producers, plus return signals of plan fulfilment from each enterprise. Anonymous market signals serve to give indications of choice within the totality of products available for use. Finally, all resources belong to the state as the seat of popular will. The rate and direction of economic and social development are kept under review by regularly revised one-year, five-year and long-term perspective plans of increasing generality.

These extremes of the economic spectrum can thus be distinguished from one another by various criteria, since they differ on basic dimensions according as they are planned or unplanned; directed by a central authority or impelled by the free play of power and choice exercised through decentralized market forces; ordered by explicit directive and response or by automatic signals of the price mechanism; and governed by reference to overriding priorities or by mindless choice of the market-place.

Let it be said at once that neither of these extreme solutions can survive unchanged in an advanced economy of today. In a complex industrialized system, coexisting alongside others in an interdependent milieu, where information and markets are worldwide, it is no longer possible, in the first place, to insulate consumers in one country against knowledge of standards and expectations in another. This is a social fact militating against the survival of extreme solutions whether fully authoritarian or fully anarchic.

Pure competition for markets cannot long survive without controls to limit concentration of power by firms and individuals, while public allocations not made by the market would not be made at all. What *in theory* is the most efficient system in the economy of means it employs would in practice lead today to a society lacking either balance or justice.

An economy that is *centrally directed throughout* encounters problems of an opposite kind. While it can (if planning norms truly reflect a popular consensus) allocate scarce resources accurately between priority needs, the multilevel information system of signals required to achieve this becomes so impossibly complicated to run that the economy becomes cumbersome, rigid, over-bureaucratic and unable to respond quickly where change is required. What has happened in practice is that most national economies are ranged somewhere between these two extremes, incorporating varying degrees and types of planning procedure, varying degrees of central control and public ownership, and with varying reliance on market motivation.

Political Economy and Human Nature

Let us now take our mixed economy system as we know it in the real world of 1982 and trace what has happened to the original theory set out in 1776. First recall the two major good points of the system. If we can assume a perfect market of equal consumers, independent workers and separate producers each too small to influence prices, then the market system could maintain an equilibrium between supply and demand, with outputs, prices and requirements adjusting to one another by means of market signals. Resources, labour and capital would automatically be applied to greatest effect by the same 'invisible hand' of competition working in a free market.

Moreover, the philosophers who propounded this system also devised a minimal non-interventionist state framework to embrace it. Since individuals are (in theory) equal self-expressing units, a principle of universal suffrage was advocated simply to protect the governed against the governing. By the mid-nineteenth century this minimal view of economics and liberal democracy had (again in theory) been somewhat humanized, mainly through the work of J. S. Mill, to embrace the idea of men and women as active agents seeking to improve society, and themselves, through the medium of a democratic process.

And so we approach the essence of today's system in real-life human terms. First, for the initial opening-up of the world, in a limitless market and with expanding transport facilities, the original system was a valid medium, if one disregards the appalling human price. Indeed, the whole point is that the system can *only* function with continuous, non-selective *expansion* of markets and output. After its middle phase, from 1930 to 1950, during which J. M. Keynes discovered how to counter the immediate problem of falling demand, a post-war era of full employment and world re-expansion appeared to have vindicated the market system. In 1952, however, the first signs of a fundamental social change began to appear and some 4 years later this started to influence economic behaviour as well. The main trade unions were becoming large-scale monopolies, the expectations of workers under full employment, with massive advertising and credit, were being fanned to demand ever-higher public sector pay from docile Labour governments. These were the economic counterparts of an era of social permissiveness that has burgeoned since the early 1950s and which, among other things, has seen a massive decline in responsibility and respect for obligations and an upsurge of crime and indiscriminate terrorism. The economic indicator of a worldwide decline in market systems has been a steady rise in cost-push price inflation to endemic proportions and a slowing down of home-based capital investment. In Great Britain, in particular, inflation has had some well-defined causes. One major cause has been a gradual concentration of union power in the public sector and a forcing of excessive pay rises, accompanied by expansion of the money supply to meet them and a falling-off of new investment. Growing unemployment once again became inbuilt into the market system and was found to be the *only* real brake on excessive wage demands. It has to be noted too that it was solely in the *market* economies that this endemic inflation originated, though it later spread to the rest of the world through export.

Another major factor in world inflation and instability was also much expanded in the 1950s. While competitive market theory still rests on small independent producers and workers, large trade unions had already become labour monopolies, while a few giant private concerns have proliferated worldwide since that time as semi-monopoly transnational corporations, until they have come to dwarf the competitive economy and even most of the nation-states as well. As I have shown elsewhere (A. J.

Dilloway, 1977) by 1976 55 per cent of employment in Britain was in large concerns and only 17 per cent remained in the competitive sector. If public corporations are included over 70 per cent of employment was in very large enterprises. If we go worldwide we find that by 1975 78 out of several hundred transnational corporations had come to ". . . produce 15 per cent of everything manufactured, mined or grown in the whole world" (T. M. Schoenfeld, 1976). This figure continued to rise, to around 20 per cent by 1977, and by 1980 may have approached one-quarter of world output. Reflect further that even in 1975 the output value of each of these same 78 TNCs exceeded the GNP of all except 62 countries. The point about these transnational giants is, of course, that they can become largely independent both of market forces and of the fiscal or other policies of government. They can adjust prices and output to suit internal long-term aims, as well as being able to switch operations and components to benefit from tax, employment or exchange-rate conditions pertaining in different areas (A. J. Dilloway *et al.*, 1976). In 1982 TNCs have first begun to be used by one government to put pressure on other governments. Their own commercial and political power can clearly be all-important today, particularly in the developing world, as is suggested by widespread marketing there of numerous products that have been banned or circumscribed in their countries of origin.

We can now try to sum up some *human* implications of our market- or mixed-economy system as it operates today in world development. The two strongly opposed views on this matter — about the role of free private enterprise on the one hand and a planned economy on the other — are well known. A similar stark contrast of view now exists about private transnational concerns, which are variously seen as ". . . a natural force beyond the power of man to halt" and ". . . the most important instruments of capitalism in our time, ultimately pointing to a world capitalist system, *sui generis*, to succeed the international one" (T. M. Schoenfeld and Johan Galtung respectively, in A. J. Dilloway *et al.*, 1976).

To get back to the subject of this chapter — the interplay between human nature and human institutions — I have tried, in Table 12, to sum up some main characteristics and human defects of each of the two extreme forms of economic system insofar as they may influence the character of their participants. The real point is that, in essence, an economic system is a co-operative endeavour but that ours have become something quite different — on the one hand a confrontation arena and on the other a managed system of priorities in which the mass of users have too little say. Note too, that in each case the rationale employed is linked either to human freedom or to human development!

Without going into more detail, I believe we can conclude, firstly, that the persistence of our market-economy system shows how deep is the survival-value of some less desirable traits in the human character; and

TABLE 12
Some Effects of the Two Main Economic Systems which Influence the Human Qualities of Participants and the Conditions of World Development

A. PRESENT MARKET-ECONOMY SYSTEMS
(As operating in varying degree in some 141 countries comprising 69% of world population of which 121 countries and 53% of population are in course of development)

1. *General Effects*
The System:
— Maximizes growth of aggregate output under free enterprise.
— Is incompatible with a stable continuity of output and employment.
— Is incompatible with effective socio-economic planning or choice of priorities.
— Leads to increasing concentration of output and power in few hands.
— Tends to accentuate intrinsic inequalities between regions and between participants.
— Has been the unintended initiator of chronic price inflation.
— By nature has to extol deceit, divisiveness, selfishness and greed as model behaviour.

2. *International Effects*
Transnational Corporations:
— Tend to promote products and activities inappropriate to needs of developing countries.
— Distort values and consumption patterns of developing countries.
— Have acted to promote political as well as commercial imperialism.
— Unintentionally contribute to a destabilizing of the world financial system.
— Operate to advance their growing commercial world power without accountability.

B. PRESENT CENTRALLY PLANNED SYSTEMS
(As operating in varying degree in 22 countries comprising 31% of world population, 15 of which are in course of development.)

1. *General Effects*
The System:
— Allows investment, output and their composition to reflect choices and priorities.
— Minimizes economic enterprise for personal gain.
— Is compatible with a relatively egalitarian distribution of income or consumption.
— In the planning process allows insufficiently for the views of the population.
— Allows insufficiently for individual choice in consumption.
— Is cumbersome in responding to changing conditions.
— Is forced to incorporate intolerance as the price of effective planning.

2. *International Effects*
— Encourage self-sufficiency.

secondly, that the system itself is a main distorting influence that holds back any real flowering of human ideals in the twentieth century. At present there is a great searching around for ways of improving human performance, but it is significant that hardly ever is the working of the economy itself called into question. Yet, as will be seen in Chapter 5, some recent investigations have shown that a quite small adjustment to our present market economy could allow it, without major upheaval, to respond to present-day needs.

Events to date have shown that the Hitler war of 1939–1945 was merely the prelude to a polarization of world ideologies based on two contrasting economic systems and their attendant interests. On both sides it is élites or 'establishments' that have sought to protect their respective dogmas. This dichotomy in turn has spawned the present arms race, which is merely a special feature of the economic struggle. So divorced from perilous reality has become the collective paranoia behind today's military–economic brinkmanship that its proponents are now being forced to confront, not merely each other but the rapid encroachment of a commonsense third force — a nascent public consciousness of human priorities and the true reality of an interdependent world.

5

The Development Prospect

Development is an outgrowth of human qualities called fully into play by a stimulating environment. The qualities in question, or rather potentialities, have emerged from an evolutionary process that has somehow produced erect gait, jointed fingers, a brain capable of dealing with concepts, of communicating, reasoning and being conscious of time — all in the context of a long period of individual nurture. This last, plus an incipient need for other-regard, has led the human species always to coalesce into group life and it is there alone that man's uniqueness and productiveness can flower, in a collective interdependence that is forged for good.

But as we know to our cost, this is not the end of the story. Progress is an anthropomorphic notion, but in the above sense development is not. As an idea that is value-free, development connotes at least some increase in scale or numbers and in shared co-operative effort, and it also implies some growth in *organized* effectiveness and freedom, the last two as the means to individual expression and fulfilment.

But when we come to consider how such development can occur, we are brought back to an unfinished look at human qualities attempted in Chapter 4. Growing effectiveness, in the sense of a better apportionment and co-ordination of functions towards collective ends, demands everywhere a hierarchy, a pyramid of organized power and administration. Here we confront the perennial problem of 'we' and 'they', where the means to secure a balance of countervailing power by the governed against the governing has somehow to become built into the system. Freedom, roughly the means to ensure that individuals can enrich the common pool of ideas or talents, must be reconciled with enough organization to secure and advance the common weal. Free co-operation is the means to a consensus on broad policy aims but this too implies some balance between harmony overall and the tensions ever present in the clash of personalities or ambitions.

This chapter will explore two important facets of our enquiry into the conditions of world order. Firstly, and pursuing the above line of argument, there is the anatomy, or rather physiology, of social development in general — how the functioning of certain links between parameters of social life can reflect the state of nations. If this sounds too abstruse I hope to show, both here and in succeeding chapters, that some new

81

thinking along these lines is called for before a clearer view of the world order problem can emerge.

Secondly, and on a more down-to-earth plane, it is time to look at some examples of major world development trends now proceeding. Three distinct areas will first be considered where the effects of human nature work in very different ways, or at least where the outcomes are likely to differ widely because of them. Comparing such broad trends of worldwide concern is quite distinct from international comparative analysis properly so-called, where it is possible, and highly rewarding, to compare developments in different countries on a common basis. For our purpose this latter method should also be used so far as possible, building on the results of new work now to hand.

Finally, building on this and preceding chapters, a minimum series of proposed measures or policy changes will be put forward, most of them designed to be implemented worldwide through the United Nations to set in train some sustained movement towards a more rational world system.

What is Development?

This question is less easy to answer than may at first sight appear. A widespread debate about what development entails for individuals and for peoples has been part of the international scene since it was first propounded as a right by K. M'Baye of Senegal in 1975, but so far there is no final consensus on what the idea includes. To the business man, perhaps, and to not a few politicians, the answer requires little thought. More of the same with all speed, until every bushman has two video recorders, two electric toothbrushes . . . and so *ad infinitum*. But to many in the developing world, and particularly to all concerned with rights and duties, a search for the essence of development remains central to the world order problem.

To reach a true starting-point one has to go back to the investigations of L. T. Hobhouse, and especially to his work *Social Development*, first published in 1924, long before the developing world had surfaced as a problem. Starting from major investigations of social evolution, and from empirical comparative studies of simple pastoral, hunting and agricultural peoples, Hobhouse defined four objective criteria which characterize developmental change in society. Social development, he argued, which is "the development of men in their mutual relations", comprises advances in *Scale, Efficiency, Freedom* and *Mutuality*. Each of these characteristics can be and is defined, but it is not merely an increase in each that is significant but also the weight of each relative to and in terms of the others. Thus freedom may exist simply because organization is loose and ineffectual. Or a social system may be well organized to pursue some particular end, such as production of wealth, but be directed by a few without enlisting the free co-operation of the population as a whole; and so on. Freedom, in this sense, is the "spontaneous devotion of intelligent energy to the common life. This is not compassed by anything so simple as the acceptance of a democratic form of government" (Hobhouse, *op. cit.*).

In practice, of course, development has often been one-sided and partial. In early history growth in organizing efficiency or in scale has usually been accompanied by growing subordination until slow material advances have led eventually to some assertion of freedom. Typically this has been followed in turn by a fluctuating balance between the two. Development overall is advancing fulfilment of human aims and qualities that are more and more successfully expressed as the key social conditions come to prevail. But this self-expression, individual and collective, requires some control over the conditions of nature, including social forces both organized and unreflective and those of human character. Moreover, since no community can be truly self-contained, its relations with other communities must be those of co-operation. Ultimately, therefore, the entire world must form a single community, however many and varied the communities comprised within it may be.

In the context of our broader investigation I shall try to build upon and advance from the standpoint of this analysis. To that end Figure 12 first

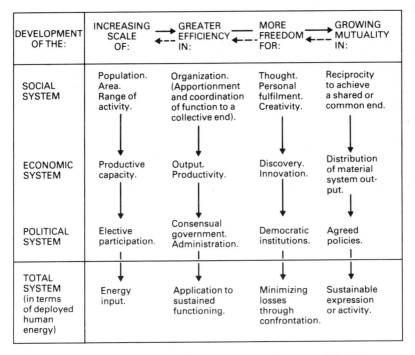

DEVELOPMENT OF THE:	INCREASING SCALE OF:	GREATER EFFICIENCY IN:	MORE FREEDOM FOR:	GROWING MUTUALITY IN:
SOCIAL SYSTEM	Population. Area. Range of activity.	Organization. (Apportionment and coordination of function to a collective end).	Thought. Personal fulfilment. Creativity.	Reciprocity to achieve a shared or common end.
ECONOMIC SYSTEM	Productive capacity.	Output. Productivity.	Discovery. Innovation.	Distribution of material system output.
POLITICAL SYSTEM	Elective participation.	Consensual government. Administration.	Democratic institutions.	Agreed policies.
TOTAL SYSTEM (in terms of deployed human energy)	Energy input.	Application to sustained functioning.	Minimizing losses through confrontation.	Sustainable expression or activity.

FIG. 12. Criteria for Appraising Scope for Development of Societies.

illustrates the Hobhouse thesis and extends it to cover the social, economic and political systems of a modern state, with a fourth line added to sum up advances within the different categories in terms of human energy applied. Each of the four categories at the head of columns 2–5 of the Figure is to be seen as interacting with that next to it, and the same is true of items pertaining respectively to the Social, Economic and Political Systems. Similarly, when reading vertically, each component of the Social and Economic systems is to be seen as having links with that immediately below it. The whole diagram thus shows twelve interacting facets of development which follow from increases in the four main development categories.

Contrasts in Three Worldwide Development Sectors

As we experience them, problems of social development are not seen as matters of philosophical balance. Aggravated as they are by mass poverty and ignorance, conflicts arise out of an urge to power and one-upmanship on the part of those in strategic positions. Then again people are suggestible, liable to feel fear and thus aggressiveness against out-groups which either pose a potential threat or are different enough to seem to do so. There is, too, a strong animal urge to selfish greed, a yen to outdo rivals in a scramble to satisfy needs by means that are either scarce or are made to seem scarce. Today this urge is sustained by a strong feedback from our market-economy system, which depends on maintaining the idea of scarcity as an incentive.

Today's ever more perilous world situation is a clear tribute to the strength of these various urges and the mechanisms that continue to sustain them. But here there is an important distinction to be noted. Development can be mainly intrinsic, co-operative, consensual and emergent; or it can be impelled simply by the motivated play of social or technical forces outside conscious control. Let us call the latter type of trend extrinsic. We now come to the important point, since in our own experience these extrinsic developments too can have variants which produce very different results. One type, for instance, can eventually prove self-correcting since it may bring into play equally strong motives that can stabilize the trend at a higher level or even reverse it. These emergent motives, in turn, can also be of two kinds. The first are produced by results which bring countervailing self-interest into play, while in the second case it is humane ideals that are brought to bear, mainly through a perceived discord between knowledge and action. In either event it is a mixture of common self-interest and idealism that becomes the countervailing motive force. However, it is also true from current experience that development trends need not be self-correcting. Where motives are reinforced by confrontation, for instance, there may be no 'point of inflexion', so that behaviour on one side stimulates that on the other through a mirror reaction until all sense of real priorities is lost, perhaps for good.

It happens that these different types of development can be exemplified very clearly at the present time in three distinct fields of worldwide concern. These are, respectively, the trends of population growth; concern for world environments; and the nuclear arms race. Looking at these three preoccupations in turn may serve to bring the development theme more clearly into focus.

Growth-trends of World Population

An outstanding fact about the human animal, and one with the most far-reaching consequences for life on earth, has been his expansion in numbers since 1850. Up to that time, from the dawn of human-kind some millions of years earlier, the cumulation of the species had produced a total of about one billion. In the next seventy-five years, between 1850 and 1925, world population doubled again, reaching some two billion in the latter year. A third doubling occurred between 1925 and 1975 and it is probable that the total will be doubled again by 2010, reaching about 6200 million in the year 2000.

Demographic trends are more complex to unravel than these figures suggest. Not only do they involve a balance between births and deaths, but age and sex composition are factors in the future growth in numbers, as are other indicators such as the reproduction rate — roughly the number of female children per 1000 women of child-bearing age on standard assumptions of fertility and mortality. If trends in numbers are vital for understanding world development, it is because of endless ramifications between population size and the parameters and prospects of human society — food and shelter; health, life expectancy, literacy and education; migration, social services and the work force; economic activity and the urban–rural balance — the last two pointing to yet further interrelations between production, transport, the size of cities, environmental pollution and waste or conservation of the earth's natural resources. These linkages and some main facts about world population, are portrayed in various other tables and diagrams in this book, and most directly in Tables 3–7 in Chapter 3.

The present demographic position illustrates the fact that there can be a time-lag between growth in numbers and declining *rates* of growth, so that population can go on rising long after percentage rates of increase have started to fall (see Table 13).

From 1980 on, these figures are medium projections. They have been adapted and rounded from a United Nations assessment of World Population Trends and Prospects made in 1978. The increase in numbers depicted in columns 2–4 will continue for a good time to come, but it is the

Is World Order Evolving?

TABLE 13

Growth of World Population and Rates of Increase, 1950–2000

Year	Population (billions)			Annual % Increase (5 year averages)[a]		
	World	More developed areas	Less developed areas	World	More developed areas	Less developed areas
1	2	3	4	5	6	7
1950	2.5	0.8	1.7	0.8	0.8	0.9
1960	3.0	0.9	2.1	2.0	1.3	2.3
1970	3.7	1.0	2.7	1.9	0.9	2.3
1980[b]	4.5	1.1	3.4	1.8	0.7	2.2
1990[b]	5.3	1.2	4.1	1.8	0.6	2.1
2000[b]	6.2	1.3	4.9	1.6	0.5	1.8

[a]Fifty-year average for 1950.
[b]Projected figures.

reversal of a long-term rise in rates of increase that occurred around 1965 (columns 5–7), and more particularly in the developing countries, that is important in the present context. Only very recently has it become clear that the decline in growth-rates is a real, and probably a continuing tendency that will operate even more fully as time goes on. The causes should be understood, for they are a vital condition for worldwide advance.

The fact is that some specific reasons for slower population growth are now coming to the fore. With a gradual advance in living standards comes an opening-up of horizons. Pressures grow to improve elementary conditions of food, shelter, water supply, medical care, etc. Since about 1965 the overall world death rate has been falling annually by some 3 per thousand but at the same time the corresponding birth rate has slowed down even more quickly — by about 5 per thousand. Not only do prospects open up for more people but a higher expectation is accompanied by greater enlightenment, a rise in literacy and access to education. Wherever these tendencies emerge traditional practices tend to be undermined. Notwithstanding a way of life that is commonly eased by an abundance of family labour, there comes a time when sights can be set higher in providing for the next generation. As was noted in Chapter 3, if birth rates for many developing countries are compared with their Physical Quality of Life indicators the results suggest that a fairly sharp fall in the birth rate tends to occur where the PQL index reaches a value of just over 70. This level of the composite PQL index, in turn, will often correspond to an average GNP per inhabitant in the region of 500–1000 dollars per year.

Such a process of slow-down is being greatly aided by UN population agencies such as the Population Commission and the UN Fund for Population Activities, which are helping some governments to promote policies in line with the idea that existing rates of increase are a serious brake on development. Population policies of varying effectiveness are becoming more acceptable as an aid to development, one of the most radical being China's State Family Planning Commission set up in 1980.

Because this trend in slowly falling birth rates now seems to be gaining ground, efforts are being made to estimate prospects for population slow-down in different countries as a major long-term factor. Such an exercise is carried out and kept up-to-date for 124 countries by the World Bank. Calculations are worked from national totals, fertility and mortality rates being projected for 5-year periods until age- and sex-specific mortality rates become stable while the age-specific fertility rates remain at replacement level. At that stage the net reproduction rate is sufficient only to replace the population (NRR = 1), birth and death rates are equal and age-structure constant.

I have prepared Table 14 to show some main features of such an evolution for 12 countries which together comprise some 60 per cent of world population. It can be seen that the period required to reach a stable

TABLE 14
Examples of a Hypothetical Time-span for Population Slow-down[a][b]

Country	GNP per head (1980) ($)	Population:		Year of Reaching:		Hypothetical stationary population (millions)
		Millions (1980)	Av. growth-rate 1970–80 (%)	NRR rate of 1.0[c]	Stationary population	
1	2	3	4	5	6	7
Bangladesh	130	89	2.6	2035	2125	321
Ethiopia	140	31	2.0	2045	2135	160
India	240	673	2.1	2020	2115	1694
China	290	977	1.8	2005	2070	1570
Indonesia	430	147	2.3	2020	2110	376
Nigeria	1010	85	2.5	2035	2105	528
Brazil	2050	119	2.2	2015	2075	281
USSR	4550	266	0.9	2000	2060	353
United Kingdom	7920	56	0.1	2000	2025	60
USA	11,360	228	1.0	2000	2030	284
Sweden	13,520	8	0.3	2000	2000	8
Switzerland	16,440	7	0.3	2000	2005	7

[a]Based on World Bank data and calculations, 1982.
[b]Countries are arranged in increasing order of GNP per head in 1980 (column 2).
[c]Briefly, a Net Reproduction Rate of unity is the rate at which, on average, child-bearing women bear only enough children to replace themselves in the population.

population may vary from about 150 to only 20 years, depending in part on earlier growth-rates. As the Table shows, this also means that the time taken to reach a hypothetically constant population tends to vary inversely with present levels of economic development as summed up by GNP per head (column 2). Even if present tendencies are confirmed and population growth *is* a valid example of a social trend that is self-correcting, the net result will still be that an effective slow-down will not occur before the number of people in the world has reached 10,000 million, or more than 2.25 times the present total.

Environment and Development

Concern for the environment was already being expressed over 2000 years ago. Early in this century it became fully explicit in the work of Patrick Geddes and then began to receive attention in international programmes in the late sixties. Since 1972, when environmental concern was first examined as a candidate for world action, the United Nations Environment Programme has gone far to energize governments, although not yet far enough. The net result of a decade of action has been a new consciousness that development ought to be made sustainable, but usually is not. Up to a few years ago there were few restraints on discharging wastes into air and water, while land and natural resources could be exploited freely without concern, for that was how the individual entrepreneur could best limit costs to himself. Today much of this is still happening, and such environmental and genetic damage as comes, say, from destroying a tropical forest still lies well outside anyone's economic balance sheet. But the reality that environmental assessment, management, and conservation offer a positive gain to mankind is now at least visible. On average the economic cost of pollution damage in more developed countries totals some 3–5 per cent of GNP while its abatement, and resource protection, probably costs only around 1–2 per cent. In developing countries enormous gains can be realized, in terms of infectious disease prevention, improved health and productivity, simply by devoting 0.5–1.0 per cent of GNP to constructing simple water and sewage systems.

The United Nations Environment Programme was envisaged not as an operating agency but as a Programme of the World Community, to focus attention, to co-ordinate special knowledge and to stimulate action. In the words of General Assembly Resolution 2997 the guiding principle is ". . . to safeguard and enhance the environment for the benefit of present and future generations of man". What this means in practice can be glimpsed from Table 15 and Figure 13, in which I have tried to suggest the range of global concerns covered by the Environment Programme, its Global Environment Monitoring System and the related World Conservation Strategy, the last a reasoned scheme drawn up by the International Union

TABLE 15
Outline of Some Major Aspects of the United Nations Environment Programme

Type of Environmental Activity	Undertaking or Project	Special Bodies Involved
1	2	3
ASSESSMENT		
Climate-related:	World Glacier Inventory (750 stations)	UNESCO
	Baseline Atmospheric Pollution (CO_2, turbidity etc. — 12 stations)	—
	Background Atmospheric Pollution (110 regional stations)	—
	Coordinating Committee on the Ozone Layer	—
	Long-range Transport of Air Pollutants (110 stations)	ECE
Renewable Resources:	Soil Degradation and its Risk	FAO
	Tropical Forest Resources (76 countries)	FAO
	Tropical Rangeland Network	—
	Wild Living Resources	IUCN
	Species Conservation Centre	—
Ocean-related:	Regional Seas Programme	—
	Open Oceans Background Pollution	—
Pollution and Health:	Air Quality Monitoring (200 stations)	
	Water Quality Monitoring (300 stations)	WHO
	Monitoring Human Body Fluids (DDT, cadmium, lead etc.) (10 countries)	WHO
	Reviewing Effects of Atomic Radiation	UNSCEAR[a]
	International Register of Potentially Toxic Chemicals	—
General:	Outer Environmental Limits (plant productivity, etc.)	—
MANAGEMENT AND LAW		
Pollution:	Five Conventions (Global and Regional) on Marine Pollution	—
	European Convention on Long-range Trans-boundary Air Pollution[b]	ECE
Protection of Nature:	Four Global Conservation Conventions	UNESCO etc.
SUPPORTING MEASURES		
	Regional Advisory Teams	UNESCO
	Education and Training	IMO[c], UNIDO, ILO
	Disseminating Information	—
	State of the Environment Reports	—

[a]United Nations Scientific Committee on the Effects of Atomic Radiation.
[b]Operative from 16 March 1983.
[c]International Maritime Organization, the former IMCO.

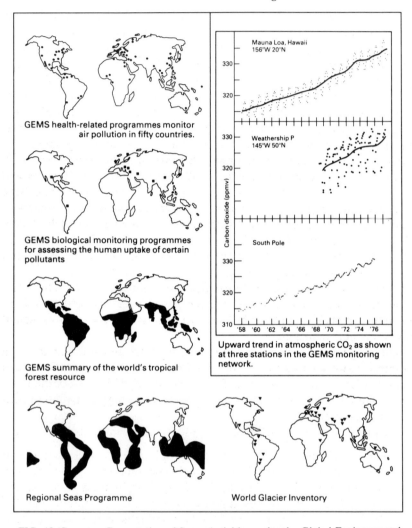

GEMS health-related programmes monitor air pollution in fifty countries.

GEMS biological monitoring programmes for assessing the human uptake of certain pollutants

GEMS summary of the world's tropical forest resource

Upward trend in atmospheric CO$_2$ as shown at three stations in the GEMS monitoring network.

Mauna Loa, Hawaii 156°W 20°N

Weathership P 145°W 50°N

South Pole

Carbon dioxide (ppmv)

Regional Seas Programme

World Glacier Inventory

FIG. 13. Summary Presentation of Some Activities under the Global Environmental Monitoring System (Collated from Material in the Publication *GEMS*, by John Reader, United Nations Environment Programme, 1982).

for Conservation of Nature and Natural Resources with the support of UNEP and the World Wildlife Fund.

Now that commercialized technology is being exploited freely in a gainful market that has become virtually worldwide, the intricacies of unforeseen and previously unknown linkages of forces affecting not only human health and well-being but the entire human future are spreading throughout the global habitat and its eco-systems. Possible dangers to health are being uncovered several times a year — the latest, as I write, being a disclosure that Britain's water supplies are being exposed to the likelihood of causing an increase in stomach cancers, already one of the commonest forms of the disease, through a massive and growing use of agricultural fertilizers from which nitrates are being drained into rivers and ground water sources. At a more global level some of the complex links between natural and artificially created phenomena now pose questions which can threaten irredeemably the entire human habitat if new efforts at measurement and understanding are not translated into curbs on commercial freedom. Table 15 suggests some of the trends being monitored worldwide. These range from a rapid destruction of tropical forests — in several countries probably halving or obliterating them in 25 years and leading to such likely effects as degradation of soils and a decline in genetic diversity through loss of dependent flora and fauna — to prospects of inadvertent major change, e.g. by depleting the ozone layer which absorbs ultra-violet light and shields the earth's surface from lethal radiation; or perhaps by creating an atmospheric blanket of carbon dioxide — natural and artificial — which by slowing the escape of terrestrial heat, can raise temperatures and average sea-level, with highly unusual results. There are, in short, real limits to the adaptive capacity of our biosphere just as there are limits to the capacity of human societies to observe rules of sound environmental management.*

Summing up this expanding but still puny effort to make human living sustainable, we see that to old norms of immediate cost and profit have to be added far-reaching new ones. The whole conception is comprehensive, science-based, humanistic, and far removed from a single-minded pursuit of industrial advantage.

To quote from some definitions of the World Conservation Strategy:

> Humanity's relationship with the biosphere . . . will continue to deteriorate until a new international economic order is achieved, a new environmental ethic adopted, human populations stabilize, and sustainable modes of development become the rule rather than the exception . . . For development to be sustainable it must take account of social and ecological factors, as well as economic ones; of the living and non-living resource base; and of the long term as well as the short term advantages and disadvantages of alternative actions . . . Thus conservation is positive, embracing preservation, maintenance, sustainable utilization, restoration, and enhancement of the natural environment.

For reasons already discussed, this kind of thinking requires a revolution in political and economic behaviour and it is not yet certain that such a

---

*There is now a glimmer of hope in respect of the ozone layer — the belt of rarefied gas located around 10–50 km above the earth's surface — since a United Nations Convention for the Protection of the Ozone Layer was finally adopted on 22 March, 1985.

revolution will occur. But it is already true that the underlying ideas have captured, in a surprising way, the enthusiasm of millions of uncommitted people, and this perhaps is because *Homo economicus* still yearns unknowingly for the natural roots of its existence. We can conclude that if mankind's burgeoning of pillage and waste is not a self-correcting trend, it can still call forth a strong backlash of idealism that may yet bear visible fruit.

Armed Confrontation and Development

Warfare, and the 'verdict of war' as a resolver of conflict, has accompanied the rise of civilization from prehistoric times. Many have been the causes of past wars but in our day three new features of armed confrontation have brought the threat of annihilation not merely to the doorstep of every citizen of the earth, but to the entirety of the world's natural and social environment as well. These three factors are, respectively, the accelerating pace of the development of high technology; a new involvement of non-expert politicians in ultimate direction of war policy; and the rise of a polarized ideology which, for two major world protagonists, combines in one all-powerful theme the separate motives for conflict that existed in earlier days.

Faced with a daily cliff-hanging wrangle about nuclear life and death, is there anything new that the analytic style used here can contribute towards understanding this ultimate dilemma? Every permutation of known elements, and of the disputed statistics, has long since been explored. Perhaps it may prove useful to look at just those simple facts that are *rarely or never mentioned* to see if they can offer any guidance.

Let us start from the situation of everyday experience. All we know of the confrontation is from the statements of leading politicians on either side and some pressure groups, plus abundant press comment. In liberal democracies, however — and, with some differences, in centrally planned states — there are four main fields of interest affecting policy and practice, innovative or reactive.

These are illustrated in Figure 14. Together they exert a powerful pressure on governments anxious to retain popular esteem. First are the influential backers, who may have ensured the election of the party and its leader. Both the leader and his recruited colleagues and staff will tend to mirror the views of these backers, who strongly desire to maintain the security of their interests against what are perceived as external threats. The electorate too — the fourth component — demands security and full employment, but it has also to feel that policies to induce these are fair and credible. A more decisive sector is the military hierarchy and its planning and administrative staff. On the one hand this force is given high priority and prestige as the defender of security, while in many smaller states it may

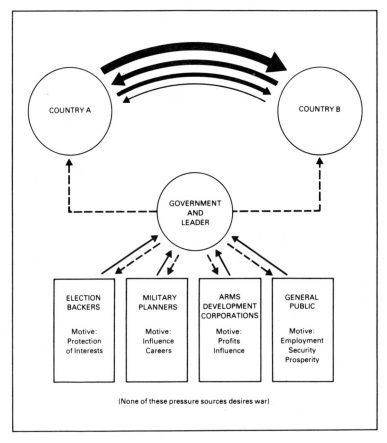

FIG. 14. Reciprocal Pressures for Warlike Confrontation.

offer the source of effective power in government. However, this prestige is not in itself enough to secure continuing privilege and career prospects, since absence of war is a negative experience. To sustain personal and collective power and prospects by securing high budgets the military planning machine must maintain and magnify a continuing sense of menace from outside (which it will already feel), and must demand ever-new technological advances to counter an opposing 'threat'. This brings us to the final category shown in the figure, the innovators, suppliers and exporters of advanced technology for military and associated space programmes. These are powerful transnational corporations. They receive preferential contracts from government and have an equally strong interest in perceiving an outside 'threat' and in devising ever-new techniques to counter or upstage it.

Above, and receptive first of all to this barrage of highly technical advice, stand the political leaders and the inner government. These also observe the reactions of opposite numbers elsewhere, and they may be forced by alliances into collective policies forged under a barrage of military counsel, as well as being exposed to crude political pressures from powerful neighbours, exerted in the form of implied blackmail.

This situation is common to most of the developed liberal states. A similar but rather simpler milieu can be expected in centrally planned systems, where a primary aim must be to ensure steady advance in a hostile encircling world. In this way the two main protagonists together, with a mere 11 per cent of world population, have come to spend one half of the world's military budgets and to export nearly 60 per cent of all the arms entering international trade. At the present time (March 1983) their own armed might remains roughly in balance.

The mental climate enveloping these two major opponents prompts three considerations. Firstly, the motive for confrontation, though in itself artificial and unnecessary, has an appeal which combines all the motives for war throughout history — power, religion and economics most of all. Secondly, the economic motive for more and better arms is uniquely reinforcing, since demand comes to beget demand without any point of saturation. Thirdly, and perhaps most importantly, the whole structure is erected on a premise that is always assumed but never demonstrated. This unseen premise is that the adversary's purpose is to invade, conquer and subdue. Puncture that assumption and the whole edifice falls to the ground.

Clearly our world development situation is now dominated by this nuclear-conventional 'reflecting game of fear' across Europe. But virtually all states, including in some degree the 101 members of the non-aligned group, are now forced into a grudging choice between one set of interests or the other. For over 20 years all five continents have in addition been demonstrating that the Security Council remains impotent. Sixty-five wars of some magnitude, including invasions and civil wars, have been waged since January 1960. Ten have occurred in Latin America, two in Europe, nine in the Middle East, five in Southern Asia, eight in the Far East and no less than seventeen in Africa. From incomplete statistics gathered by Sivard (R. L. Sivard, 1982) it would appear that civilian and military deaths from such conflicts have been rising at a fairly constant rate. Around 5,216,000 deaths in all have occurred from this cause in the decade 1960–1970 and a similar number — 5,485,000 — in the period from the end of 1970 to mid-1982.

In many countries military forces are attractive to strong-arm military governments as a means of maintaining power. In certain developing regions competitive arming has been built up between adjoining states or regions with strong antipathies — religious, ethnic, tribal, political or territorial — when military aid from outside has appeared to favour one side. Then again, authoritarian rulers, in developing countries in particular, are dazzled by prestige gadgetry — especially where nuclear power is concerned! In nearly all countries it would seem that nuclear fission power for civil use is attractive for its technical sophistication, its supposed export potential — and its promise of atomic weaponry. Despite its appeal as an image-builder for the budding statesman, the fact is that nuclear energy as a source of supply for a developing country is at once uneconomic, irrelevant and forever criminally dangerous.

How far is it possible to get an overall picture of modern warmindedness as a factor in world development? In Table 16 I have collated and calculated some summarizing world indicators for the period 1960–1980 from average data brought together by Ruth Leger Sivard (R. L. Sivard,

TABLE 16
Some Summarizing Indicators of World Confrontation in Development, 1960–1980[a,b]

Category	1960	1970	1980
WORLD (141 countries)			
Gross national product (billion constant dollars)	4380	7289	10,792
Military expenditures (billion constant dollars)[c]	298	411	495
Armed forces (millions)[d]	18.55	21.48	24.64
WORLD			
Population (billions)	3.05	3.71	4.48
GNP (dollars per head)	1437	1964	2409
Military expenditures (dollars per head)	99	111	112[e]
Armed forces per '000 population	6.1	5.8	5.6
Index of yearly price inflation (%)	1.5	7.0	9.5
DEVELOPED COUNTRIES (28)			
Population (billions)	0.88	0.98	1.06
GNP (dollars per head)	4077	5950	7803
Military expenditures (dollars per head)	320	354	366
Armed forces per '000 population	11.2	10.4	9.0
Index of yearly price inflation (%)	1.7	7.0	9.4
DEVELOPING COUNTRIES (113)			
Population (billions)	2.17	2.74	3.42
GNP (dollars per head)	367	540	743
Military expenditures (dollars per head)	13	23	31
Armed forces per '000 population	4.0	4.2	4.4
Index of yearly price inflation (%)	−3.0	6.0	9.9

[a]All financial data are expressed in US dollars at 1979 prices and exchange rates. Inflation indicators shown for 1960 are those for 1961.
[b]Basic data used in making the calculations shown in this Table are from Ruth Leger Sivard, 1982 (Statistical Annex).
[c]Refers to current and capital expenditures to meet the needs of the armed forces, including military assistance to foreign countries and the military components of nuclear, space and R and D programmes.
[d]Refers only to manpower in the regular forces, including conscripts.
[e]Provisional.

1982). These show trends in world population, gross national product and price inflation, all related to growth of military forces and expenditure on arms.

From figures in the upper part of the Table we can deduce that in real terms arms spending has grown on average by 2.6 per cent per year over the 20-year period — at the same rate, in fact, as gross national product per head. Total GNP has of course risen somewhat faster than this, since world population itself has increased by 48 per cent between 1960 and 1980.

The period in question is the one in which price inflation has mushroomed to the dimensions of a top world problem. Its steady rise, as shown in the Table, though closely linked with certain socio-economic trends, can in part be explained by arms spending, which is both essentially unproductive and subject to rapid obsolescence.

The same Table shows that in the developed world the proportion of population in the armed forces has fallen somewhat over the period, whereas it has been rising elsewhere. Real military expenditure per inhabitant, by contrast, has been on the increase in the developing as well as the developed group, the difference reflecting greater 'productivity' and scale of weaponry in the latter.

Military expenditure, including research and development, accounted for about 4.6 per cent of total world product in 1980, or about 500,000 million dollars. Contrary to common belief it is by no means a 'necessary' source of employment. Under United States conditions (1980) it can be estimated that about 36,000 new jobs could be *created* for every one billion dollars by which arms spending was reduced. This compares with a total of 122 billion dollars spent on arms in that country in 1980. What such figures mean in terms, say, of health foregone brings out even more clearly how heavy is the tax now levied on development. The World Health Organization's entire budget for 1983–84 has been set at 520 million US dollars, which at present is one-third of one day's world spending on arms. This organization managed to eradicate smallpox from the earth over a ten-year period by devoting only 83 million dollars to the task. Had funds been available, a mere 450 million dollars would have been spent in the same way to conquer malaria.

Endemic military spending and endemic price inflation emerge as two of the major follies of mankind. But, unlike the trends of population growth and environmental waste studied earlier, this obsession with mass-suicide technology is not a self-correcting trend. It remains very uncertain, and even perhaps unlikely, that a sufficient counterblast of public reality can arise to cry 'halt' to our harassed politicians. The point is that there is here no natural saturation in demand. For the combined urges of economic ideology act to upstage every new excess by a fallacious call for 'deterrence' against an imaginary 'threat'. If technology has made the modern world it would seem that technology may well be due to end it.

In case the above account is thought over-dramatic, may I add a post-script. As I write (9 March 1983) the head of state of one of the two main world protagonists has described the opposing side as "the focus of evil in the modern world", going on: "I urge you to beware of the temptation . . . to declare yourselves above it all and to label both sides equally at fault, to ignore the facts of history and the aggressive impulses of an evil empire, to simply call the arms race a gigantic misunderstanding . . ."*

An Overall View of Development

People are obliged to stay together in communities — and in our day in nation-states — in order to live and transmit their human qualities. In the process of living they acquire skills, both material and social. They also pursue anti-social behaviour, perpetuate injustices and fail to use their mutual opportunities to best advantage. The net result of this mix we call development and in these pages much of our search is simply for means to make the process a humanly viable one.

It is possible to gain a bird's eye view of differences in basic social advance for a sample of countries. As discussed in Chapter Three, average GNP per head is a poor measure to use for the purpose since it records wealth as a flow rather than a stock and omits a great deal of useful effort, such as work in the home, and a great deal of unattributed debt too, simply because neither has any measured value or cost in market terms. A better indicator is one like the Physical Quality of Life Index devised by the Overseas Development Council, Washington, which summarizes several basic aspects of well-being and the level of success in meeting basic needs. A companion index, the Disparity Reduction Rate or DRR, introduced subsequently by the ODC, is designed to measure the *rate* of change in meeting basic needs (Overseas Development Council, 1980).

We shall use the ODC data for these indicators, as well as average GNP, to present changes in a varied sample of states. The PQLI, it will be recalled, combines three indicators — infant mortality, life expectancy at age one, and adult literacy — into a single composite index, with each component indexed on a scale of 0 (the least favourable performance anywhere in 1950) to 100 (the best performance expected by the year 2000). The final index is calculated by averaging the three indices, giving them equal weight. In its composite form, the DRR measures the rate at which the gap between a country's overall level of performance according to PQLI and the best performance expected anywhere by the end of the century, is being closed.

Table 17 shows the results given by these two indices, and that given by gross national product per head, over the period from 1960 to the latest

*Reported by Harold Jackson (*Guardian*, 9 March 1983).

TABLE 17
Some Indicators of Development for Selected Countries

| Country | Governmental type[a] | GNP per head | | Physical Quality of Life Index[b] | | Disparity reduction rate[b] (%) |
		Dollars (1982)	Rate of increase 1960–82 (%)	1960	Current	
1	2	3	4	5	6	7
Under $350 per head						
Benin	RA	310	0.6	12.6	38	1.3
Haiti	AC	300	0.6	20.9	43	1.8
India	LD	260	1.3	30.0	46	1.4
Sri Lanka	LD	320	2.6	73.2	85	2.7
Tanzania	P	280	1.9	20.1	61	3.3
$350 and under $1000						
Egypt	P	690	3.6	35.3	57	1.9
Honduras	AC	660	1.0	41.6	63	2.2
Indonesia	P	580	4.2	35.3	58	2.6
Morocco	LD	870	2.6	30.5	49	1.4
Philippines	AC	820	2.8	58.6	75	3.2
$1000 and under $5000						
Algeria	P	2350	3.2	29.2	50	2.0
Ecuador	P	1350	4.8	53.2	73	2.8
Korea, Rep. of	AC	1910	6.6	64.5	86	5.7
Malaysia	LD	1860	4.3	60.0	73	2.9
Romania	RA	4660	8.6[c]	78.4	92	5.2
$5000 and over						
Finland	LD	10,870	3.6	90.3	98	4.0
Japan	LD	10,080	6.1	89.0	99	8.6
Kuwait	TC	19,870	−0.1	63.8	78	3.1
Singapore	P	5910	7.4	69.1	89	5.4
USSR	RA	6350	4.0[c]	88.9	94	2.0

[a]Refers to the situation at 1 Jan. 1982, according to the classification of Prof. J. Blondel. RA = Radical Authoritarian; LD = Liberal Democratic; P = Populist; AC = Authoritarian Conservative; TC = Traditional Conservative.
[b]For the description of this indicator, see text (period of coverage as in Fig. 15).
[c]1960–1980

available year in respect of 20 widely differing countries. Anticipating a later analysis, the form of government in each current at 1 January 1982 has been added, using a classificatory system devised by Professor J. Blondel and data especially revised by him. This same information is presented graphically for the same 20 states, plus 41 others, in Figure 15, thereby affording a panoramic view of the development process in action.*

*On Figure 15, however, the latest GNP and PQL indications refer to 1978.

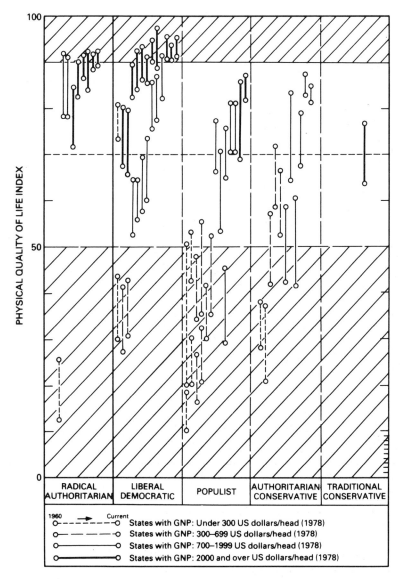

FIG. 15. Systems of Government, Rates of Development (since 1960), and Average Income.

A word on the method of presentation. First, for each country the lower circle marks the PQL standing for 1960 and the upper one the position reached in the latest available year. Of the two shaded areas, the upper one marks the level reached by states regarded as developed (i.e. those with a PQLI of at least 90 and GNP per head of 2000 US dollars or more), while the lower shaded area includes most of the countries considered least developed within the UN system. Finally, a broken line shows that level of PQLI which is the threshold at which rising basic levels of health and education begin to produce a declining birth-rate, and so reinforce the development process.

Careful study of Table 17 and Figure 15 discloses many contrasts between national income and elementary well-being. One of the better-known cases is that of Sri Lanka, which can be compared, for example, with Benin. Similarly, Morocco can be contrasted, say, with the Philippines, or Algeria with Romania or Cuba (the last with PQLI of 95). A similar contrast can be noted when Japan or Finland is compared with Kuwait. So far as the Disparity Reduction Rate (not measured by Figure 15) is concerned, there is a marked difference between a country like Tanzania, say, and Mali (latest PQLI 27.0, with a DRR of only 0.6), or Benin. It is easy to spot examples of countries in the middle range which are pushing ahead rapidly, like Singapore or the Republic of Korea, a group which also includes Hong Kong and some larger states.

This first look at the development process at work does not disclose any clear correlation between type of government and rate or level of social advance. This is a question that will be addressed more fully in the next Chapter.

Creating Practical Conditions for World Development

What are the practical steps now needed to create conditions for moving towards a more viable international climate? Because it is still too soon to contemplate a single world enforcement agency, the search must be for steps to promote a loose world community of nation-states that can allow individual states to function in the economic, social, monetary and political spheres as well as through a broad consensus about the earth as a delicately balanced resource and conservation unit. On this purely practical side — that is, before considering the human rights aspect — one can at once list a range of short- or medium-term objectives for concerted international action, mainly within or associated with the UN system, that emerge from what has been discussed so far.

A selection of fifteen such basic aims is listed in Table 18. The first three follow fairly obviously from earlier analyses in this chapter. Thus, reducing the present state of armed tension implies mobilizing world opinion still further to enforce inter-governmental action aimed at freezing, destroying

TABLE 18

Fifteen Selected Measures to Promote a More Rational World Development[a]

No.	Measure or Initiative[b]	Nature	Purpose	Coverage	Present Situation
1	2	3	4	5	6
1	End the arms build-up	EP	PI	ID	EC
2	Reduce the world's high birth-rates	S	P	D	PR
3	Protect world natural/social environments	SE	PI	ID	PR
4	Control transnational concerns	EP	PI	ID	EC
5	Raise the role and status of women	S	PI	ID	EC
6	Modify both political–economy systems	E	PI	ID	E
7	Monitor science/technology development	ES	PI	I	E
8	Reverse decline of 35 poorest countries	ES	P	D	PR
9	Raise output of world's agrarian work-force	ES	P	D	EC
10	Replace national aid by global tax system	ES	PI	ID	E
11	Create stable world monetary system	E	P	ID	EC
12	Move towards a true World Information Order	SP	P	ID	E
13	Create world urban/rural development policies	SE	P	ID	CE
14	Upgrade conservationist energy policies	E	PI	ID	PR
15	Universalize Law of Sea Convention	PE	PI	ID	E

Symbols shown above have the following meanings:

Column 3: E = Economic   Column 4: P = Practical
         S = Social   I = Inspirational
         P = Political

Column 5: I = Industrial and   Column 6: E = Entrenched
         D = Developing countries   C = Complex
                                     PR = Potentially responsive

[a] Other than those required to strengthen observance of human rights and duties.
[b] For a fuller statement of proposed measures see list included in the text.

and then reducing arms output and export, creating a European nuclear-free zone and outlawing more types of weaponry. The aim throughout must be to *reduce* an opposing threat rather than seeking to upstage it.

The second item is equally clear. It implies aiding and intensifying schemes for birth-rate reduction in the developing world while encouraging all social measures to promote that elementary level of well-being at which birth-rates begin to fall sharply.

Item three involves getting the UN Environment Programme scaled up to a truly global effort, with high priority for protecting the atmosphere and its upper limits, restoring man-made imbalances in biosphere and lithosphere and limiting production factors affecting urban and rural health.

The fourth area of concern, like the first, requires a mobilizing of pressure on governments — in this case to adopt stronger controls over the activities of transnational corporations, in their countries of origin as well as in those where they locate, and to adopt a strong binding Code of Conduct for TNCs.

With the fifth item we reach a field which raises both practical and normative considerations. Concentrating at this point on the former, a practical aim must be to seek a worldwide ratification and observance of the relatively new UN Convention on Elimination of Discrimination Against Women so that women can play a greater part both in humane decision-making and in framing international policies.

Objective number six has been discussed in the previous chapter but will need further attention at the end of this one. Here it suffices to say that the purpose of this proposal should be to initiate a serious investigation and active debate, firstly on modifying the market economy system so as to make it truly accountable and sustainable without serious upheaval; and, secondly on adapting centrally directed systems to make them more responsive to their own public opinion. Some notes on possible ways of achieving the first aim will be included at the end of this Chapter.

The next reform, number seven, would entail seeking widespread backing to implement the call of the world's scientific leadership (first made at the UN, Geneva in 1975) for international machinery to monitor basic scientific and technological developments, drawing attention to possible dangers as well as potential benefits and perhaps considering means to control any new developments which pose a threat to human safety.

Item eight is a relatively short-term measure: to halt and reverse the deteriorating position recognized in some 35 countries which, being both poor and often disadvantaged by geographical position, have in the last decade suffered a decline in elementary conditions of life. International efforts now being made to remedy this situation need to be intensified.

The next reform, listed as item 9, is directed to raising both food supplies and living conditions in many parts of the developing world by stimulating labour productivity of the agrarian work-force through small-scale activity, by land reform and by improved practices. Existing international programmes need to be stepped up and given high priority.

The tenth proposal is more radical. It entails the setting up of a UN Conference or other body charged to work out a scheme for a global taxation system which would replace much tied national aid and other variable assistance and secure the financing of essential worldwide development and conservation projects.

A similar and even more radical type of initiative is that listed as number eleven. This might best start from a high-level standing inquiry, under UN auspices, that would be charged to define essential conditions for creating a stable world monetary system.

Yet another necessary worldwide objective is that aimed at removing some of the grosser distortions from the flow of information. It should go beyond a recent UNESCO undertaking, for one aim would be to loosen the stranglehold of TNCs in advertising and media information and to promote a supply of straightforward material, freer from political or commercial slants, to the world's emerging and under-informed publics.

The tasks subsumed under item thirteen present truly staggering problems of investment and allocation to most of the rapidly developing states. How, among other things, to confine the proliferating shanty fringes of already vast urban areas is a question that demands priority and resources far greater than those now available to the UN Habitat programme.

Item fourteen can affect virtually all countries but needs an international impetus. Sustainable energy policies, using abundant renewable resources plus real conservation measures, are now becoming more and more feasible but are still largely disregarded by governments and supply undertakings. Conservationist policies alone can now reduce energy use in the developed world by up to 20 per cent and they need to become the norm rather than the exception worldwide.

Finally, the UN Law of the Sea Convention is unique in its provision for a supranational administering Authority to manage the resources of the world's oceans. United Nations efforts have to be redoubled to secure both full ratification and a widespread respect for its priorities and its ideals.

This list of basic objectives is not meant to be exhaustive. It is set out in the full knowledge of the many awesome barriers that stand in the way, themselves a measure of the odds against world order. The function of each item in this corpus of reform is suggested in columns 3–5 of Table 18 and in column 6 an attempt is made to compare their likely strength of resistance to resolute action.

It ought to be clear that these fifteen fields of effort are not to be seen as isolated endeavours. Thus items 1, 3, 6, 7, 9, 13, 14 and 15 at least are all connected in various ways with the natural environment. Similarly, numbers 1, 4, 6, 7, 9, 11, 12 and 15 equally impinge on problems raised by transnational corporations.

I promised to return at the end to the question of how item 6 might be tackled. While many reasons are advanced for the poor showing of mankind in the face of our ever-growing knowledge, there is one factor that is never called seriously into question as a *cause* — that of the economic machine itself. Let us then consider the claims of such a diagnosis.

Market economy theory entails the pursuit of growth with a calculus of scarcity. In theory it allocates impartially according to relative costs, but can say little about absolute costs — about rational behaviour in the face of limits set, for instance, by exhaustible natural resources. Market theory has to be indifferent to any rational non-market choice because it must work through personal divisiveness and, more importantly, must force competing nation-states to act likewise, forgetting their true inter-dependence.

In recent years many have observed the dire *effects* of this consumerism. But only since 1977 have ways been sought from within of *changing* the system that still rules most of the world. Two proposed changes lately put forward in the United States could go a good way in this direction without even having to eliminate the market factor. The first, developed by Dr. W. Halal and others, rejects the concept of the corporation as responsive simply to shareholders, managers and workers and, briefly, would use a social accounting model to arrive at the net cost–benefit return on inputs from *all* transactions between the working concern and society, and not just return on invested capital — i.e. public and private investments, employees, customers, the public at large and other trading concerns. In principle, this framework would thus allow organizations to become publicly accountable in terms of resource use, pollution control, use of human capital and total use of social facilities.

A second and more radical correction involves keeping the activities of private concerns within acceptable limits. As proposed by H. E. Daly (H. E. Daly, 1977), this can be done by setting various limits within which market forces can be left to allocate resources and distribute incomes 'within imposed ecological and ethical boundaries'. A first such boundary could be provided by a government system of auctioning depletion quota rights on scarce material resources, internal or imported, so as to confine aggregate economic growth within defined and acceptable bounds. Revenue from this arrangement could, if necessary, be used in part to maintain upper and lower boundaries to income distribution.

This idea, which is based on sophisticated reasoning at the conservation level, is probably the most painless way of making mature market economies fit into a rational world development with a minimum loss of business or personal freedom. Ways of dealing equitably with transnational concerns can be, and clearly would need to be, worked out.

Finally, a comprehensive set of purely economic adjustments, designed to bring the market-economy system into line with present-day realities both internal and international, has now become available. See *The New Model Economy*, by P. G. Elkan (Pergamon, Oxford, 1982).

PART II

An Emerging Frame of Rights and Duties

6

Development and Democracy

Many are the patterns of our contemporary world. If those dictated by climate, terrain and natural resources can explain much of today's geopolitical layout, we are equally concerned with how expectations and desires are satisfied or thwarted across the globe in the diverse situations of national politics.

In this chapter important new ground has to be broken in at least two respects. Firstly, after trying to clear up some confusion about what can now be meant by the term 'democracy', we shall look at how the world's developing states are faring, in their unique cultural settings and styles of government, as their peoples strive to move towards a better life. Secondly, it is time to come to grips with the new international norms that are coming to delimit acceptable human performance — those enacted under the United Nations machinery for disarmament and for protecting human rights respectively. How far can these new curbs on governments — for their history as a world force spans a mere 35 years — hope to create legitimate restraints on the one hand and acceptable freedoms on the other?

From now on the theme of human rights and duties will loom much larger in this investigation. In the present chapter we shall simply examine how far three of the main human rights international instruments are being accepted in the developing world as a part of contemporary life but in later chapters the many ramifications of human rights thinking will have to be looked at more carefully.

New Views of Democracy

For a very long time now democracy has been under revision. In its original sense — what we would call 'direct democracy' — the term meant that those citizens of a small state who were free men took part in deciding what was to be done. Much later, after slowly shaking off the 'monocratic' idea of the divine right of kings, the notion of a liberal state emerged in Britain in tune with the first hesitant stirrings of capitalism and industrialism. This new liberal state implied that a government retained only minimal powers, individual freedom being protected by safeguards against excessive government encroachment. Freedom of choice was the criterion both politically and economically but it applied only to a wealthy few. Slowly, and after long debate, voting rights were gradually extended from the original wealthy landowners to more and more groups, until parliamentary representative government as we know it finally became the liberal democratic norm in western-style developed states.

Over the last 65 years this familiar institution has been rivalled by two important variants that seem to have little in common with the original meaning of democracy. The first, the type adopted in what we shall call the radical authoritarian, or centrally planned, systems, arose from criticisms of liberal capitalist society made by Karl Marx and Frederick Engels in the mid-nineteenth century, and from the new egalitarian economic vision that Marx advocated to replace it. This critical diagnosis predicated a logical collapse of the current system under its own inconsistencies — a mounting imbalance between classes already highly unequal in their access to wealth despite a rising productive potential that promised an end to scarcity as the engine of economic effort. However, the accident that Marxist theory was taken up by Lenin and applied as a practical programme in a society not yet advanced enough economically to absorb it meant that the system introduced in the USSR had to rely on a minute 'vanguard' of committed members to carry it through. That vanguard, exercising power in the name of the people, became and has remained a single party machine whose mandate is approved periodically in a general election.

How far can this be called democracy? We may agree that formally its object is democratic in the sense that it seeks the well-being of an entire people without class discrimination. Whether it is democratic in electoral terms, allowing polices to reflect a popular consensus, must depend on conditions to be considered below.

We thus have the individualist liberal capitalist and the non-liberal or misnamed 'communist' versions of democracy. But since 1950, with much of the developing world gaining independence from colonial rule, new forms of democracy have arisen which now make up a clear majority of all governments. Why these so often differ from what we regard as the democratic tradition is simply because in many areas — for example, in Africa — a newly emancipated people has little traditional experience of the competitive liberal work ethic and few occupational or class divisions. What it does have is a greater common interest, and possibly some consensus, in favour of sustained advance. Any contrasts are likely to be tribal, ethnic, religious or linguistic rather than due to stratified classes. What will be termed a populist state, commonly with a single-party system but perhaps with none at all or with two or more parties, may well seem to offer a more natural forum for concerted development than one split by opposing factions alternating between public or private control.

How far can this same argument be applied to the centrally directed system? In the states of eastern Europe, at least, there is more economic maturity than in most of the developing world, a far more complex division of labour and thus more variety of interests. Here, then, provided we can take it that class exploitation has been removed, the criterion of democracy in a one-party state must rest on whether or not party membership is open to all; whether the party itself is democratically run; and whether the exercise of membership is feasible for an average citizen faced with other commitments. So far it is by no means clear that these requirements are fully met, but if they can be perhaps the democratic label should be accorded some meaning in this context (C. B. Macpherson, 1966).

All this means that in theory we have to envisage three main forms of democratic rule at work in the contemporary world. In practice the position is even more complex than this and it is important that we appreciate the real differences that exist.

To begin with, we can distinguish two common features of the democratic principle. These are, firstly, an equal right of citizens to contribute in some way to the reaching of consensual choices on matters of national policy; and, secondly, their rights to equal treatment, not only under the law but also in respect of those basic means to fulfilment that are secured by the state as the outcome of a common endeavour. These same two facets of the democratic idea also underlie the United Nations code of rights and duties, as will become clear when we dig a little deeper.

It follows from these principles that, for any kind of democracy, the governmental or political basis of the state and its economic basis are interlinked, and indissolubly so. Because the liberal democracy started out as a liberal market state based on free or non-arbitrary choice for an exclusive minority, and only later had democracy and popular enfranchisement tacked on to it through force of circumstance, this essential link is now minimized or forgotten by the modern marketeer. There is an even more fundamental reason to keep the link in mind when we recall that the very qualities that make people human at all are a product of society, and that society itself rests on the interdependence of unique personalities co-operating to meet their common needs and individual wants within a consensual frame of perceived justice. That is the reality behind any form of democracy, and indeed any form of society, whatever the conflicts of motive that may appear to divide it.

The liberal democratic state, and the capitalist market economy that is its economic counterpart, both of which developed in Great Britain from the eighteenth century onwards, have now spawned several variants that range between the British style of liberal democracy at one extreme and the USSR-type radical authoritarian solution at the other. In addition, there is the populist market state, found in many developing countries, which has embraced some attributes of the two extremes and rejected others; and then the traditional conservative and authoritarian conservative types, both market-oriented but varying widely in their democratic content according as they embrace highly personal or military rule or possess working assemblies and perhaps even several parties.

Figure 16 illustrates, first, how systems of government and economic systems are related to one another in some specific national examples which range between the extremes of liberal democratic and centrally directed states; and second, how the five main forms of government can be distinguished from one another according to the classificatory scheme of political systems developed by Professor Jean Blondel, which has been adopted here (J. Blondel, 1972).

Figure 16A requires a word of explanation. Here I have tried to distinguish between seven relatively advanced states as they differ in their governmental and economic components along what we may call the liberal democratic–radical authoritarian axis. We start at the top left-hand corner with the United Kingdom and its system of countervailing power with opposing parties, plus free market enterprise. Coming next to systems with degrees of consensual administration, the first case shown is that of Switzerland, still with a market-type economy and opposing parties but possessing a unique form of fairly direct and decentralized democracy, including frequent referenda at national and local levels. By contrast the case of France also retains an opposing party system, but its market economy is to a considerable extent concerted through official and indicative economic plans, plus various links between government and private activity. Different again is Japan, still with opposing parties but with a fair degree of consensus thinking and consultation throughout its entire national life, including its power structure, and with a market system which likewise reflects in its productive process the traditional but weakening tendency of the populace to seek harmony rather than confrontation.

With Yugoslavia we reach the single-party system, and national resources vested under public control. However, the economy is still somewhere near to the idea of concerted enterprise, since the productive system, in this particular case, is based on worker control of state-owned enterprises. A different variant again is found in Hungary, where a single-party planned state now coexists with a fair measure of private enterprise incorporated into the command economy. Finally, with the USSR we reach the true single-party system, with unified control and a centrally planned economic framework which, although it now embraces greater scope for initiative within constituent enterprises, tolerates a true market only to a very limited extent.

Figure 16B requires less comment. Retaining the classificatory scheme developed by Professor Jean Blondel, it shows that the five principal types of government in force today are each to be identified near to one end or another of three major 'axes' — the liberal authoritarian, the radical conservative and the democratic monocratic. While the liberal democratic

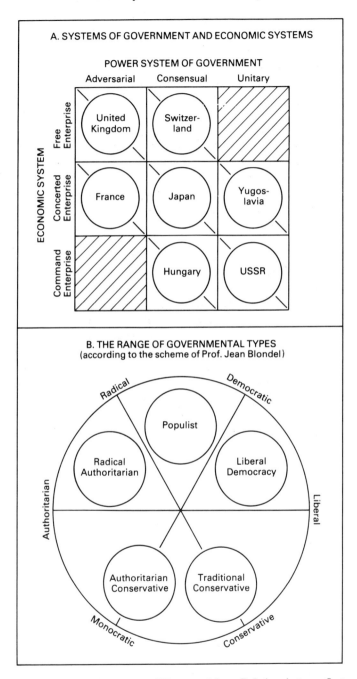

FIG. 16. The Range of Governmental Types, and Some Relations between Systems of Government and Economic Systems.

style always has two or more parties and the true radical authoritarian a single party and a planned economy, the other three may function with no parties at all or with one or more, and may differ fairly widely as a result. All will remain near the market end of the economic spectrum but the conservative types may have less claim to democratic status than the rest.

Politics and Government in the Developing World

How far can one appraise the effectiveness of government in its respect for or disregard of humane values? It is possible to compare countries, and regions, not merely in terms of their socio-economic indicators but equally by looking at their types of government, by the extent of repression or regard for democracy, by frequency of coups or civil wars, by arms spending, or again by considering respect for humane standards as reflected in adherence to UN human rights Conventions or Disarmament Agreements. Probably a composite index of some kind could even be worked out on such a basis.

All this is in line with the kind of thinking employed in Chapter 4, in looking at human character. Respect for human rights and duties is not merely a potentially sensitive development indicator but it is also a common measure of aspiration and achievement that is understood by nearly everyone. This is one important reason why human rights concerns are central to the whole world order issue. At this point, nonetheless, we are mainly concerned to see the domain of human rights and duties in its developmental context — to seek an overview of how the worldwide effort mounted in this field is being received.

Where, then, to start? For the present purpose we shall concentrate on the developing world — not, in all conscience, because more advanced states do not have problems, for they have far more than normal human frailties could justify. Neither is the developing world to be seen as a homogeneous assembly of ignorance and barbarity. The truth is far more complex than that. After 35 years of contact with international problems I am convinced that the whole development process entails a slow unconscious *mental* evolution towards an achieved web of stable institutions within which needs for conflict and consensus can be sufficiently contained. That evolution has to be a lengthy one and it will not be by-passed simply by rapid economic growth.

From this it follows that the functional effectiveness of developing states must be looked at from somewhere near the analytical standpoint sketched earlier in Chapter Four. But the method must also encompass a diversity compounded of languages, religions, ethnic divisions, cultures, social structures, standards of living, resources, situations and development prospects. Most of the developing states are poor overall but with gross inequality, though some too are oil-rich and one is theoretically the world's richest. An exceptional few are endowed with high technology while others, uncharacteristically, have reached a high level of social integration. In many countries ethnic or other minority problems obtrude themselves to complicate an already pronounced disparity in wealth or way of life.

There are means of reducing some of this variety to more manageable proportions. Knowledge of the literacy rate, for instance, suggests how far a society may already be integrated in a common field of communication, as well as marking the success of its education services. Common elements of culture, historical experience, frames of law and tolerance are in some degree subsumed under four major geographical groupings of developing states that can be identified also with a main language and religion. The quality of political leadership is less easy to measure on its own, but by looking at regional characteristics alongside forms of government, accessions to UN Conventions and so on, some fundamental world patterns may come to light.

An Outline Political Analysis of the Modern World

To set the scene for this mini-survey it is instructive to look first at how the main political systems are distributed throughout the world. This is possible because Professor Jean Blondel (J. Blondel, 1972) has analysed their distribution comparatively and has now revised and enlarged his original survey to record the situation ten years later. We can thus see how far governmental types are liable to change under present-day conditions — a point of some moment where prospects for democracy and human rights are concerned.

Table 19 sums up the data gathered by Blondel in respect of the situation at 1 January 1972 and 1982 respectively, with twenty-four more states being included in the later survey. We can see that a fair degree of stability exists worldwide in the composition of governmental styles but that some developments have occurred during the decade. Liberal democracies have retained their place in just over one quarter of the world's states. In Sub-Saharan Africa and in Latin America Populist systems have advanced during the decade, while Authoritarian and Traditional Conservative governments have declined — a fact that has reduced the latter's contribution to the world's total of states. This trend reflects the popularity of single-party populist styles of government in newly independent countries, where there is a strong impetus for rapid advance as a common goal, even for economically disadvantaged majorities. It can be seen that there has been a small increase overall in states with two or more parties and those with Assemblies; and a decline in no-party states. The proportion of military governments and states characterized by highly personal rule has remained roughly constant in the world distribution, the former now being present in a little under a quarter of all states.

TABLE 19
World Distribution of Basic Governmental Systems — 1972 and 1982[a]

Category	W. Europe & N. America[b]	E. Europe & N. Asia	S. & E. Asia	M. East & N. Africa	Rest of Africa	Latin America	World No.	%
1	2	3	4	5	6	7	8	9
Countries included								
1972	23	13	20	21	38	24	139	100
1982	23	13	26	22	46	33	163	100
Governmental type (%)[c]								
LD 1972	87	—	25	14	6	25	36	26
LD 1982	96	—	21	18	4	33	44	27
RA 1972	—	100	20	—	—	4	18	13
RA 1982	—	100	8	9	9	4	22	13
P 1972	—	—	—	43	55	21	35	25
P 1982	4	—	25	32	78	33	61	38
AC 1972	13	—	25	—	26	42	28	20
AC 1982	—	—	17	5	7	30	18	11
TC 1972	—	—	30	43	13	8	22	16
TC 1982	—	—	37	36	2	—	18	11
No. of parties (%)								
None 1972	4	—	45	53	31	12	36	26
1982	—	—	42	41	13	18	31	19
Single 1972	9	100	20	33	45	25	49	35
1982	—	100	23	32	63	15	60	37
Two+ 1972	87	—	35	14	24	63	54	39
1982	100	—	42	27	24	67	72	44
With Assembly (%)[d]								
1972	96	100	90	53	69	83	110	79
1982	100	87	96	64	76	76	133	82
With military government (%)								
1972	4	—	30	25	37	17	30	22
1982	—	7	21	18	41	27	38	23
With highly personal rule (%)								
1972	—	8	5	5	10	8	10	7
1982	—	20	8	18	15	12	20	12

[a]Information refers to 1 January 1972 and 1 January 1982 respectively. For the former date figures have been calculated and adapted from data compiled by Professor Jean Blondel (J. Blondel, 1972). Figures referring to 1982 have been newly revised by Professor Blondel, and relate to states with populations above 50,000 inhabitants.
[b]Includes also two states of Oceania (Australia and New Zealand).
[c]LD = Liberal democratic; RA = Radical Authoritarian; P = Populist; AC = Authoritarian Conservative; TC = Traditional Conservative.
[d]Refers to the percentage of states possessing Assemblies with one or more Chambers.

We are now in a position to attempt an outline of the world political situation. Grouping together all those states classed as developed according to the definition cited in Chapter 3 (Table 7), the world's sovereign entities can be placed in five major regions — or four plus the so-called developed world — the entity comprised within its European and north Asian heartland plus large 'islands' of advanced living in north America and Australasia. We shall concentrate first on the four distinctive world regions that make up what is called the developing world, and on as many as possible of the countries comprised in each.

These four world regions are not simply geographic entities,* but each reflects a certain unity or consistency in its history, culture, languages and main religions, as is shown by the following grouping:

TABLE 20
Regional Groupings of Non-European Developing States

Cultural/Religious Regions	Continental Area	Samples of states considered	Number of governmental types
Islamic	W. Asia and N. Africa	26	5
Latin Catholic	S. and C. America	24	4
African 'Syncretic'	Sub-Saharan Africa	35	5
Hindu–Buddhist	S. and E. Asia	16	5

For the purposes of our comparative outline it is thus possible to bring together details for an extensive sample of 101 developing states. To that end we can collate forms of government, economic data and quality-of-life indicators, such as literacy, with the existence of Assemblies or the presence of military or highly personal governments. States classed as highly repressive or repressive under explicit criteria, or those subject to civil wars or frequent coups, can be weighed in the balance sheet. Against all this the frequency of ratifications or signings of UN Conventions — e.g. human rights Covenants or accessions to ten Disarmament Agreements — can also be allowed for. By bringing together these negative and positive attributes of states we can look for any regularities that may appear when cultural or religious uniformities are brought into the reckoning.

With this exercise completed, and data brought together for each of the governments in all four of the distinctive cultural/religious regions, we get the results that are summarized on a percentage basis in Table 21. Before considering this Table there are a few points, mainly about interregional comparisons and matters of definition, to be borne in mind. First, there are

*A similar grouping system has been used for a different purpose by Manouchehr Ganji in a report prepared for the Commission on Human Rights. (*The Realization of Economic, Social and Cultural Rights: Problems, Policies, Progress*, United Nations, New York, 1975).

a few countries, particularly in the Hindu–Buddhist region but also in some others, which do not fall too easily into the character of the region in which they occur. This is true of China, Mongolia and the Philippines, which are located in S.E. Asia; while Mauretania, for example, is also not fully typical of the Islamic region in which it is placed.

On matters of definition in Table 21, a few questions may involve a measure of interpretative judgement where evidence is incomplete or the matter is open to dispute — for example with some military dominated, highly repressive or highly personalized governments. For the first and third of these categories we have used the Blondel interpretation where differences arise. Definitions are thus important and two of those used by Sivard (Ruth Leger Sivard, 1982) are clear-cut. Thus military governments may involve a state of martial law; civil leadership by the military; recent creation of regimes by military coup; a legal system based on military courts; and links between military forces and political police. Governments, too, are highly repressive if they consistently violate rights to personal safety, as by torture or similar extreme forms of physical abuse. They are simply repressive if they ignore civil liberties by resorting to, for example, arbitrary arrest and imprisonment, denial of public trial or invasion of the home. Each of the definitions has been used by Sivard in conjunction with a variety of reference sources and those defining high repression and repression in particular have been adopted here.

While Table 21 presents summary political profiles of each of the world's four cultural–religious developing regions, Tables 22–25 show how this same mode of analysis can be used to sum up the character of each region when countries are assigned to Blondel's five governmental types.

We can thus compare regions according to the following six parameters:

— cultural–religious character;
— make-up of governmental types;
— economic and level-of-life indicators;
— special political characteristics;
— degree of political stability and harmony;
— record of accessions to binding international agreements.

The first conclusions from such a review are somewhat surprising. Each region does show a special array of governmental types and its own typical level of life, but there is no clear-cut correlation between style of government and either political characteristics, stability, or even adherence to international agreements. Some resemblance does appear between levels of accession to human rights conventions and agreements on disarmament.

So far as the data can be considered representative and not seriously affected by subjective judgement, and remembering that we are dealing with developing states, the survey can throw useful light on at least two

TABLE 21

Summary Political Profiles of World Cultural–Religious Development Regions

	Cultural–Religious Development Regions			
Category	Hindu-Buddhist (S. and E. Asia)[a]	Latin Catholic (S. and C. America)	Islamic (N. Africa and W. Asia)	African 'Syncretic' (Sub-Saharan Africa)
1	2	3	4	5
Number of states in sample	16	24	26	35
Special characteristics				
Percentage of states (1982) with:				
Assembly	87	75	66	82
Military government	19	33	35	40
Highly personal rule	19	17	15	20
Stability				
Percentage of states experiencing:[b]				
Highly repressive rule	25	54	46	26
Two or more coups	12	33	19	23
Civil war	31	37	39	34
Level of life				
Gross National Product (dollars/head 1978)[c]	740	1041	1710	330
Physical quality of life index (%)[d]	64	71	41	35
Adult literacy (%)[d]	68	72	34	32
International agreements				
Accessions and accessions/signings:[e]				
UN human rights covenants:				
Economic social and cultural	37(43)	58(62)	35(39)	32(35)
Civil and political	31(43)	54(62)	35(39)	32(35)
UN Convention:				
Discrimination against women	37(49)	38(80)	4(19)	6(46)
Ten UN disarmament agreements	42(51)	47(64)	34(46)	30(43)
Total rank-order score of regions	22(20)	24(24)	35(36)	39(40)

[a]The region includes China, Mongolia and the Philippines.
[b]Refers to period January 1960–mid–1982 and to data of R. L. Sivard (1982).
[c]Unweighted averages.
[d]Unweighted averages of latest available national data.
[e]The first figure refers to all accessions only and the second to accessions plus signings: by 1 January 1983 for covenants; 1 July 1982 for the convention; and 31 July 1982 for disarmament agreements. All figures are percentages for each group.

Category	Type of Governments:[a]					Sample:	
	Liberal democratic	Radical authoritarian	Populist	Authoritarian conservative	Traditional conservative	Number of states	Percentage
1	2	3	4	5	6	7	8
Composition of sample							
Number of states	4	6	2	2	2	16	100
Percentage of states	25	37	13	13	13	100	—
Level of life[b]							
GNP/head 1978 (dollars)	725	480	1700	835	305	—	—
PQL Index — latest (%)	69	49	70	77	52	—	—
Adult literacy — latest (%)	60	65	71	89	51	—	—
Special characteristics							
States with assembly (%)	100	67	100	100	100	14	87
States military-dominated (%)	—	—	50	50	50	3	19
States with highly personal rule (%)	—	17	50	50	—	3	19
Stability							
Judged highly repressive/repressive (%)[c]	25(75)	—(83)	—(100)	100	50	4(13)	25(81)
Two or more coups — 1960–82 (%)	—	—	—	50	50	2	12
Civil or internal war 1960–82 (%)	25	33	50	50	—	5	31
UN covenants or conventions[d]							
Economic, social and cultural rights (%)[e]	50	50(67)	—	50	—	6 (7)	37(43)
Civil and political rights (%)[e]	50	50(67)	—	—(50)	—	5 (7)	31(44)
Discrimination against women (%)[f]	25(50)	67(84)	—	50	—	6 (8)	37(49)
Ten UN disarmament agreements (%)[g]	47(59)	40(45)	35(45)	35(55)	50(55)	7 (8)	42(51)

[a]Refers to the situation at 1 January 1982.

[b]Figures are unweighted averages.

[c]First figure refers to highly repressive states and second figure refers to highly repressive and repressive states, according to criteria of R. L. Sivard (1982).

[d]First figure refers to accessions and second to total of accessions or signatures.

[e]As at 1 January 1983.

[f]As at 1 July 1982.

TABLE 23

Political Profile — Latin Catholic Development Region (S. and C. America)

Category	Type of Governments:[a]				Sample:	
	Liberal democratic	Radical authoritarian	Populist	Authoritarian conservative	Number of states	Percentage
1	2	3	4	5	6	7
Composition of sample						
Number of states	6	1	7	10	24	100
Percentage of states	25	4	29	42	100	—
Level of life[b]						
GNP/head 1978 (dollars)	1520	810	1230	835		
PQL Index — latest (%)	80	92	73	59		
Adult literacy — latest (%)	85	96	76	57		
Special characteristics						
States with assembly (%)	100	100	85	50	18	75
States military-dominated (%)	—	—	—	80	8	33
States with highly personal rule (%)	—	100	25	20	4	17
Stability						
Judged highly repressive/repressive (%)[c]	33(50)	—(100)	14(57)	100(100)	13(18)	54(75)
Two or more coups — 1960–82 (%)	17	—	29	50	8	33
Civil or internal war 1960–82 (%)	17	—	29	60	9	37
UN covenants or conventions[d]						
Economic, social and cultural rights (%)[e]	100(—)	—	43(—)	50(60)	14(15)	58(62)
Civil and political rights (%)[e]	100(—)	—	43(—)	40(60)	13(15)	54(62)
Discrimination against women (%)[f]	33(100)	100(—)	43(—)	30(60)	9(19)	38(80)
Ten UN disarmament agreements (%)[g]	42(58)	50(60)	50(63)	45(65)	11(15)	47(64)

For key to notes, see Table 22.

TABLE 24

Political Profile — Islamic Development Region (N. Africa and W. Asia)

| Category | Type of Governments:[a] | | | | | Sample: | |
	Liberal democratic	Radical authoritarian	Populist	Authoritarian conservative	Traditional conservative	Number of states	Percentage
1	2	3	4	5	6	7	8
Composition of sample							
Number of states	2	2	12	2	8	26	100
Percentage of states	8	8	46	8	31	100	—
Level of life[b]							
GNP/head 1978 (dollars)	870	330	920	720	7275		
PQL Index — latest (%)	57	23	38	49	42		
Adult literacy — latest (%)	48	19	32	40	32		
Special characteristics							
States with assembly (%)	100	50	100	—	25	17	66
States military-dominated (%)	—	—	58	100	—	9	35
States with highly personal rule (%)	—	—	33	—	—	4	15
Stability							
Judged highly repressive/repressive (%)[c]	50(100)	50(100)	66(100)	100(—)	—(50)	12(22)	46(85)
Two or more coups — 1960–82 (%)	—	50	17	50	12	5	19
Civil or internal war 1960–82 (%)	50	—	50	50	25	10	39
UN covenants or conventions[d]							
Economic, social and cultural rights (%)[e]	100(—)	—	50(58)	—	12(12)	9(10)	35(39)
Civil and political rights (%)[e]	100(—)	—	50(58)	—	12(12)	9(10)	35(39)
Discrimination against women (%)[f]	—	—(50)	8(25)	—	—(12)	1(5)	4(19)
Ten UN disarmament agreements (%)[g]	50(75)	50(60)	34(46)	45(65)	24(33)	9(12)	34(46)

For key to notes, see Table 22.

TABLE 25

Political Profile — African Development Region (Sub-Saharan Africa)

			Type of Governments:[a]			Sample:	
Category	Liberal democratic	Radical authoritarian	Populist	Authoritarian conservative	Traditional conservative	Number of states	Percentage
1	2	3	4	5	6	7	8
Composition of sample							
Number of states	2	3	27	2	1	35	100
Percentage of states	6	8	77	6	3	100	—
Level of life[b]							
GNP/head 1978 (dollars)	475	185	325	385	280	—	—
PQL Index — latest (%)	34	21	34	37	52	—	—
Adult literacy — latest (%)	22	9	29	45	59	—	—
Special characteristics							
States with assembly (%)	100	67	82	100	100	29	83
States military-dominated (%)	—	33	48	—	—	14	40
States with highly personal rule (%)	—	—	22	50	—	7	20
Stability							
Judged highly repressive/repressive (%)[c]	—	33(66)	26(74)	50	—(100)	9(24)	26(69)
Two or more coups — 1960–82 (%)	100	33	19	—	—	8	23
Civil or internal war 1960–82 (%)	100	100	26	—	—	12	34
UN covenants or conventions[d]							
Economic, social and cultural rights (%)[e]	—	—	41(45)	—	—	11(12)	32(35)
Civil and political rights (%)[e]	—	—	41(45)	—	—	11(12)	32(35)
Discrimination against women (%)[f]	—(50)	33	4(48)	—	—(100)	2(16)	6(46)
Ten UN disarmament agreements (%)[g]	55(65)	13(23)	30(44)	30(35)	40(50)	11(16)	30(43)

For key to notes, see Table 22.

Is World Order Evolving?

TABLE 26
Characteristics of States with Different Party Systems[a]

Region and party system	Special characteristics			Stability			Number of states in sample
	Assembly	Military rule	Highly per- sonal rule	Highly repres- sive	With coups (2 or more since 1960)	With civil wars (since 1960)	
1	2	3	4	5	6	7	8
HINDU–BUDDHIST							
One-party system	6	1	2	—	—	3	8
No-party system	2	—	1	1	—	1	2
Two+ party system	6	2	—	3	2	1	6
Total number of states	14	3	3	4	2	5	16
LATIN CATHOLIC							
One-party system	4	—	2	2	1	1	5
No-party system	—	4	—	4	2	2	4
Two+ party system	14	4	2	7	5	6	15
Total number of states	18	8	4	13	8	9	24
ISLAMIC							
One-party system	8	5	3	5	2	3	9
No-party system	3	3	—	3	2	3	11
Two+ party system	6	1	1	4	1	4	6
Total number of states	17	9	4	12	5	10	26
AFRICAN 'SYNCRETIC'							
One-party system	19	8	7	6	3	8	20
No-party system	—	5	—	1	2	—	5
Two+ party system	10	1	—	2	3	4	10
Total number of states	29	14	7	9	8	12	35
All One-party systems	37	14	14	13	6	15	42
All No-party systems	5	12	1	9	6	6	22
All Two+ party systems	36	8	3	16	11	15	37
Grand Total	78	34	18	38	23	36	101

[a]Refers to the situation at 1 January 1982.

points — for example: How far do different cultural–religious settings affect the functioning of political systems? Or again: How far are arbitrary rule, high repression and instability associated with different types of system? In other words, to what extent do the culture and type of system affect the effective human quality of political performance?

To elucidate these questions let us begin by taking the four cultural–religious regions shown in Table 21 and see how they fare when each is accorded a rank order from 1 to 4 on performance under each of the criteria in lines 2–7 and 9–14 of the Table, the rankings then being summed to give a total score. The score for each region is in fact given on line 15 of the Table, which shows that the order in which the regions are listed is that of their overall best performance. Here it might be objected that the criteria differ in kind and in accuracy, while some may be more relevant than others. If, however, we eliminate quality-of-life criteria (lines 9–10) the ranking remains unchanged. The same thing happens if we omit accessions to international agreements (lines 11–14) or, again, if we omit special characteristics (lines 2–4). It would thus appear that on this very simple rank-order method the region of S.E. Asia (loosely described as the Hindu–Buddhist region) comes first in its quality of life and political effectiveness, ahead of the somewhat more economically developed region of Latin America and, indeed, of Islam or Sub-Saharan Africa. This purely statistical result is surprising when one recalls the appalling anti-human conflicts suffered of late within South-East Asia. On the other hand, bearing in mind the pacifist nature of the region's belief-systems, one may feel a little less bemused by this result.

What, then, of the effect of different political systems? While some differences can be seen by inspection of the Tables, it may be of interest first to compare one-party, no-party and multi-party systems of all types in terms of stability or special characteristics such as military or highly personal rule. When states are grouped on this basis, as is done in Table 26, the links between number of parties and political 'quality' are given by the figures in each cell which, as it happens, are virtually percentages also of the total number of states considered. For example, 13 per cent of all single-party states have been rated highly repressive as compared to 16 per cent of multi-party states, but these two groups comprise an equal number (15) that have suffered civil war. We see that there are no single-party states classed as highly repressive in the S.E. Asia sample, whereas there are several in the Islamic region and in Sub-Saharan Africa.

It might be objected that because Table 26 groups together data for five types of governmental system the figures in terms of parties are not decisive. From this standpoint it is perhaps more instructive to look at the prevalence of high repression, coups and civil wars in liberal democracies and radical authoritarian states. When this is done, however, the totals for developing countries do not suggest any marked change or superiority either way, as the following figures show:

TABLE 27
Relative Stability of Governmental Types

Governmental type	Highly repressive	Two or more coups	Civil war	Total of states
Liberal democratic	4 (29%)	3 (21%)	6 (43%)	14 (100%)
Radical authoritarian	2 (17%)	2 (17%)	4 (33%)	12 (100%)

The evidence on cultural–religious regions brought together above supports a general conclusion that is negative, but highly significant nonetheless. If we are looking for signs that the widespread conflict, blatant inhumanity and disregard for elementary rights witnessed through-out the developing world are linked in some way to the political systems in force, no such general link can be discerned. In particular regions, it is true, certain styles of government may tend to be associated with massive abuse of human rights. But if anything two factors — the cultural–religious traditions and level of development — prove to be of greater overall weight in this regard than any special governmental type. As might perhaps be expected, discord does tend to become more marked as intermediate development levels are reached.

In stating these conclusions two qualifying remarks are in order. First, because conditions in some states may change fairly quickly, possible errors due to any lack of identity in reference dates must be kept in mind. Secondly, major political change sometimes leads to a situation where earlier accessions to international conventions are repudiated, even though temporarily, by an incoming administration, thereby changing a country's apparent standing with respect, say, to human rights. This in fact explains the lack of such accessions by China, since much earlier ratifications have been cancelled and are still subject to review. Practical limitations of this kind are inherent in any attempt to survey development problems in countries experiencing rapid change.

A last word to explain why states described as 'developed' (roughly those of Europe, N. Asia, N. America and Australasia) have not been included in this particular analysis. This is mainly because the indicators used would not suffice for comparative purposes. Governments are usually Liberal Democratic or Radical Authoritarian, stability is fairly high and accessions to international instruments are usually fairly consistent. This does not imply that such states present no problems for their citizens, but simply that the gravity of those problems merits special treatment.

Getting to Grips with Human Failure

Ideals of the international community — such as the notion of a peaceful world, the quest for a real code of human rights, respect for the natural environment and accelerated advance for the poorest peoples — all arise from a conviction that man's ability, knowledge and power now give the human individual a legitimate right to life, to a state of peace, and to tolerable chances of self-expression within the limits of his social milieu. While this conviction grows as development proceeds, the conditions that limit its satisfaction now seem to be deteriorating, and doing so in a new way. First, armed conflict is now ceasing to be a local means of settling irreconcilable disputes and is assuming an inbuilt momentum towards a dreadful finality which threatens to end the adventure altogether. Secondly, major ills that had to be suffered as 'acts of God' less than a century ago can now be remedied or avoided altogether — but are not. It is in these two senses that we can speak of a deteriorating world prospect.

Let us try to get to grips with the inhumanity manifested in collective social practice. Despite a good deal of uncertainty about human motives, perhaps five main sources of trouble can be distinguished. First of all, both individually and in the group, humans act massively in ignorance. Thus they are driven to ingest and diffuse man-made chemicals, and to spread indestructible nuclear waste, without knowing the consequences of their creation either on themselves or their outer environment. Then again they may be both ignorant and powerless, as when highly nurtured crops are devastated by abnormally fluctuating weather.

A more serious defect arises from an urge to hold tenaciously to beliefs for which there is no evidence. Men will kill, torture or violate without remorse for completely erroneous reasons, where creeds, ideologies or commands so demand. The catalogue of arbitrary executions, systematic torture, involuntary disappearances, genocide and harsh unfounded discrimination considered annually by the UN Human Rights Commission in Geneva runs to hundreds of thousands of cases in many countries, yet it is nowhere near complete.

To this kind of motivation we must add those that arise from self-seeking urges, displayed in varying degree but on an enormous scale in nearly all countries. These may include the exercise of arbitrary or self-assumed power, as by dictatorship or bureaucratic tyranny on a large or small scale; or involve the ruthless pursuit of self-advantage or one-upmanship either as seller or producer, or in social life. Much of this behaviour arises from the competitive, adversarial nature of democratic politics and liberal economic systems; while bureaucratic tyranny and monolithic secrecy are the concomitants of radical authoritarian systems. Authoritarian conservative states likewise will tend to encourage political dictatorships, often supplemented by military power.

Finally, human beings *en masse* are highly susceptible to suggestion and thus easily moved to irrational and inhuman acts by a sort of group hysteria. This may easily be sparked off by hostility to out-groups, or whipped up by a charismatic leader. All these are familiar examples of basic anti-social weaknesses, pursued by resort to violence, deceit, deception and crime, that arise without any need to postulate psychotic or other abnormal mental states.

The combined effect of these limits and flaws of character on daily life and life chances, although they differ in their impact at different stages of development, are now visible always as acute misfortune or injustice. By virtue of his or her membership of a cumulating society the equal rights of a human being to life, to food and shelter, to knowledge and to some elementary impress of personal potential — rights conferred by his essential human quality — are thereby trampled upon, reduced or terminated by arbitrary maltreatment.

Let us recall in barest outline how this basic life problem is experienced at each stage. Among many millions living in the poorest countries even the search for enough food and water, much less shelter or medical care, presents for most a horrendous problem, attended with mass affliction by disease, blindness and early death. From FAO data, about a quarter of all the people in developing countries are undernourished, more than 30 per cent of them in the Far East. In Chad, Ethiopia and Haiti some 40 per cent or more of the population is in the same plight. It is therefore no surprise that in some states only 10–20 per cent of the adult population is literate, while average life expectancy at birth may be little over 40 years. In such conditions expectations are unsurprisingly low so that ignorance, corruption and superstition may reign almost unchecked. Political conflict may be minimal, although hatred of more privileged or successful minorities, or immigrants, can be stirred up. In the poorest countries, however, idealism can still exist amid shared misfortune, and in fact accessions to international conventions there can be surprisingly high.

At an intermediate level of average income, developing states may still show ample signs of hunger, disease, poor shelter and illiteracy, even in large and progressive states. If India has 200 million undernourished people, Indonesia has over 30 million, Nigeria some 14 million, Brazil and Pakistan nearly as many. In these intermediate countries, however, knowledge and technique are more readily to hand and economic advance may well exceed population growth. If corruption still reigns, expectations will be higher than in very poor countries, so that an active opposition to authoritarian rule and privilege may bring large-scale internal conflicts and coups. Ignorance, and the reign of religious or other dogma, may still delay popular emancipation, while easy imports of arms from the government-aided export industries of the developed world too often seek to ensure that authoritarian rule remains secure. If any kind of rule appears 'anti-business', attempts may be made to topple it in the interests of foreign 'security' by agents acting for more powerful states.

Countries at the intermediate stage thus contribute enormously to the more glaring human rights abuses posed by the developing world. Every year major violations on a mass scale are investigated by the UN Human Rights Commission in Geneva in respect of some 12–15 countries, usually located in Latin America, Asia or Africa. In such countries systematic torture by police or security forces is usually endemic, while involuntary disappearances have been investigated in 21 countries in 1982–83, twelve of them on a large scale. Some two million arbitrary or non-judicial executions are estimated to have occurred since 1968 and detention without trial, often on doubtful grounds, is commonplace. Slavery and slavery-like practices remain also widespread in several countries, particularly in Africa, and harsh treatment of indigenous peoples, which in the Americas may comprise many millions in various countries, is widespread. If some of these offences are largely associated with the ruling or religious élites in repressive regimes, many are more diffuse in origin and are common to developed and developing countries alike. This is true also of a new breed of counter-activity, including cross-frontier abductions, indiscriminate terrorism and hostage-taking.

So glaring is this cumulating catalogue of offences against common humanity in the developing world, where life itself is excessively cheap, that it seems incongruous even to broach the mental and emotional anguish that lies hidden beneath these blatant but unheeded crimes. In any event the data available do not allow us to do so. But when we turn to the so-called developed world, where battles rage around the scope for freedom rather than about freedom to exist, it is something of a paradox that the contrast between power and achievement seems more glaring and more ominous. For it is the developed world that sets the global norms, and if its standards are false then the consequences are likely to be magnified grotesquely for all in the years to come.

In the 'developed' world there is less room for *persisting* failure due to popular ignorance or lack of expertise, but in other respects the main sources of human failing, though pursued through more subtle means, are equally in evidence. Rewards for personal ascendancy through wealth, corruption and/or wire-pulling are both enormous and widely sought. If the role of myth and mistaken beliefs seems less justified than in the developing world, it is no less widespread. For all societies are governed through a ruling élite. As wealth and expertise become more widespread, as the scope for direct rule is weakened, so a widely diffused establishment view or tradition has to arise and create sufficient consensus to replace the more direct force of arms. This 'invisible conditioning' becomes part of what was earlier described as 'the social character' and 'the social unconscious'. It has to be highly successful over a long period, for it must rationalize not only the practice of government but that which has become far more open to contention — the economic system itself, with its highly differential rewards. Thus it is that our final human frailty — susceptibility to mass persuasion — is in part transformed in the more developed state by a wide use of highly developed skills aimed at influencing people *en masse* — on the one side by an appeal to self-interest, and on the other through a sense of national purpose backed, where thought necessary, by coercion.

How, then, should we evaluate that fateful dichotomy that is the developed world? First, we have two alternative economic systems. To keep each system intact its ruling élite must fill its citizenry with a deep conviction of the unimaginable horrors on the other side. The systems themselves, although theoretically opposite in their working, have been forced to move towards each other, so that the mixed economy has had to embrace a considerable measure of technical planning, and a rising public sector, while the command system has had to resort to some private initiative and a growing market sector. Far more than is realized by the public at large, both sides have been linked together in cooperation through transnational and state enterprises (Levinson, 1978).

What, then, of life chances and basic rights in the developed world? While access to most essentials is assured through state action, problems of human rights persist, though in a far less blatant form. There is still room for complaints by individuals — in liberal states because of problems of discrimination, e.g. in respect of sex, religion or ethnic origin; or, in either regime, against the petty obstructive tyranny of bureaucrats, for rampant bureaucracy is the price that has had to be paid for a complex, legislated life. If we have to sum up the main violations on both sides in a few words — which is dangerous, for much remains to be said — command states impose greatly excessive coercion because of a fear of free opinion as a disintegrating force; while liberal states enjoin excessive business freedom in deference to the myth of free competition.

The consequences, in terms of life chances and basic rights, are for the many far from ideal. In the cumbersome command state a planned material evolution is secured at the price of incarceration and exile if opinions run counter to party dogma. In liberal states, by contrast, elected governments have to placate the sources of party finance, and retain power and votes by playing safe with privilege. These are the states where questions of rights arise from an over-free commercial exploitation of science and technology; where the future is mortgaged to the profitable present; and from where home-based transnational concerns are free to export proscribed products to countries of the developing world. No one has a monopoly of vice or virtue where human rights and duties are concerned.

But beyond bureaucracy, and overt violations of rights, the citizens of advanced states pay a hidden price for their throw-away gadgetry that still negates humane development. That price can only be measured by rates of psychosis, neurosis and *anomie*; by drug-taking in various forms; by s· icide; by economic dependence; by occupational hazards and accidents; and by cardiovascular diseases and tumours. In the outer habitat, too, the price must be assessed — here by obsessive ugliness, a gobbling up of resources and a fateful violating of natural systems.

But, on the other side, and against all this, it has to be remembered that very many are now aware of these ills and are seeking to counter them. This is true even of that single country whence originate most of the consumerist distortions that afflict the rest of the world. Not only is mankind aware of the ills of civilization in 1984 but it has long since discovered a key that might open the way to their solution. That key is a worldwide code of human rights and duties as a practical embodiment of humane ideals. The discovery of such a code's significance in a world frame was made by H. G. Wells in the London of 1940, and Wells's first statement has since been broadened to a worldwide campaign pursued through the United Nations. Our analysis so far has led us directly towards this point, and in the next two chapters it is the elements of a world code of rights and duties that will have to be explored.

7

Human Rights and Duties:
The Substance and the Shadow

Consciously or not, those of us who have lived through the four decades since the Second World War have witnessed a silent revolution in human affairs. That revolution was, and is, simply the beginning of a new way of thinking — a dawning acceptance that people everywhere are linked to each other through a worldwide nexus of rights and duties. This nascent idea of an interdependent world sprang from two sources: firstly, from a heightened public awareness of comradeship in the face of perceived common peril; and secondly, from a realization that two world conflicts in 25 years must bring forth new global institutions to match the power of science and technique at work in a shrinking habitat.

As we now know, that hopeful vision proved to be only a patchy and inconclusive first step so that here, less than four decades later, we confront once again a need for climactic change — this time as the condition for continuing to exist, yet also without any urge to a common purpose.

In the present chapter we shall start from the revolution of 1940–48, which sought both to codify human rights thinking in a world context and to create a world community of sovereign states united by a shared environment and a common interest in development. The second part of that endeavour was not unique since it sprang from an embryonic framework that emerged from the end of the First World War — the founding of the League of Nations in 1919. In Chapter Two we have already touched on the organizational frame of the United Nations as a world economic and political conception. What has to be done now is to draw out the still-hidden implications of a revolution in thinking that lay behind that conception — the recognition of interdependence in diversity that came into view in 1945 with the UN and its code of human rights and duties — and it is to that endeavour, and its continued flowering, that we shall now turn.

The Modern Conception of Human Rights

While the roots of our modern social rights are to be found in those events that occurred first in England, in 1215, 1679 and 1689, then in Britain's American colonies in 1776, continuing in France in 1789 and so to various ensuing developments in the nineteenth and early twentieth centuries, the idea of a world code of human rights and duties first saw the light, appropriately enough, in the London of 1940. It began, quite inauspiciously, when H. G. Wells, after a wartime conversation with the late Lord Ritchie Calder, wrote two letters to *The Times* on war aims and human rights which he followed with a draft Declaration that was refined by the eminent and specially convened Sankey Committee after a month-long debate in the national press. Micro-film copies of the Declaration were dropped to the Resistance movement in occupied Europe. The Declaration was then translated into ten languages, and distributed worldwide to 300 editors in 48 countries. In 1942 Wells produced a revised, amplified and definitive version of the Declaration — the Rights and Duties of the World Citizen — that in some respects remains unequalled to this day.

From this point events moved swiftly. The term 'United Nations' itself was first used in 1942. Following proposals worked out by representatives of China, the United Kingdom, the USSR and the United States at Dumbarton Oaks in 1944, the United Nations Charter was drawn up in 1945 by 50 countries and finally came into existence on 24 October 1945, after it had been ratified by the four founding states, plus France. It was the Charter that brought an all-pervasive purpose to the UN organization when it identified the functions of the UN General Assembly and the Economic and Social Council with ". . . the purpose of promoting respect for, and observance of, human rights and fundamental freedoms for all". In several provisions of this kind the UN Charter thus recognized, and focused on, the individual human being and ". . . the dignity and worth of the human person". It also assumed the existence of a world community. But its main thrust, in keeping with the earlier history of international law, lay in constraining the actions of states as the components of that community.

To return to the post-war rise of human rights, the first part of the first UN General Assembly, held in London in January 1946, some months before the death there of H. G. Wells, had before it a Draft of Fundamental Rights and Freedoms. In the same year the UN Commission on Human Rights was set up and in 1947 began work on what became the historic Universal Declaration of Human Rights of the UN, finally adopted on 10 December 1948. The provisions of this Declaration are supposed to govern the actions of all member states, but more specific and, where ratified, fully binding Covenants — those on Economic, Social and Cultural Rights and on Civil and Political Rights respectively, plus an Optional Protocol — were completed by 1966 and entered into force early in 1976 (see Annex 1).

Although nobody has acknowledged officially the pioneer role of the Wells Declaration, the Universal Declaration of Human Rights did encompass nearly all the substance of its predecessor of 1942, though a few major points remain to this day unmentioned and still unattainable. There are other points of seeming paradox: for instance, that the rights both of individuals and states are covered in the UN Bill of Human Rights (i.e. Declaration plus Covenants) although international law still does not recognize the individual. To understand how thinking evolved from the happenings during and immediately following the Second World War, we have to go back to various international instruments forged between 1940 and 1949.

These are:

— the Wells Declaration on the Rights of the World Citizen (1942);
— the UN Charter and the Statutes of the International Court of Justice (1945);
— Charter of the International Military Tribunal (Nuremberg Trials, etc.) (1945);
— the Universal Declaration of Human Rights (1948);
— the UN Genocide Convention (1948);
— the Revised Geneva Conventions for Protection of Victims of War (1949).

Three UN international instruments in the above list, plus some 35 main ones enacted over the next three decades and others still under study in 1985, have defined the spirit and purpose of post-war governments in respect of human rights and duties. Broadly they affirmed that ". . . recognition of the inherent dignity and of the equal and inalienable rights of all members of the human family is the foundation of freedom, justice and peace in the world". States were mainly responsible for assuring such rights, but special instruments designed to deal with a post-war military situation — such as the Charter of the International Military Tribunals of 1945 — introduced the new idea that in some circumstances individuals can be held responsible for acts which may have international consequences. The two binding covenants introduced later, in the light of a post-colonial evolution, added some further concepts not contained in the Universal Declaration: namely that people collectively have a sovereign right to self-determination, in the sense of deciding their political status and development, and can freely dispose, for their own purposes, of their natural wealth and resources without prejudice to obligations arising from international co-operation. Other innovations have likewise arisen in response to changes in the later post-war scene. One that will certainly demand some attention is the emergence of a supposed 'right to development' in the years following 1975.

The reader, very understandably in view of the records of many governments and many politicians, may well feel, from what has been said so far, that notions of human rights and duties are hopelessly idealistic, with little practical place in the real world of violence, power-wielding and cheating. I hope to show otherwise. Because the whole subject has a strong evolutionary character, probably the best place to start is at the beginning, with the 1942 Declaration of H. G. Wells.

The Essential Rights and Duties

What are legitimate, inalienable rights that can be applied worldwide? If we begin with their original formulation, in the Rights of the World Citizen — the World Declaration of the Rights of Man as defined between 1940 and 1942 by H. G. Wells and the Sankey Committee of eminent men and women which he brought together for the purpose (see Annex 1) — we find that the eleven articles apply to everyone without distinction of age, sex, race, colour or professed beliefs or opinions. Following a brilliant Preamble which, in true Wellsian fashion, pinpoints the world situation today as closely as it did in 1940, and should be studied, these articles deal respectively with the *Right to Live* — that among other things every man, equal in the eyes of the law and as joint inheritor of all the natural resources and of the powers, inventions and possibilities accumulated by our forerunners, is entitled, within the measure of these resources, to various specified means to realize his full possibilities of physical and mental development from birth to death. Succeeding articles deal with the *Protection of Minors*; with *Duty to the Community* (including the idea that ". . . it is only by doing his quota of service" — without conscription — "that a man can justify his partnership in the community"; with the *Right to Knowledge*, including access to all necessary information and adequate education; with *Freedom of Thought and Worship*, which includes freedom of expression and association; with the *Right to Work*, which specifies freedom of occupation and legitimate remuneration but excludes as unlawful any speculative buying and selling simply for profit, whether by private individuals or public bodies; with *Right in Personal Property*; with *Freedom of Movement* about the earth — other than within the private and personal domain; with *Personal Liberty* and freedom from restraint except under closely specified conditions; with *Freedom from Violence*, including torture, mutilation and vicarious punishment as a hostage; and finally with the *Right of Law-Making*, including the idea that all laws should be made openly, with the active or tacit acquiescence of every adult citizen: "The fount of legislation in a free world is the whole people, and since life flows on constantly to new citizens, no generation can, in whole or in part, surrender or delegate this legislative power, inalienably inherent in all mankind."

Comparing the full provisions of this Declaration, as set out in Annex

1A, with its successor, the Universal Declaration of Human Rights adopted on 10 December 1948 as a basic instrument of the new United Nations Organization (Annex 1B), we find that the two are in strong agreement. While the Universal Declaration has 30 articles and spells out some of the basic rights in more detail, it is unable to refer at all to a few key ideas set out in Wells's World Declaration of 1942 (A. J. Dilloway, 1983). This is not because the ideas in question are irrelevant. On the contrary, it is a measure of their key importance in the world that neither in 1948 nor today would it yet be possible to gain their common acceptance. For the moment it will suffice to note that the main concepts it does not embrace are those set out in Articles 3, 6 (sixth sentence onwards) and 11 of the Rights of the World Citizen. The idea contained in Article 3 is in the process of being acted on by the Human Rights Commission and some brilliant work has been carried out in this area (see Mrs E. I. A. Daes, 1983).

Despite this caveat the Universal Declaration of Human Rights is a truly historic achievement, attained without dissenting vote and now backed by binding Conventions framed in more specific detail. All the rights and freedoms it enunciates apply regardless of race, colour, sex, language, religion, political or other opinion, national or social origin, property, birth or other status.

Broadly, two kinds of right are recognized. First there are civil and political rights, which have evolved over the long development of democratic society; and then economic, social and cultural rights, recognized when it was seen that any effective use of civil and political rights must depend on the possibility of enjoying other rights of an economic and social nature.

Civil and Political Rights

Firstly, everyone must have the right to life, liberty and security of person and all should be equal before the law. No one should be held in slavery or punished in an inhuman or degrading way. Neither must individuals be arrested nor exiled at someone's whim. They should be entitled to a fair hearing if someone charges them with a crime and must be presumed innocent until proved guilty. Everyone's privacy, family, home and correspondence must be protected against arbitrary interference. If anyone is persecuted he should be able to seek asylum in another country. Everyone should have the right to a nationality and should be able to marry and to start a family and that family should be entitled to protection. Everyone should have the right to own property.

There are certain freedoms too that are fundamental, i.e. freedom of thought, conscience and religion; freedom of opinion, expression and information; and the freedom to join with others in peaceful assembly and association. It is important that no one, however, should be compelled to join an association. Everyone should have the right to take part in the government of his country through elections and through equal access, with others, to jobs in the public service.

Economic, Social and Cultural Rights

These include the right to work, to free choice of jobs, to just and favourable conditions of work and to protection against unemployment. All men and women should be entitled to the same pay if they do the same work. All should have the right to rest and leisure. Another right, whose application must clearly depend on a state's level of development, is to an adequate standard of living, by which is meant enough food, clothing, housing, medical and social services, as well as social security. Mothers and children should be entitled to special care and assistance. Everyone should have the right to education and the right freely to participate in the cultural life of the community.

Reference to Annex 1B will show the full moral power of this Universal Declaration, which is far more wide-ranging than this bald outline is able to suggest, as a common standard of achievement for all peoples. To render the articles binding on member states nearly all the rights and freedoms enunciated therein are set out more specifically in two covenants dealing respectively with civil and political rights and with economic, social and cultural rights. By 1 June 1985 the first of these had been acceded to by 80 states and the second by 84. As legal instruments both covenants comprise operative clauses setting out their rights and freedoms in considerable detail (Parts I–III); and procedural sections defining means for international review of the way states carry out the obligations they undertake.

A brief word on the implementation of the Covenants. All countries ratifying them are obliged to report to a United Nations body (the Economic and Social Council for the Economic Covenant or a special Human Rights Committee where Civil Rights are concerned) on measures taken and progress made. The Committee may also, by agreement, report on the facts of an inter-state dispute if a disagreement on civil rights observance cannot be resolved through its good offices. For the Covenant on Civil and Political Rights there is also machinery for complaints by individuals. This Covenant contains an Optional Protocol which, if ratified by a state, ensures that where individual rights have been violated without adequate redress, the aggrieved citizen can ask the Human Rights Committee to take up the case on his or her behalf. By 1 June 1985 35 states had ratified or acceded to this Protocol (Annex 2).

It is a weakness so far that no international body can formally override the authority of the supreme organs of any national state. In addition to the *moral* power of world opinion and the possibility of collective international action efforts are now being made to mobilize public opinion nationally by strengthening national bodies for promoting and protecting human rights. Regional intergovernmental organs already exist, too, for Europe and for Latin America, and the decision to create a human rights organization for Africa was taken in 1979. Apart from signs of increasingly more humane policies at the national level, some practical successes have already been gained through the existing United Nations machinery, aided by the efforts of international non-governmental organizations, and this is notably true of gains in human rights observance being achieved in such situations as have recently arisen in Chile. Communications alleging gross violations of human rights in particular countries are considered annually by the Human Rights Commission. As already mentioned, there is a system of periodic reporting by states as to developments and progress achieved under their jurisdiction, although this stimulus to voluntary reform, which relies on unwelcome publicity and moral opprobrium, inevitably works very slowly.

Human rights concern is now impinging on the world scene as a powerful but still grossly insufficient countervailing force against violations, including in many cases the most gross and violent affronts to elementary human dignity, that currently persist in widely varying severity in something like three-quarters of all member states. Yet we should also do well to remember that the new stress on rights is an effect as well as a cause of social change; that overmuch stress on rights in a newly permissive climate dominated by ambiguous notions of 'freedom' and 'liberation' *can* become an aid to international terrorism and, even in mature societies, can stimulate the appeal to self-assumed standards. This is a possible by-product of the human rights 'industry' that has received little attention.

The Nature of Rights and Duties

Propositions about human rights may at first sight appear to be trite and self-evident, or else utopian. Such a view would be both misleading and misplaced. The truths proclaimed in human rights statements are first of all the shorthand indicators of a particular view of the nature of people in society. That view is one of social and economic justice based on the perceived interdependence of unique personalities developing in common and co-operating as citizens in a democratic milieu. The first purpose of a human rights code is thus to protect the individual against violations of his or her irreducible rights by others and to protect both individual citizens and groups of citizens against an arbitrary exercise of power by persons granted delegated authority within governing bodies. Conversely, the obligations of citizens to the state and to society must equally be proclaimed if the community is to cohere. By analogy with individual rights, and because new states are still being created, the rights of sovereign collectivities within the world community are now coming to be defined also, so that the rights of citizens relative to a world community may equally be envisaged and, in fact, are implied by a Declaration on the Right to Development that was nearing completion in 1985.

If human rights of any type are to be meaningful and are to be observed they must be capable of being codified in law — either national or international law — and one must be able to establish means of monitoring and enforcing the law. Even in advance of successful enforcement, however, declarations of such rights diffused through a global milieu can still have a massive influence. Why is this? It is because such proclamations can disclose to the world community the size of any gap between social achievement and the growing power societies now possess. This is one of the reasons why observance of human rights advances, or ought to advance, roughly in line with the vistas opened up by new knowledge of the consequences of acts and policies and in line too with a growing power to satisfy real human needs and to enforce by law the essential relations governing life in a viable democratic community.

Because statements of valid rights commonly become enshrined in law, it tends to be assumed that such rights are immutable. That this idea does not always hold true follows from the fact that key institutions can change as societies develop. In principle, therefore, some human rights can still be evolving. At all events, human rights concepts are today becoming more numerous as interdependence becomes more complete, although a few can equally fall into disuse as institutions undergo change. Even so it must also be recognized that complete objectivity and full collective efficiency is an impossible aim for people, that in large measure we are all the prisoners of our culture, our interests, our powers and the intellectual horizons of our time.

The only test of the validity of a right, whether individual or collective, is that its exercise is possible without restricting the same or other rights of other individuals or collectivities. From the nature of things this condition does not everywhere exist and in such cases laws may properly be enacted which curtail the universality of a right. It may be, for example, that the right to strike is excluded by law from certain occupations — e.g. the police force — since its exercise in such conditions may endanger the essential fabric of society on which all depend. Today, at a time when economic society has become so complex that a stoppage in any vital part can bring breakdown to the rest and misery to all, it might equally be maintained that the same principle should be applied to all essential work in the public sector and public services and that adherence to a legal contract of uninterrupted service might be a recognized condition in accepting such jobs.

From this example it is clear that, to maximize freedom in a modern technological society that works, the real rights of the individual, although fundamental, must be finite and closely delimited. This is true for various reasons. In the first place it follows from the fact that the acceptance of nearly any right implies a corresponding obligation. Further, the history of the last two centuries is one of the slow psychological conditioning of the individual to internalize an enormous and growing range of constraints, from laws and restrictive regulations at one extreme to the physical imperative of traffic lights at the other. This is the price that the civilizing process entails and it is that process — with some short-cuts now attainable by controlling or modifying counterproductive institutions — that has to accompany any further true development. There is another reason why individual rights are limited. We have to distinguish between two kinds of right — those following directly from the essential dignity of the unique personality, and which in principle can be realized everywhere; and those which, like the right to a given standard of living, depend for their fulfilment on the power of the state to satisfy them — in other words on the state of economic and social development already reached.

Finally, we can discern a further possible restriction on apparent personal or collective rights. In a developed state of today we ought to recognize (but so far do not) that communities exist in time as well as in space. This implies that policies to improve our lot today ought always to be weighted to allow for their effects on the rights of future citizens. This is a limiting consideration that may invalidate, or put seriously in question, some familiar productive schemes — for instance, projects for near-perpetual storage of highly toxic waste from nuclear installations. That this question, like many similar ones, has not so far been discussed in a human rights context is a tribute to the fatal attractiveness to governments of nuclear fission for military purposes, since the true economic and safety aspects of civil nuclear fission can no more be sustained today than can the argument from human rights.

Recognition and Acceptance

When we speak of movement towards world order we are implying several different sorts of order — movement towards a loosely functioning but more rational and equitable economic and monetary system; towards a world organization for preventing armed aggression and for protecting the earth's total environment; and towards a rational system of information, among many other things. All this should promote an end-product that we can call a world order of basic law and human rights — a situation that would afford tolerable life-chances and means of self-expression for the individual citizen. Before such a state can be attained, however, several more things would be required. The first is that national constitutions or legal systems must contain a basic code of essential rights for the individual. The second is that governments, in their public and inter-national conduct, must have the integrity to respect the human rights commitments enshrined in their laws and constitutions. The third is that citizens must from birth be imbued with a sense of the duties or obligations that have to be assumed if true rights and freedoms for all are to be maintained. These, the 'first and last things' of world order, are still proving unnecessarily difficult to attain, and particularly the last two. I will therefore take each of these three elements in turn, and try to evaluate the position.

Figure 17 gives a pictorial view of world accessions or signatures to the two basic United Nations Covenants on Human Rights as at 1 January 1983. In this map the area of each country is proportionate to its population, so that it is the human rights coverage in terms of population that is illustrated. If we compare this map with a similar one prepared by A. O. Herrera and others (A. O. Herrera, etc., 1976), which shows how basic food requirements are being met worldwide, no clear correlation can be seen between hunger on the one hand and human rights accessions on the other. While some states with large populations, such as China (98), Indonesia (104), Brazil (36), Nigeria (78), Pakistan (113) and Turkey (118) have not acceded to the basic Covenants and some others, such as India (103), and Mexico (47), have ratified them fairly recently, only two of these countries (103 and 104) are shown to be experiencing serious food problems, with both calorie and protein deficiencies in their average consumption, although three others have since developed sizeable under-nourished populations.

I have taken this investigation somewhat further by classifying accessions and signatures to ten main international instruments on the basis of population and economic level of the peoples involved as at 30 June 1979 (Table 28). This study shows that half the world's population is covered, at least by signatures to two basic covenants, while the figure rises to over 60 per cent for certain other conventions, such as those covering slavery, the political rights of women and racial discrimination. Although these percentages are far higher among the 'developed' than the developing countries, the number of people in the latter group is of course three times as high.

It is a striking fact that the poorest third of the world's people (1350 million) has been more fully represented by signatures to the two basic UN covenants than a similar group comprising the richer developing countries. That the world picture remains very confused is further shown by the fact that, while nearly 60 per cent of people in the world's poorest group live under governments that have ratified or signed the two basic UN covenants, these same two covenants had not (by June 1985) been ratified by such a country as the United States. At recent rates of advance, moreover, with accessions increasing annually by some 3–5 per cent, the main UN instruments may not be fully ratified until the end of the century.

What, then, of the second of our concerns — respect by governments for

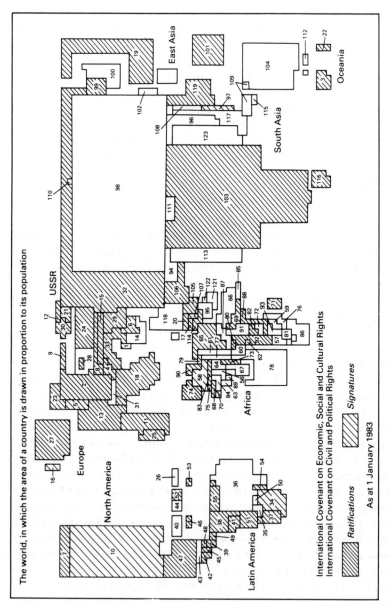

FIG. 17. The World Distribution of States that had Ratified or Signed the Two Basic Human Rights Covenants by 1 January 1983.

the binding agreements they have signed? If all countries *had* ratified the main human rights Conventions, how far would they abide by them? Every year the Human Rights Commission looks into special situations of alleged large-scale violations of human rights in up to fifteen countries. Some of these situations — e.g. in Chile and South Africa — have remained on the agenda for many years while others, like that in El Salvador or Iran, have arisen more recently. In some cases, as with Bolivia in 1982–83, Governments have responded to the approaches made and some promise of normality has been restored.

It can be quite misleading to take the list of accessions to human rights instruments as indicating the situation in a particular country at any given time. Thus, Bolivia, Chile, El Salvador and Iran are all among the 70-odd ratifiers of the Covenants (1 January 1983), while China and Switzerland, say, are not. What may be more important than mere recorded acceptance is the date of ratification. If democratic regimes have acceded to the instruments before being overturned by force, recorded acceptance may no longer reflect present practice. It is the extent to which international treaties have been incorporated into domestic law and/or national constitutions, and the priority they receive in applying domestic law, that has to be the true criterion of human rights acceptance by government and judiciary.

What can be said about our third condition — the internalizing by the individual of respect for rights and duties? In the light of what emerged from some earlier chapters there is a distinction to be drawn between the channelled conduct of administrators within a framework of laws and visible curbs which can motivate conduct and prevent or remedy abuse, and the spontaneous conduct of individuals not so constrained. Prospects for the rule of law, where demand for public control exists, may be far more positive than prospects for a free acceptance of mutual rights and duties in everyday life. Some reasons for this have already been suggested. Without going into weighty questions, simply consider the role of selfishness in current behaviour, or ponder what would happen if you offered a car and a picnic to one hundred Europeans under 45? Insofar as the last thirty years have seen an unequalled breakdown of every kind of personal restraint, the chances of maximizing freedom as a development aim seem, paradoxically enough, to have been correspondingly weakened. If there is at least some prospect of control over the tyranny of governments, what are we to conclude about the protection of individuals against each other?

TABLE 28

Accessions to Selected Human Rights Conventions in Relation to Distribution of World Population and GNP per Inhabitant

Gross National Product — 1976 (dollars per head) and Region	Number of Countries	Population 1978 (Millions)	Covenant on Economic Social and Cultural Rights	Covenant on Civil and Political Rights	Optional Protocol on Civil and Political Rights	Prevention and Punishment of Genocide	Elimination of all forms of Racial Discrimination	Convention on the Political Rights of Women	Slavery Convention (as amended)	Abolition of Slavery, the Slave Trade and Similar Practices	Suppression of the Traffic in Persons	Protocol Relating to the Status of Refugees
1	2	3	4	5	6	7	8	9	10	11	12	13
			Number of accessions ( ) and % of populations covered[a]									
Poor (under $300)	45	1331.2	(10) 57	(10) 57	(3) 3	(17) 69	(30) 77	(19) 78	(18) 70	(22) 71	(12) 63	(16) 11
Africa	28	241.8	51	51	17	66	82	46	62	74	28	60
Asia	15	1084.4	59	59	0	74	76	85	73	71	70	0
Latin America	1	4.8	0	0	0	100	100	100	0	100	100	0
Less Poor ($300–699)	38	1277.9	(11) 9	(11) 9	(7) 7	(15) 14	(21) 20	(18) 16	(9) 12	(14) 15	(9) 10	(12) 10
Africa	17	137.0	20	20	5	23	88	34	70	84	16	86
Asia	6	1078.5	5	5	4	8	8	12	5	5	8	0
Latin America	11	56.5	74	74	72	99	82	47	14	33	19	19
Europe	1	2.6	0	0	0	100	0	100	100	100	100	0

Region	No.	Pop.	1	2	3	4	5	6	7	8	9	10
Medium ($700–1999)	38	505.4	(22) 41	(21) 41	(10) 8	(23) 86	(25) 85	(21) 71	(16) 70	(23) 86	(12) 72	(18) 60
Africa	6	53.5	45	45	0	45	45	11	97	46	86	46
Asia	8	90.5	67	67	0	67	67	5	24	78	61	39
Latin America	16	264.0	26	26	12	99	98	99	74	92	83	63
Oceania	2	0.7	0	0	0	85	85	85	85	85	0	85
Europe	6	96.7	56	56	11	89	90	90	89	100	45	77
Rich ($2000 or over)	48	1101.8	(29) 92	(29) 92	(9) 12	(29) 87	(35) 87	(31) 96	(28) 81	(33) 87	(19) 54	(23) 55
Africa	2	3.3	85	85	0	0	100	15	85	0	85	15
Asia	11	136.0	87	87	0	9	4	87	9	11	89	3
Latin America	5	18.1	78	78	72	74	80	7	7	7	72	0
Oceania	5	17.8	98	98	0	98	98	98	98	98	0	98
Europe	23	684.6	90	90	15	99	99	99	91	100	68	49
North America	2	242.0	100	100	10	100	100	100	100	100	0	100
Developing Countries	141	3163.7	(47) 35	(46) 35	(21) 6	(60) 50	(86) 55	(63) 51	(50) 47	(66) 51	(38) 42	(49) 19
Developed Countries	28	1052.6	(25) 94	(25) 94	(8) 12	(24) 88	(25) 88	(26) 99	(21) 83	(26) 89	(14) 55	(20) 56
World	169	4216.3	(72) 50	(71) 50	(29) 7	(84) 59	(111) 63	(89) 63	(71) 56	(92) 60	(52) 46	(69) 28

aFigures in parentheses refer to the number of countries in each group which had ratified, acceded to or signed the international covenant or convention in question by 30 June 1979. The lower figure in each column represents the percentage of total population in each group covered by these national accessions up to the same date. Titles of the Conventions are partially abbreviated.

8
The Farther Reaches of Human Rights

The last chapter sketched out those more basic rights and duties which stem from the UN Charter of 1945, the Universal Declaration of 1948 and the two associated UN covenants which entered into force in 1976, all of which were preceded by a Declaration on the Rights of the World Citizen worked out by H. G. Wells in 1940–42. In essence five kinds of rights or duties are comprised within these various instruments. Firstly there are personal rights to life, liberty and security of person. Next are rights founded on personal relationships between individuals. Thirdly there are political rights, including freedom of conscience, speech and association, which follow from the idea that government derives from the will of the people. Fourthly there are rights and responsibilities of an economic and social nature which underlie the material well-being of persons and communities alike. Finally we may distinguish those rights, rules and responsibilities which stem from the need for a viable international order if self-expression, security and development are to have any assured meaning.

If these basic codes are the foundations of individual and collective well-being, they do not at all exhaust the frame of rules required for either citizens or states to coexist in harmony. Many more international instruments are needed in today's world to counter the effects of warfare and civil strife, genocide, terrorism and hostage-taking; to regulate the position of stateless persons and refugees; to combat the massive persistence of slavery and slave-like practices such as debt bondage and child labour; to limit the systematic use of torture, arbitrary execution and involuntary disappearances in repressive regimes; and to improve the abject condition of women in large areas of the world. These are the areas of gross violation but even they do not complete today's vista of concern.

We face a seeming paradox in that many of the world's new constitutions either include the substance of the Universal Declaration or are strongly influenced by it, yet nearly all member states still tolerate human rights violations of wide-ranging severity. It may thus be worthwhile to restate the problems in terms of the situations in which such violations arise.

Firstly, and most clearly, come those in countries underdeveloped both

146

economically and socially, where brutality, corruption, superstition and illiteracy may be primary ways of life which coexist along with extremes of well-being. Next come the states, more sophisticated civically and mentally, where military or other dictatorships may depend on an apparatus of official ill-treatment to counter subversion, where religious bigotry is commonly inbuilt and where indigenous or other minorities may suffer harsh discrimination. Finally, in the mature states, unresolved problems of human rights remain which may be far less obtrusive and even go unnoticed by the casual observer.

Let us consider these last problems. First, some radical authoritarian states possess a wide range of institutions for protecting human rights internally. But these rights must always be exercised within the confines of party ideology. Views which stray beyond those confines are liable to be stifled by direct detention or internal exile, or else treated as aberrations to be corrected in psychiatric institutions. Likewise in mature parliamentary democracies, much provision is made in the law for protecting and promoting human rights. But here the content of acceptable opinion is more subtly filtered — in this case by a free private press and other media — so as to maintain an establishment viewpoint, which is predominantly that of major leaders in business, government, the press, the Church, the civil service, the armed forces and the law. I do not here mean to imply that this is a sinister or even, collectively, a deliberate arrangement. Variations in government can be absorbed without major difficulty so long as aspirants to power do not seek to modify the established order in any radical way. This system ensures a slowly adaptable continuity of tradition but, by definition, it is self-preserving for those who set the scene. In the context of human rights the system is relevant because it ensures the continuity of extreme freedom for business interests and, in theory, of competition — but for others. Some of the main offences against the rights of the individual emanate, therefore, from abuses by private business — mainly big business — and these abuses, not surprisingly, are difficult to combat. As I have mentioned earlier, this is the climate where human rights questions can arise from an over-free commercial exploitation of science and technology; where the future is mortgaged to the profitable present; and from where home-based transnational concerns are free to export inappropriate or proscribed products to countries of the developing world.

The Rights of Man in Growing Detail

In contrast with the very few international instruments prior to 1948, nearly every year since then has seen new human rights conventions or declarations adopted. In 1983 many more instruments are still in preparation or under study within the Human Rights Commission, a trend which certainly reflects an ever-growing complexity in human affairs.

The following list of subjects — which is itemized in part, with dates of adoption, in Annex 2 — sums up the types of question dealt with by conventions, declaration or other instruments introduced by the United Nations' family of organizations since the UN Charter of 1945 and the UN Bill of Rights:

A. Prevention of discrimination (against minorities or members of special groups).
B. War crimes and crimes against humanity, including genocide.
C. Slavery, and similar practices.
D. Protection of persons subjected to detention or imprisonment.
E. Nationality, statelessness, asylum and refugees.
F. Freedom of information.
G. Freedom of association.
H. Employment policy.
I. Political and other rights of women.
J. Marriage and the family, childhood and youth.
K. Social welfare.
L. Right to development.
M. The economic rights and duties of states.
N. Terrorism and hostage-taking.

Some 50 major conventions, declarations and other instruments have been brought into force within these broad human rights categories in the post-war period. Most of them are aimed at putting an end to gross or serious violations that have emerged with or been accentuated by the political and economic evolution of the post-war world — e.g. genocide, problems of refugees, people seeking asylum or youth problems; or else have arisen from new situations created by fast-developing technology, as in means of waging war and certain other problems considered later. Most of the codes have thus elaborated in closer detail on the safeguarding of human rights already recognized in the basic Bill of Rights.

Groups A–E are clearly of this type. Those concerned with Discrimination go more deeply into the conditions needed to end abuses that have proliferated of late as economic standards have risen and mobility has increased. New instruments, adopted or under study in this field, cover such questions as racial discrimination or all forms of discrimination against women, persons born out of wedlock, indigenous populations, ethnic or other minorities, or aliens.

Then there are other standard-setting declarations designed to concentrate attention on urgent or newly-recognized areas of common concern outside human rights which nonetheless underlie the conditions for their observance. Examples include those on the Human Environment (1972) and on Eradication of Hunger and Malnutrition, the latter adopted in 1974 by the World Food Congress.

In 1983 a varied series of new international instruments is in preparation or under study within the Human Rights Commission and its Sub-Commission on Prevention of Discrimination and Protection of Minorities. These include a Convention on Torture* and other Cruel, Inhuman or Degrading Treatment or Punishment; a Convention on the Rights of the Child; and a body of principles for Protection of all Persons under any form of Detention or Imprisonment. A Declaration (perhaps later a Convention) on the Elimination of All Forms of Intolerance or Discrimination Based on Religion or Belief has been adopted. Other Conventions adopted outside the Commission on Human Rights included one on International Terrorism and the Taking of Hostages.

Many more important matters are under study through the Human Rights Commission, including that of Conscientious Objection to Military Service and the many-sided problems of human rights opened up by developments in science and technology. One of these last being acted on in 1983 is the preparation of guidelines, principles and guarantees to protect persons detained on grounds of mental ill-health or suffering from mental disorders. Nothing has been said about special human rights efforts in situations of a local or regional character, such as the Middle East, South Africa's apartheid policies, or other world trouble-spots.

As well as standard-setting in these multifarious fields the protection and promotion of human rights are equally receiving much attention. It is too soon to arrive at any conclusion on the rate of impact on human rights observance in the world. A good deal can be expected from departures embarked on during the thirtieth and thirty-fifth anniversaries of the Universal Declaration, when a quite new stimulus was given to ways of organizing and legislating for human rights protection within individual states — firstly by an exchange of experience and a drafting of guidelines at a Seminar on National and Local Organizations for the Promotion and Protection of Human Rights held at Geneva in September, 1978; and, secondly, by a similar inter-governmental exchange of experience in implementing international human rights standards.

The Rights of Man as a Humanist Conception

If we strip away all circumlocution, what is the essential base on which human rights are founded? What are the 'first and last things' that must justify all rights of man in the real world?

Secondly, and remembering that it is politicians and civil servants who send lawyers and other experts to reach agreements, what would remain if

---

*Adopted in December 1984.

there were no mixed motives to consider — no politicians seeking power, no bureaucrats to prevaricate, no business men or trade unionists to be placated, no privilege to preserve? More importantly, perhaps, what would be there that isn't?

Let us take the first question first. If we look carefully at the text of basic instruments, such as that set out in Annex 1, we can soon sense their origins and the true conception of human beings that lies behind them. That conception had its roots in the Renaissance and in eighteenth century rationalism, but in modern parlance the rights of man, human rights and their corresponding obligations or duties, rest on a humanistic conception of society, with 'man as the measure of all things'; on a vision of men and women as unique personalities seeking self-expression while co-operating as citizens in an interdependent community. Even the existence of *humanness* itself is an irreducible outgrowth of such a community. Only in a pre-existing society, in other words, can the genus *Homo* develop uniqueness and become human at all.

Let us move now to the second question: What would be the content and coverage of human rights instruments if they fulfilled the pure theory and logic of their foundations without regard for political or other constraints? We can admit straight away that the main drift of today's acceptable ideals has been truly captured by human rights concepts so far as we now see them codified. The world would clearly be a much better place if they were more fully observed. What is noteworthy about the post-war rise of human rights is not so much what is included as what is avoided or left out of account. In the present universe of discourse it would appear that certain matters are either assumed to be so far beyond doubt as to be axiomatic, or else are studiously avoided because they are not conducive to producing an agreement. *The conventional field of application is thus defined empirically rather than through sensing an inner cohesion in the functioning of society such as emerges from an explicitly humanistic viewpoint.*

This explains some notable omissions and conflicts of view. It explains why a whole corpus of economic and social rights has been erected without any attempt to delimit those conditions of permissible economic conduct which are the only means to safeguard those rights society seeks to protect. There is, for example, no attempt to contrast purely commercial and self-interest criteria which dominante so much of economic activity with the human rights of existing, much less future, citizens. Here, too, is the explanation for a marked lack of enthusiasm in considering proposals from the world's scientific leadership to set up international machinery for assessing new technology from the human rights standpoint, possibly calling also for controls upon any new developments which pose a threat to human rights. As standards for protection human rights criteria are so far our only modest safeguards against the freedom accorded to those commercial pressures that impel most of the process of technology and, indeed, most of economic life as well. But this basic source of conflicting behaviour remains completely unremarked.

It is precisely in the same economic field that Wells's 1942 formulation of the Rights of Man remains unique to this day (A. J. Dilloway, 1983, *op. cit.*). Wells was not an economic specialist and since his time we have learnt much that is new about the springs of economic development. But his declaration remains the only attempt so far to attack the common sources of human folly that fire so much of human rights abuse while, at the same time, resisting all moves towards a real world order. It is largely for this reason that the brief Declaration of the Rights of the World Citizen perfected by Wells between 1940 and 1942 remains unsurpassed in the breadth of its perception of the rights and duties of modern men.

Wider Limits of the Rights of Man

We have still not fully explained how the concept of 'human rights' implies an explicitly humanist view of the legitimate *range* of human rights concern. Earlier it was maintained that the notion of human rights arises as a corollary of the perceived essence of humanness itself. By 'humanness' I here mean that gift for language and abstract thought; for looking inwards to the self as well as outwards; for being aware of the past and of the need to foresee; and for drawing ethical ideas from our dependence on others. The point is that this human quality can arise only in a pre-existing society. To extend the scope for human potential requires a cumulating *economic* society that enshrines human rights concepts and bring forth ideas of mutual obligation. People are bound up in a division of labour which seeks to apply available resources as effectively as knowledge and technique will permit to meet the common needs and individual wants of citizens within a consensual frame of justice. It follows that economic society is part of the total community and not, as we are taught by market competition to believe, something separate that obeys its own rules. It also follows that the purpose of production is to meet our needs without being counterproductive, a situation that clearly does not obtain today. *More generally, then, we can conclude from any thoroughgoing humanist analysis that the basis of human rights and obligations is or should be bound up with the working of the entire economic and social system and not simply with an adequate distribution of its results.*

Discovering the Wider Unity of Human Rights

I am now going to examine, in a way that, so far as I know, has not previously been attempted, some farther reaches of human rights and duties which follow from, and only from, the way of thinking set out above.

One can start from the proposition that different types of basic right so far defined can be derived in a logical sequence from each other. First there are some accepted principles that are absolute and unconditional — the rights to life and security of person and to freedom of thought and conscience (e.g. Articles 1, 3 and 18 of the Universal Declaration) — that follow directly from a distinctive quality of humanness in the genus *Homo*. These rights immediately imply other rights — to basic means of life such as food and shelter and the elementary protection of the community (e.g. Article 25). Behind these rights again are those which fundamentally delimit the relations between individuals in social life (e.g. Articles 2 and 4–7). Life, sustenance and social rights having been provided for, an individual's right to contribute to community life is next assured by what are in the nature of political rights (e.g. Articles 20 and 21, etc.) Finally, as a consequence of his citizenship of a state, come an individual's international rights and duties in respect of the world community.

We thus see that there is a logical linkage between currently established rights and duties. In 1983 efforts were being made to establish the content of a newly proclaimed and more generalized right — a right to development. One argument employed to this end is that just as there are individual rights and collective rights, so one must distinguish a hybrid class of 'solidarity rights', to which this new right belongs.

Some major consequences ensue from this proposed new departure, some of them still unrecognized. Having participated as an observer in the group of experts created to draft a Declaration on the Right to Development, I have seen how opinion has evolved in the matter. The right to development is felt to apply both to entire populations and to all individuals, the human person being the central subject of the development process, with development construed not merely in economic terms but as a 'comprehensive economic, social, cultural and political process' aimed at improving the well-being of all individuals and entire populations on the basis of their free and meaningful participation and a fair distribution of benefits arising therefrom.

In its connotation for states, which are seen as responsible for creating favourable conditions for development, the right is based on the Covenants and on various instruments enacted over the last decade, e.g. the Charter on the Economic Rights and Duties of States, the Declaration on the Use of Scientific and Technical Progress in the Interests of Peace and for the Benefit of Mankind, a Declaration on Preparation of Societies for Life in Peace, and several others.

From such instruments certain principles of international law and international economic relations are recognized which impose on states such duties as to formulate suitable development policies and to co-operate in promoting development for nations and for individual citizens by accepting such principles as:

— sovereignty, territorial integrity, political and economic independence and equality of states;
— non-intervention in domestic affairs;
— avoidance of hegemony and spheres of influence;
— non-aggression and peaceful settlement of disputes;
— international co-operation for mutual benefit;
— fulfilment in good faith of international obligations;
— free access to the sea by land-locked states;
— permanent sovereignty over national wealth and resources;
— respect for human rights and fundamental freedoms.

Although these principles are meant to be treated as consistent with each other, it can be seen that any such programme presupposes an indefinite continuation of near-absolute sovereignty of states over their territorial entities. It depends, in other words, on an analogy between individuals, co-operating of necessity and for mutual benefit within a single state, and a world community of individual states co-operating with each other for mutual advantage. This may be a practical necessity at present, when there is a prevailing global dichotomy arising from two opposed philosophies of development — the one based mainly on collective responsibility and the other mainly on the doctrine of individual enterprise. But to assume this to be the permanent state of mankind is to assume that mankind has no future — unless, indeed, we can posit some convergence between the economic philosophies of East and West.

The current obsession with matters of sovereignty, independence and non-interference in a climate of *de facto* interdependence arises from the present voting majority of non-aligned and often newly independent states, and in some degree from a defensive stance by radical authoritarian states as well. In suitable circumstances international agreements do recognize that at least some parts of the world environment are 'the common heritage of mankind'. This is true of the ocean bed beyond the limits of national jurisdiction, it is probably true of outer space as a common resource and of Antarctica also. There is thus at least a hint of dual criteria in the thinking behind many present-day international agreements arrived at by governments.

If we pursue this line of thought, looking somewhat beyond the purview of a right to development, an entirely new vista opens up. In earlier Chapters some account has been given of the United Nations' programmes on population, the world environment, food, health, weather, telecommunications and many other world enterprises gathered together under the Economic and Social Council, the Security Council, etc.

There are many quite distinct but vital activities subsumed under these heads. Work to provide health for all by the year 2000, work to improve the world's urban settlements, efforts to ensure adequate drinking water for the world's peoples are examples. *Human rights conventions, because they start from the essential equality of rights and duties of the human person, are in the position of forming, both logically and in fact, a common basis underlying and linking those multifarious international efforts.*

We can go further. Just as there are human rights agreements, so there are international agreements on arms control — including the sea bed and outer space; on the protection of the environment; and on many other matters. It is impossible to accede, say, to an agreement on environmental protection — for example, the Convention on Long-range Transboundary Air Pollution of ECE — without underwriting limitations on the untrammelled use of a state's productive facilities or natural resources. It is primarily the purpose of all such conventions to delimit the permissible sphere of national activity in the common interest of all signatories. Whether it be peace, population control, health, environment or postal services, some specific degree of *de facto* limitation of sovereignty is required which in its turn extends a state's potential scope for promoting human rights and development.

What has not so far been recognized is, first, that in *all international agreements concluded to advance the common interest it is precisely the protection and promotion of human rights that is the ultimate end.* Further, if this proposition is once accepted, then a second corollary seems to follow: that, far from depending on an adversarial system that is distinct from community life and follows its own rules, economic life too is in reality an integral field in the whole corpus of human rights and duties. This in turn means that legitimate concern for human rights, including the 'right to development', should logically be conceived, not on an *ad hoc* basis as at present, but as *ramifying through the total field of human co-operative endeavour.* Not only is this true within the nation-state, moreover, it is also true of the world community.

For the human rights specialist let me summarize some logical steps in this humanistic case. Whether or not we recognize the fact, national societies rest on the interdependence of unique personalities co-operating in a division of effort to meet their common needs and individual wants within a consensual frame of perceived justice. This means that the economic frame of society, national and global, is in reality part of the total community and not something apart that obeys its own rules.

We thus arrive at the core of our subject. A true code of basic rights and duties marks out the acceptable shape and relationships of a just society. To some extent, therefore, human rights and duties can still evolve, while a few now proclaimed may become redundant as development proceeds. To implement many individual rights requires a considerable development of *economic* society, since elementary rights to well-being and self-development are feasible only when the state can assure some essential conditions. On the other hand, in the mature state we have to recognize that communities exist in time as well as in space, so that today's policies have to allow for the rights of future citizens.

The final justification for a code of human rights is, firstly, that it defines the true conditions in which human potential can develop in an interdependent milieu; and, secondly, that such a code, for the individual and for interstate relations, offers *the only frame of common ideas that can span the diversity of cultures, religions, living standards, political and economic systems* to bring a common nexus of humane practice to an emergent *world* community.

PART III

The Prospect for An Humane World

9

The Scope for Human Potential

I. POPULATION, SOCIETY AND GOVERNMENT

This is the point where we have to draw together various threads from an over-brief probing into man's further potential in today's world — his net balance of positive traits and negative limits. If this is meant to be an unemotional and even an objective appraisal it is not designed as an exercise in crystal-gazing. Interesting though such an effort might be, there will be no attempt to project, say, *per capita* use of micro-chips in 1995, or the length of the working week 30 years hence. Rather we have been at pains to discern facts, relationships and underlying tendencies mostly deeper than those which preoccupy ephemeral market man or his political ambitions. Some negative and positive factors and their resilience having been recognized, the problem is to assess what the net balance might offer and how far it can meet the challenge that imperatives induced by human beings have now created.

We are not, therefore, in search of sensational disclosures in any popular sense. Some of the significant facts about people, economics and world society in its present parlous state are not especially new in themselves but are too often disregarded, or overlain by the power of conventional wisdom that holds sway simply because it satisfies the interests not of the truth but rather of those best able to give it credence.

I believe that before venturing into weighty and often controversial conclusions in a study such as this the writer owes it to the reader to lay bare the origins of his own position. If the standpoint adopted here is meant to be original this is not merely because it rests on sympathy with the scientific attitude, but rather because the analysis is believed to break much new ground by extending *humanistic* thinking in a systematic way. If one adds practical experience of international matters in a life free from attachment to any political party throughout the span of our century since 1910, these facts may suffice to identify the writer's standpoint even if they do not lessen his presumption.

Thus the synthesis to be attempted is at once ambitious, selective and humanistic, but otherwise free from loyalty to special interests. There is a further point. This first drawing together of threads — for any final conclusions should follow separately — must itself be evolutionary in that its successive themes should arise out of and follow from one another so as to create a textured fabric of understanding. If any kind of balance *is* achieved its verdict can be only a tentative one, such being the nature of humankind and the gaps that remain even in some elemental knowledge about the genus *Homo*.

The Frame of our Conclusions

It may have struck any reader who has persisted thus far that the years since 1945, although marred by some apparent decline in human effectiveness, have also witnessed the early stages of at least two convergent revolutions in awareness that could mark the beginnings of a new era. These are, first, a dawning sense of the unity of all natural phenomena, human and non-human; and, next, the rise of a common code to assist worldwide behaviour in human relations. As a corollary of the first of these the singleness of our planet, and even its solar system, has finally been acknowledged — the reality of one world, that is, in terms of human organization through international institutions as well as the unity of mankind with its total habitat, on which not only man but all living systems equally depend. There exists, too, a common code of human rights and duties — a cementing bond of reciprocity that can hold together the entire human order if its rule can be successfully internalized.

These world order concerns seem to form part of a slower, deeper, all-embracing move towards unified thinking in general. Such a change appears likely to encompass within its scope not merely all human phenomena but all other interlinked processes which permeate the phenomena of nature. Evidence brought together in this book thus seems broadly to confirm a far-reaching theory elaborated by L. L. Whyte in 1948 — that there is in human affairs a slow trend towards a system of unified thought as the "next development in man" (L. L. Whyte, 1948).

This brings us to the heart of a central concern informing this whole inquiry — that is, to understand the salient features of that unique product of *humanness* which arises from an interplay between the being *Homo sapiens* and its social system — features that are illumined still farther when the lessons of the last 10,000 years of social evolution have been allowed for. It is not useful to repeat what has been said on this theme in earlier Chapters except to recall, first, the latent capacities for abstract thought, language and reasoning; then a long period of dependence for socialized learning; and finally a growing interdependence that springs from the common need of a pre-existing community — these together producing unique individuals and unique societies that have gradually coalesced into technically powerful states.

But the human brain, although it is a key factor in the rise of human qualities, is not a single homogeneous entity since it seems to combine within itself vestiges of some earlier evolutionary stages. These include a primitive brain, a 'palaeo-cortex' and limbic system which govern much emotional behaviour, and then the familiar neo-cortex with which we tend to associate our more rational thought-processes. Here, we have to assume, is a reason for all-too-well founded doubts about human potential, a duality in our make-up that has persisted throughout human history.

When we look at the human story as a whole over the last 10,000 years we find that the main process of social evolution has been compassed within some 400 successive generations, or say 200 average lifetimes. This staggering fact about the rise of human potential must be one key detail to ponder when development prospects are appraised. If, despite many deviations, only two hundred lifetimes separate today's television addict from Palaeolithic man, have we still to conclude that nuclear arms must spell the end of our species?

There are perhaps three cardinal points about humanness that we ought to bear in mind. Firstly, that the bases of man's governmental, social and economic order — that is, a hierarchy, a code of law, a socializing process and a system of education, a division of labour, a field of shared beliefs plus consensual co-operation based on reciprocity; and a democratic form of government — all these are *irreducible* facets of the human adventure. It follows, firstly, that an entire economic society can be logically humane and fully sustainable only insofar as it can seek to optimize the meeting of attainable human needs and individual wants *within these parameters of humanness*, i.e. without being humanly counter-productive.

Secondly, human development, however it is rated by our standards, necessarily follows a compound-interest law determined by growth in numbers and/or communication and by rising interaction, experience and cumulating knowledge or technique. Thirdly, human nature comprises two conflicting clusters of propensities, plus an ability to learn. In the long term ignorance and selfishness have been in slow retreat against enlightenment and mutuality because enlightenment and mutuality are built into the strong social potential of human beings. Mutuality is kept alive in the form of a struggle for human rights and duties. Yet human rights can flower only through effective legal and economic frames assured by government. And governments are too often fallible if not venal, enshrining the predilections of politicians, their judgements apt to be coloured by unreal images of the world situation. . .

The Relatedness of our Main Themes and its Implications

If we list some of the major themes discussed in these pages we find that they can be arranged in a logical order or sequence. Looking back to Chapter 1 and some formative discoveries of the nineteenth and twentieth centuries which helped to create a new awareness of the nature of man and his time-scale, we see that those discoveries, too, follow an interlocking sequence. We can go even farther, and view the whole cultural evolution of humankind — notwithstanding its setbacks, its disasters, its conquests and intrigues — as expressing a developmental logic that arises from a two-sided process of discovery and enlightenment. It is well-known that scientific discoveries, like early advances in basic technique, arise in a step-by-step sequential order from which new understanding or technical power can open further new vistas, often in unrelated fields. When new technical knowledge is applied under present conditions, social practices may quickly be affected and behaviour modified, for good or for ill. In this way a cumulative process of enforced enlightenment flows from an opening-up of what had been unforeseen consequences of acts and policies triggered by new technology, itself the result of innovation in pure science. The net result of this process is twofold — to disclose both an ever-widening web of newly-perceived relationships between natural phenomena and a slowly growing interdependence within socio-economic life.

What does all this imply for our inquiry? By bringing together some separate threads it should allow one cardinal, new and positive principle to be proclaimed — one that underlies the various distinct concerns that are here under study.

To elaborate this idea, Table 29 puts into general form a recent 'discovery' by ECOSOC — that it is not useful to consider, say, problems of world environment or natural resources apart from population, economic trends or, even more to the point, the arms race. Whether at national or world levels, all main categories listed at line A of the Table (that is, items 1–6, or beyond) are closely interrelated with one another through such connecting problem-areas as Aa, Ab, Ac, etc. The condition of humanly sustainable Development (line C) is not merely that Human Rights observance (B) should sufficiently permeate category A2, or even A3, but that *all* national legislation and *all* international agreements reached under categories A1–6 or beyond and their subsidiaries (a–e, etc.) should be seen to conform to existing codes of human rights. Table 29 thus serves to illustrate an important principle — established in detail in Chapter Eight — that now needs to be absorbed into United Nations practice, and which can be stated briefly as follows: *While all major sectors of human activity pose problems for the peaceful development of mankind, solutions adopted by the international community by way of technical or other treaties should everywhere be consistent with the Universal Declaration and the two Human Rights Covenants.* This is simply because the proper domain of human rights extends throughout all human affairs. Such an idea, although it goes far beyond what is accepted today, is already being recognized in a piecemeal fashion in some fields of international action. That human rights principles can be generalized to extend to all

TABLE 29

Selected Systemic Relationships between some Major Categories of National and World Activity

		1 POPULATION	2 SOCIETY	3 ECONOMY	4 GOVERNMENT	5 ENVIRONMENT	6 SCIENCE
A	a	Food	Health	Work	Education	Work	Information
	b	Health	Education	Food	Information	Health	Health
	c	Education	Food	Information	Health	Food	Resources
	d	Information	Work	Resources	Work	Resources	Food
	e	Resources	Information	Health	Resources	Information	Education
B		Human Rights	Human Rights	Human Rights	Human Rights	Human Rights	Human Rights
C		Development	Development	Development	Development	Development	Development
D		(Negative) Proliferating Armaments	(Negative) Proliferating Armaments	(Negative) Proliferating Armaments	(Negative) Proliferating Armaments	(Negative) Proliferating Armaments	(Negative) Proliferating Armaments

Notes:

Main system categories (capitalized) pose major constraints for development that is inconsistent with human rights criteria. All categories are interrelated with each other both at national and world levels, but subsidiary items are selected and cover some main relationships only.

Population: Comprises all demographic aspects, including urban life and habitation.
Society: Includes all major aspects of national or world community, other than economic and governmental.
Economy: Comprises all aspects, including monetary system, trade and international division of labour.
Government: Refers to all aspects, including electoral, legislative, executive and judicial.
Environment: Includes conservation and covers the habitat of man and the natural habitat of all life.
Science: Refers to science and technology.

Human Rights: Refers to human rights and duties as involved directly or indirectly.
Development: Refers to social and normative as well as economic aspects, but does not connote growth.
Armaments: Refers to production, sale and export, as well as to military deployment of nuclear and conventional weaponry.
Information: Includes objective communication as well as diffusion of textual material.
Resources: Refers to natural resources of human concern, including energy.
Work: Comprises all aspects of work-related activity, including human implications and effectiveness.

international agreements that limit national freedom is an idea that must follow from any acceptance of a Right to Development.

With this preamble the rest of the chapter, and the following one, will take in turn the respective items of Table 29 (lines A and B) and consider in a national context what scope exists for their further development in the future. The global prospects opened up by a final synthesis will be the subject of a concluding chapter.

The Future of Population

The menace of an already excessive world population that still grows and urbanizes at a rapid rate, and is increasingly mobile, is now our prior human problem after inflamed nuclear one-upmanship. This is true because it will hold back a rise in physical well-being for two-thirds of the world's people; it will put a near-intolerable strain on the earth's unused natural resources and its artificially created amenities; it will increase the dangers of international tension; it will add to the enormous burden of capital outlay required to meet rising real needs; it will threaten to outrun food production capacity by the year 2000 in some 65 developing countries; and it will endanger, to an all but impossible degree, the natural balances of biosphere and atmosphere. In short, world fertility rates offer a clear case of 'more means worse'.

Positive population policies for the developing world seek mainly to reduce birth rates, family size and infant and child mortality. Large families, while due to cultural and religious reasons as well as ignorance and lack of means, are in developing countries sought above all for economic reasons, i.e. to help with subsistence. This means that reducing infant mortality is a good way to lower the birth-rate, since the number of children stated to be desired ranges mostly from around 3.7 to 4.7 whereas both completed and current fertility rates are much higher than this, as is illustrated by the following figures for five selected countries:

TABLE 30
Actual and Desired Fertility Rates in Selected Countries

Country	Year	Completed Fertility	Current Fertility[a]	Desired Fertility
Jordan	1976	8.64	7.83	6.30
Bangladesh	1975	7.06	6.10	4.10
Peru	1977	6.58	5.14	4.40
Jamaica	1975	5.53	5.00	4.00
Indonesia	1976	5.27	4.73	4.10

[a]i.e. assuming a constant rate throughout reproductive life.
Source: The State of World Population 1983 (United Nations).

At present, of some 122 million infants born each year worldwide, more than 12 million will die in under one year and nearly five million more in under five years. High mortality rates occur in the poorest countries, as is shown in Figure 18, where areas are shown proportionately to number of births and infant mortality by graduated shading. High rates are usually associated with insufficient primary health care as well as with lack of food and education. Most deaths will occur from such ailments as curable diarrhoea, measles, whooping cough, poliomyelitis, tetanus, diphtheria and tuberculosis as well as from pneumonia, malaria (by no means under control) and schistosomiasis (bilharzia). This list shows that much of the developing world's ill-health, disablement and premature death arises from a simple and removable cause: a lack of clean and adequate water supply. The many water-related diseases that take a major toll include those that are water-borne, like diarrhoeas, polio and typhoid; others, like round-worm, leprosy and whipworm, that are known as water-washed; and a third group, which is either water-based, like bilharzia, or else water-related like sleeping sickness, malaria and river blindness. The list ends with hookworm, due to inadequate waste disposal. A special UN programme to provide safe water supply is thus one that can pay huge dividends, although it suffers at present from insufficient funding.

If population presents the most pressing international concern after war control it is also, with environment and human rights, perhaps the one where UN action has so far shown most success, as may be suggested by the following figures covering a thirty-year span:

TABLE 31
*World Trends in Infant Mortality and Life
Expectancy — 1950–1980*

Category	1950	1980
Infant mortality (‰)		
Developed countries	56	19
Developing countries	164	100[a]
Life-expectancy at birth		
Developed countries	65.2	71.9
World average[b]	47.0	57.5

[a]By 1982 this figure has been estimated at 90‰.
[b]Refers to periods 1950–55 and 1975–80 respectively.
Source: The State of World Population 1983 (United Nations).

On present evidence (and barring a 'solution' by nuclear means) one can assume that a day will come when this self-defeating proliferation will be halted; but that day seems unlikely to arrive before 2095 at the earliest, when world population will have reached some 10.2 billions. It can thus be concluded that all plans for a more humane world — whether for economic

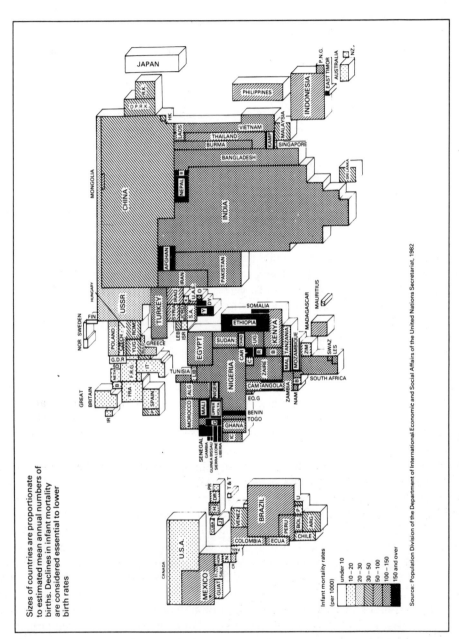

FIG. 18. World Distribution of Estimated Infant Mortality Rates — 1975–1980.

development, environmental protection or any other facet of world order — must accommodate to the heavy constraint of an ever-more excessive pressure of numbers on the finite resources of our planet. What *can* be done is to lessen much impairment of the living by better primary health care, education, immunization programmes and measures for disablement prevention.

Social Existence in the Future

How do you measure the well-being of a population living as a community? Some basic indicators of physical health, food and shelter are to hand, while school enrolment and literacy can also be measured. Given the statistical data one can equally determine an average income; the range of wealth or poverty; the level of gainful employment; or again seek to appraise political harmony in terms of, say, prevalence of civil conflict, relative expenditure on armed forces and police, or the extent of arbitrary rule. Attempts are being made to devise even more sensitive indicators to summarize the *quality* of life. In effect such indices refer only to the *state of our social environment*, which is indeed a prime factor in the well-being of people but not a full measure of human effectiveness as such.

Indicators of human rights observance come close to what is sought. Ideally they define all the essential practical *conditions* for mutual harmony, although not the actual degree of fulfilment that people as individuals should derive from an effective functioning of their communities.

How far these physical, economic, environmental, political or human rights measures suffice to appraise social well-being must depend first of all on the general level of development. If your co-citizens are ill, starving, overworked or ignorant, social harmony remains of little moment. From this standpoint it is useful to make at least a threefold division between the conditions in poor, medium and rich developing societies. In the first — which must be distinguished from true indigenous communities — most people are never far from starvation, are ill-sheltered, ill fed, lack adequate water supply and receive little money income. They are largely illiterate, have low expectations, are fatalistic and may be governed by traditional dogmas. Qualities of fellow-feeling survive largely through the extended family. Opposition to arbitrary rule is correspondingly low, civil service corruption is inbuilt at a low level of authority and most of the population works in primitive agriculture. Finally, climate and geographical position are unlikely to inspire effective economic performance. Here, be it noted, we speak of low levels of development where advance *is* intended, and not of the true indigenous community with little social change, where rules and institutions may work more efficiently in human terms.

At a second or medium stage, prosperity and elementary physical well-being are at a correspondingly higher level. Both physical and social mobility have increased, while a larger and more dynamic opposition to authority is on the march. Bureaucrats, experts and a potential élite class are all becoming more numerous. Charismatic rulers may be looking for further prestige from western technology or influence. Corruption and inefficiency are likely to inhere as business and civil service élites become integrated and involved with foreign firms.

It is only in the third, or 'rich' group of states, that food, shelter, health and elementary education move towards what they should be. By this time, however, the economic division of labour has commonly become excessively fragmented, with perhaps two-thirds or more of the work force engaged in giant concerns, both public and private. Work efficiency has again deteriorated, price inflation is fanned by exaggerated expectations, while frequent strikes exacerbate near-breakdown of the economic machine and public services. While the whole population is enfranchised, it may be largely apathetic and disillusioned. An everyday level of fellowship and helpfulness, which persists, is in contrast with the self-seeking ethic of commerce and bureaucracy. Despite a tug-of-war between competing political parties, the nation's social character has attained a sort of 'negative stability' by recognizing certain limits to politically acceptable options which assure a steady but unobtrusive maintenance in power of an appropriate governing élite. Finally, alliances inspired by intimidation and economic threat may well have replaced national policies of independence.

Of course this account is grossly oversimplified and incomplete, but in the light of it we can revert to the question from which we started: How can one assess the well-being of a community? Looking back to Figure 12 in Chapter Five, it was there shown that the social, economic and political facets of a society should all manifest development by increasing not only in scale but in effectiveness, freedom and mutuality. Looking at contemporary development as just discussed, this is not at present happening, particularly at the third or most advanced stage so far reached — except insofar as human rights criteria have now been recognized.

What has further to be considered, then, is a society's capacity to produce properly socialized as well as rational and healthy human beings. If economic advance produces many citizens that are better fed, more literate and more healthy than before, while by the third stage human rights are better protected, it does not follow that an advance in *human* effectiveness must match or even follow the rise in economic productivity. Societies that are simpler and economically less advanced may in some senses produce people more humanly rounded — that is potentially more capable of personal fulfilment in interdependent social life — than what we call the developed societies of today. Indicators of economic advance, human rights or environment all define aspects of the *climate* in which human beings can attain humanness through social existence and dependence on one another in advancing the common weal. The final dimension we seek is thus the statistical prevalence in a population of beings with true human quality. This dimension requires indicators which measure the amount of deviation beyond what a given society currently feels to be acceptable limits to behaviour. Such data can be of three kinds — on the one hand mainly social, from homicide and other well-defined crime, indiscriminate terrorism, drug-taking (including smoking and excessive drinking), to vandalism, suicide or family breakdown; and on the other mental illness, or again socially aggravated maladies like heart disease, some malignant tumours or the phenomena of unaccounted absenteeism, strikes and sit-ins. Many conditions are not yet measured at all, such as general 'anomie' or alienation, dullness and inability to use life-chances or the tools that society can offer. What can easily be seen from everyday experience over the last 30 years is that the attentive and careful performance of useful work, far from improving with better health and education, a shorter working life and longer holidays, has fallen greatly, and even catastrophically in that period. The rise of price inflation since 1965 reflects, among other things, a substitute scrambling for wealth–power possessions to replace much of the lost wonder, purpose and enthusiasm that wider vistas might be expected to call forth. *To put this in general terms, economic life in the more developed states has come to play a grotesquely exaggerated part in the process of living.*

In the early post-war years attempts were made to define a 'sick' society as opposed to a 'sane' society, these concepts referring to communities with disproportionate numbers of citizens who exhibit unacceptably abnormal character. Such can arise from an interplay between social causes and an individual's unique make-up. Using, with some reservations, the ontogenetic formulation worked out by Halliday (J. L. Halliday, 1948), it is possible to regard some of the social aberrations listed above as in the nature of psychosocial maladies:

> A life may be frustrated. . . , even terminated, by its encountering noxious physical factors — traumatic, nutritional, chemical, microorganic — or by encountering noxious psychological factors which through their psychological, psychosomatic and psychosocial effects impede its mode of emotional development (Halliday, *op. cit.*).

On this basis a 'healthy' society is a group of individuals adequately linked by common bonds, or emotional interests, which enable them to live and work together effectively. These bonds provide the coherence necessary for the group to function socially and thus to ". . . produce its particular variety of 'social goods' ". Here questions of a group's morale, discipline and perhaps fragmentation or disintegration may enter the picture. Thus "discipline" refers to those codes and systems incorporated and internalized naturally by members of a socially 'healthy' group to reinforce the coherence it needs to function successfully. Failure to recognize or accept such a code may hasten the society's malfunctioning or even decay.

What, then, is the role of individual character? Several of its measurable elements which vary from low to high among individuals arise from nature and nurture in combination — from genes plus environment — and also follow a Gaussian or normal distribution in a population — that is, their frequency of occurrence follows a bell-shaped curve from low to medium and from medium to high values (Figure 19). This is true of height, say; of what is called the intelligence quotient IQ (and which I shall call the understanding quotient UQ); and probably also of dimensions like introversion–extroversion (I–E) and what Gabor has called an Ethical Quotient (EQ).

Figure 19 A shows that with a normal distribution some 68 per cent of the population studied will fall within ± one standard deviation (a statistical measure of a group's dispersion from the mean which, in the case of 'intelligence' as shown, amounts to 16) and some 95 per cent within two standard deviations, leaving less than 5 per cent located about equally near the extreme low and high values. The broad distribution in a population of IQ or understanding capacity — between, say, 55 for an imbecile and 145 for a 'genius', with half located between 90 and 110 — suggests even more clearly how wide may be the range of personality traits in practice.

This is the kind of distribution that quite probably applies to a number of personality variables depending on combined effects of genes and environments, including the well-known empirical dimension of introversion–extroversion. In Eysenck's view, this last seems to have an important explanatory role in personal character when combined with other dimensions such as emotion–stability.

Eysenck's theory (H. J. Eysenck, 1967) posits a physiological basis for the character dimension which ranges from introverted (reserved, un-sociable, careful, thoughtful, pessimistic) to extroverted (outgoing, soci-able, talkative, impulsive, optimistic). Introversion is seen as produced by high arousal of the cortex induced by a highly active ascending reticular formation. This last supplies a stream of signals to the cortex to stimulate sufficient arousal to deal with incoming sensory signals which pass directly to the cortex. Because it assists learning and conditioning, such arousal may account for the introvert's more ready socialization and internaliza-tion of social norms. Extroverts are easily bored, have low arousal and tend to seek sensation and stimuli. On the other hand emotional expression relates to the autonomic nervous system regulated by the 'visceral brain'. Its high or low levels seem to be correlated with measurable physiological responses and to combine with the extroversion dimension to promote other contrasts in socially conforming or non-conforming behaviour-types.

We can thus see that social and physiological explanations of human

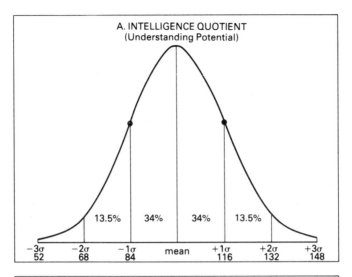

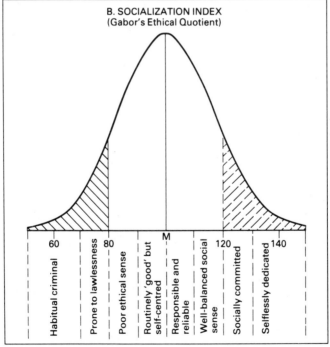

FIG. 19. Two Distinct Applications of the Gaussian Normal Curve.

behaviour can both be useful in helping to explain part of the wide variation in observance of social norms. Just as capacity for understanding varies about the mean of 100 from, say, 55 to 145 for different individuals in a bell-shaped distribution, quite probably some major dimensions of character do the same. If a society can be said to be exceptionally lacking in 'social health', or extremely 'healthy' in that sense, the shape of the bell-shaped frequency curve for some of its indicators may be skewed to one side or the other and depart from a 'normal' symmetry.

What, then, is the attainable ideal? In a responsible, forward-looking society, which presumably is the worldwide aim, one could certainly look for high rationality and awareness. If the nearest index of it we have so far is the controversial IQ (or UQ), the late Dennis Gabor, a Nobel physicist, has set out some other indicators equally needed by any sound society (D. Gabor, 1972). Although not so far investigated these, like UQ, are likely to follow a normal distribution.

First there is what Gabor calls the EQ or Ethical Quotient, roughly measuring social conscience, honesty and responsibility or its lack, which is probably well correlated with UQ and which I shall treat as the socialization index (SQ). Another is an indicator of motivation, application or diligence, which we can call AQ; and a third assesses dominance–suggestibility or DQ. An individual will score differently on each.

Figure 19 B illustrates a hypothetical and normal distribution of SQ among a population such as that of contemporary Great Britain. With crime and non-observance of earlier social norms on the increase, it may be that our bell-shaped figure will become skewed to the left of the present mean, but I know of no hard figures to support this. What we can say is that to the extent that basic character dimensions *are* normally distributed, norms of social behaviour should approximate also to something like the bell-shaped distribution shown in Figure 19.

What, then, can we conclude about the future of social existence? First, that on the whole human behaviour will remain flawed and highly fallible — a mixture of 'good' and 'bad'. This follows from the spread of personality dimensions. Codes of law and social values seek to constrain human behaviour within a limit such as that shown by a vertical line in Figure 19 B — at present with less and less success. *Early, strong and sustained inculcation of social norms within what is left of the family, plus a reinforcing but rigorous and challenging educational system, can promote a sense of personal responsibility and so extend real freedom overall; but only when government, economic system and total environment have likewise been aimed at enhancing human potential.* Such is our second conclusion. How far these conditions might be met must be deduced from the rest of this Chapter. A third conclusion is that our new world code of human rights *is* compatible — probably more compatible than national law is — with the range of understanding, and perhaps even of conduct, that is likely to prevail worldwide. This is perhaps the main plus in man's constant fight against his own ambiguity.

The Future of Government

Given the prior condition of a peaceful world, a state's scope for furthering the human quality of its citizens must rest on the effectiveness of three main components: its system of government; its economic system; and its social or cultural milieu. If this is the case it may seem strange that so little thought has been given to extending the few options offered by tradition for running a government machine. In earlier chapters it has been shown that, over much of the contemporary world, systems of government are working rather badly. Since at least some innovations are possible, we have to attribute this lack of experiment mainly to those inertial mechanisms that were discussed in Chapter 4.

Let us therefore attack this towering problem of the future of government by seeking answers to three specific questions:

— What are the proper functions of government?
— How best can the personnel of government be recruited?
— How best can governments be kept responsive to their electorates?

The first of these questions, although still thought contentious, is the least difficult to answer. Whatever type of sovereign rule we envisage, its minimal duties are to ensure security and public order for all its citizens, and to see that internal resources are so marshalled that essential needs can be met and distributed. This in turn means that governments of today must co-ordinate the state's machinery for getting essential things done and essential rights or duties protected; that they must 'hold the ring' to reconcile any clash of special interests; and that they should maintain a forward-looking function so as to provide continuity of services and accommodate to orderly change. Another cardinal requirement is to assure means for the populace to judge the acceptability of government performance and to renew or change its mandate. Beyond all this again lies a Constitution and a code of legal sanctions that have to be upheld or modified in the light of evident public need.

By government is meant the inner cabinet (or polit-bureau) which has to reach primary day-to-day decisions, plus the rest of the top power structure, which interacts with an executive bureaucracy or civil service. In practice the various elective offices of state tend to be supplemented by an outer fringe of specialized leaders who complete the frame of central government. These include leaders of the armed forces, the police and the legal machine; the heads of large producing, selling or financial concerns, whether public or private; and of the educational, scientific, health and various technical fraternities, among others. This central pyramid of elected and appointed power must include machinery for conducting relations with other states. It is, of course, matched by smaller subsidiary pyramids responsible for regional and local government. Its elected core usually owes strong internal allegiance to a party and especially to key backers, while having at the same time to appear receptive to more general but often incompatible electoral interests.

There is no space here to pursue the niceties of political science. It has already been noted that in practice all states are governed by an élite, the point being that not only does that élite share a common ideology or tradition (more or less) but that it also shares a common material interest in preserving certain features of the status quo. For these reasons, the most familiar problems of government today — outside the field of civil rights — seem to lie in dealing equitably with pressure-groups; with overall questions of distribution; and with planning and orderly change: in short, they tend to concentrate in the economic sector. New ways of selecting and running governments and new ways of assuring their responsiveness to electorates are thus central to a better future.

We shall ignore strong taboos against change by looking very briefly at three possible innovations:

— Objectifying party rule;
— Disengaging separate spheres of government;
— Making governments more responsive.

Twenty-three centuries ago Plato, in the *Republic*, dealt with the problem of bringing wisdom to government. Eighty years ago that same Platonic answer was put into modern guise by H.G. Wells in *A Modern Utopia* (H. G. Wells, 1905), when he described a state administered by a "voluntary nobility", an openly accessible élite of able, mature ascetics willing to apply their talents without conventional incentives or acclaim. It seems likely that this kind of solution, replacing monetary by other criteria of distinction, could well offer the ultimate answer to a number of fundamental problems but today, because such solutions are held to remain outside the sphere of practical politics, we need to look to some reform of party government itself as a more immediate prospect.

Political parties nowadays tend to be dominated by the sources of their finance or else by the interests of influential backers (A. J. Dilloway, 1977), while many forms of proportional representation simply produce numerous small parties necessarily linked in fragile coalitions. Must we therefore conclude that reliance on multi-party government has to rule out any effective management of human affairs? That there is at least a partial way out has been shown by John Creasey (J. Creasey, 1969) in relation to the United Kingdom's political structure. In the British system, in which a simple party majority of votes in each constituency suffices to elect a Member of Parliament while a simple majority of party Members will secure a one-party government, all governments have for many years been elected by a minority of votes. Calling this "government by dictatorship masquerading as democracy", Creasey proposes a simple change, potentially of wider application also in other states. The leader of the party with most national votes would become Prime Minister, while each party would be free to nominate members of his government proportionately to their share of the national vote. Each party would also be eligible to propose bills for debate in accord with their part of the total vote. All such bills would be submitted to a free vote in Parliament, and Parliament would be submitted to a General Election at fixed intervals. There would be national referenda on major issues of public concern.

Closer study of the scheme shows it to be both equitable and fully democratic. If there are any problems they would seem to arise mainly from the need for compromise on party issues. This is why the system — known as the All-Party Alliance — would ideally be accompanied by a further scheme — Alliance in Industry. This last provides for an equal four-way ownership of the share capital invested in all industrial concerns, public or private — i.e. between the State, private investors, management of concerns and their work forces. The author of the APA scheme has already tested its potential acceptability by standing for Parliament in four by-elections and has secured up to 3300 votes for the system without help from the press or any party machine.

One question remains. How far can such a scheme as this surmount the difficulty that politicians, while they may do tolerably well in handling political questions, show up rather poorly where economic issues or planning are concerned? A continuous forward-looking process, although never a panacea and always full of pitfalls, is needed more and more as big investments have to accommodate to structural economic changes and their resulting social echoings. Economic planning and policy need to be objective, continuous and co-ordinated (A. J. Dilloway, 1977) and are thus ill-adapted to the politician's day-to-day juggling with pressure-groups to ensure re-election. Even without agreement on that point the essential difference between the legislative/political realm of Parliament and the economic domain has been stressed by a series of writers, from the Webbs to Firmin Oulès (F. Oulès, 1966). The latter, pointing to Montesquieu's well-known doctrine of separation of powers, long accepted in dealing with authorities responsible for legislative, executive and judicial functions, has reinforced this rule by the following: "Separation of economic and political institutions should be a fundamental principle of modern organization", an idea that has been developed elsewhere with regard to the British system (A. J. Dilloway, 1977 and C. B. Purdom, 1941). See also the second reference cited in a footnote on page 184.

We thus arrive at a final key question: How best to protect the conduct of affairs from inbuilt self-seeking by aspirants to political power? Here the answer must lie in a simple fact. In a democracy, above all, it should be the strength and clarity of public opinion that ultimately decides what kinds of policy are pursued. *Careful study of opinion sampling carried out over the last fifteen years in Great Britain, and supported by results in other mature states, shows that public opinion has long remained remarkably objective, and ahead of government policies even in such contentious areas as controls over pay, union freedom and nuclear power issues. So convincing is the evidence that any continuous planning organ would certainly be much aided by the inception of a regular, independent system of polling to monitor the state of public opinion.*

But there is, too, impressive evidence of another sort to show that *appeals* to public opinion are also a vital safeguard of democracy. Politicians argue against referenda because they blunt the use of words to beguile and persuade. But when referenda are built into the constitutional process at national and local levels, as in Switzerland, the results are indeed impressive. On any local or national issue — from whether to preserve a noted building to changes in immigration law — a referendum can be sought by a specified number of people and its results will be allowed for in framing policy. Perhaps it is no accident that in the state where this practice is most fully developed the conduct of government provokes little turbulence or charisma. There are few sensational rewards to be gained and even nominal leadership enjoys only a fixed term.

If the objective force of public opinion is a key to responsible government in the future we can conclude that in newly developing countries there should be an evolution in the quality of government as education, health and average income advance above the stage where dedicated paternalism is the best that can be hoped for. This, then, is the direction that development policy should seek to follow. But much has been happening of late in the more dynamic economies of some middle-range developing states that is not encouraging in this regard. For in practice there has been a counter-evolution in the development dialectic as expanding, educated élites are seduced by western prestige technology and consumerism, so that the state becomes top-heavy or bankrupted by business excesses before any real gains can become firmly rooted in the wider populace. This is the constant dilemma of development, and one which international co-operation must seek to resolve.

What has been shown in this section is that even in the conventional practice of government within a democratic state some room for sensible innovation does exist. Even within the existing climate there can be scope to make modest improvements which could well lead to more effective and responsible government in some more mature states.

Nothing has been said so far about the arrangements that would be needed if and when a loose form of global administration has to be set up to handle an incipient world consensus. This will be touched on in the final chapter. Suffice it to say here that experience already gained and techniques now to hand could offer the means for some standing form of world overview to be maintained. The problem lies less in finding a method than in crossing the divide that separates old ways of thought from new realities.

10

The Scope for Human Potential

II. ECONOMY, ENVIRONMENT AND SCIENCE

While Chapter 9 was concerned with three facets of the human prospect where there may be scope for human nature and human institutions to become better matched, the present chapter will complete the process, again using as a frame the conspectus of human activity distinguished in Table 29. Attention will now be focused on the economic system, the environment and science, ending with a similar look at the future of human rights.

There is an important point to be made at the outset. Both Chapter 9 and the present chapter are concerned mainly with the expression of human nature in spheres where it has so far been confined — that is, within the nation-state. But even from the case of population we can see that in varying degree these different facets of activity have already spread beyond the orbit of national problems to become areas of global concern. As well as in their national setting they have come to affect human beings everywhere through their global ramifications. In the present chapter three of the items to be considered are at different stages of becoming recognizable world concerns while human rights exemplifies a contrary case — an evolving national principle that can *cement* the global interest.

We can, in fact, arrange some main categories from Table 29 in decreasing order of their acknowledged, or emerging, global status:

1 Population	5 Human rights
2 Environment	6 Health
3 Economy	7 Information
4 Science	8 Government

In this list, which is selective, the matter of armed confrontation is not included, but it too is now a global issue that quite plainly has come to constrain all others. Again, the subject of government, though like the economic framework still seen as an internal question to be settled within states, is now ripe for the international community to begin to consider how a loose frame of minimal world administration could be generalized from the alternatives and piecemeal international models that already exist. There are thus two kinds of question to be embraced in the final synthesis, and towards that end the sectoral analyses pursued here, some medium-term proposals made in Chapter 5, and many other probings throughout this whole inquiry have been leading. How far can human potential be stretched to accommodate those new demands its restless ingenuity has imposed? More specifically, can some containing frame of order be attained by active consensus, through a coalescence of will and ideas? Or must it await the force of human conquest, followed by natural destruction and a slow remaking from scratch? The spheres of economy and environment may point to those critical limits which must decide the issue.

The Future of Economic Society

The future of the world's economic systems has a very special importance for world order. For this is an area where links between the national and the world scene are both vital and easy to grasp. There are other pressing reasons for concern. For one thing, those beliefs that underlie today's economic practice have for so long been ingrained into social character that any suggestion for change will tend to be repressed into the 'social unconscious' as ideologically alien and unthinkable. Here lies a major problem, and any 'New World Economic Order' worthy of the name must first come to terms with it before such a concept can have any real meaning.

How, then, have national and world economies reached their present state? Leaving aside the Marxist system, which sprang from a critique of early capitalism, modern economic notions and modern parliamentary democracy both stemmed from a mental climate first set in train by the Reformation and its 'protestant work ethic'. These rested on a 'model of man' in which the governing law of nature was an insatiable desire for power, so that an implacable force was seen as driving early market society — the existence of scarcity in relation to unlimited desires. It was by allowing maximum individual freedom from government that this force could operate so that the interests of every man would best be served. This thesis in turn implied that individuals enjoyed equal competitive power, which they did not. Behind the model, therefore, lay an unspoken premise about the individual that is perhaps best summed up in the words of a well-known hymn: "God made him high or lowly and ordered his estate".

A century after the parliamentary liberal market system took off, during which it absorbed a widening franchise and other refinements, the constant expansion necessary to its working began to break down. With adjustments to maintain failing demand added by Keynes in 1936, and with the cushion of a 'welfare state', plus a new post-war re-expansion after 1950, the system moved forward with success for another decade. Soon after 1960, however, and despite efforts to widen mass consumption by expanding credit, the

machine again faltered in the 'developed' world. Price inflation began to
show a rising trend as trade unions gained greatly in coercive power,
particularly in public service occupations, while in supply and finance
private transnational corporations proliferated as well, often through
takeovers, expanding rapidly to assume advantageous positions throughout the developing world. 'Stagflation' was further aided from October
1973 by the new OPEC cartel, which raised both oil costs and inflation
worldwide for a decade until its eventual breakdown exposed how massive
had been the dislocation of finances it had occasioned throughout the
developing world.

One after another various theories were applied in the 'developed'
countries to overcome this general malaise at source. 'Incomes policies',
followed later by monetarist theories — a resurgence of the idea that
inflation depends on growth in the quantity of money circulating — and
later still 'supply-side economics', briefly the notion that supply will create
its demand, have all been tried but have failed to bring back that 'golden
age' of the first two post-war decades. The truth is more simple. It can now
be seen that 'developed' states are beset by an inherent contradiction that
arises from the internal logic of the system when it reaches a level of high
mass consumption in a non-expanding market. At this stage the system
comes to be characterized internally by mammoth labour monopolies and
externally by very large and transnational corporations that can 'manage'
their prices or supplies and are largely free from government controls.
What then is the inherent contradiction? It is simply that national systems,
as well as desiring full employment, want economic growth without
inflation, freedom for large concerns and free trade unions, a mixture that
is impossible in today's richer world of mass expectation. In the developing
world, of course, demand for essentials, though mostly unexpressed, is
potentially massive, but that is not the essential business of TNCs. What *is*
their business is, among other things, to produce in states with low taxes
and low labour costs and to export any home surpluses to Third World
countries open to mass advertising.*

The incompatibles in the present situation are thus of two sorts. If at the
national scale free semi-monopolies, whether of labour or business, cannot
be reconciled with price stability, neither can high interest rates or steady
growth in supply and demand. The free competition between equal and
independent units that is supposed to discipline the system is now a myth
and applies only to one-third of the economic machine. The mass pressure
to consume is also too great for output to support the financing of both
consumption and capital investment at the same time. Productivity of
labour has been falling for the same reason, because capital schemes have

*For a more positive aspect see Ian Steele: Corporations Fill Aid Gap. *Development Forum*,
February–March 1985, Geneva.

not kept pace with consumption while much that was consumed was gained from a misspent use of natural resources. Unemployment has become the only means of restricting inflation and consumption alike. A further source of price inflation, but not of employment or productivity, has been and is the rising military consumption of the state. To sum up in the words of Raúl Prebisch: "Market forces are not capable of controlling consumption and accumulation" (R. Prebisch, 1983). The net effect of this rise of the new social factors in economic performance, whatever sort of correction is applied, has mostly been 'stagflation' or depression, high interest rates and unemployment.

On the global scene, as we know, this pattern has been repeated, but with a difference. The world economy is characterized, firstly by a group of frustrated high-consumption states unwilling to take primary products from a stricken Third World, which is learning to export its manufactures at lower cost; and secondly, by a widely contrasting two-tier system, with a prosperous, expanding global network of transnational enterprises in oil, commodities, manufacturing and banking superimposed on a stagnating system of advanced or emergent national economies, mostly ill-functioning. The two latter systems are separate and yet linked in the sense that the first is sustained in its advance by the second without being accountable to it. A third feature of the world economy is the unstable disarray in its financial system, which is hardly to be wondered at given the independence and divergent interests of its other components.

Because governments remain silent about this phenomenon, it is time to fill in a few details. In Chapter 3 (including Table 9 and Figure 7) some idea was given of total world trade and its distribution. While the level has fluctuated over the last few years it can be said that transnational concerns account for some 70 per cent of today's total trade and at least 80 per cent when centrally-directed economies are excluded. Some 40 per cent of all trade is estimated to consist of intra-firm transfers between TNCs, which increasingly are conglomerates diversified in a range of activities. According to Levinson (C. Levinson, 1982) transnationals also account for half the world's industrial employment and nearly 60 per cent of world credit. That, incidentally, is why mature governments prefer to remain silent in view of their marked impotence in the matter.

To show how sales of manufacturing TNCs compare in size with government output, Table 32 shows a few comparisons from among the top twenty concerns.

No fewer than thirteen, or 65 per cent of these first twenty manufacturers are oil companies. But an equal dominance over the world economy exists in other sectors. Thus six corporations control around 80 per cent of the world's grain trade, set its prices and handle much of the agricultural exports of Third World states which import grains. Capital-intensive agriculture by TNCs in developing countries, and a growth of

TABLE 32

Some Major Transnational Manufacturing Corporations and their National Analogues

Corporation	Home Country	Rank	1980 Sales (000' million US $)	Nearest State in GNP
Exxon (Standard Oil NJ)	USA	1	103.1	Belgium
Royal Dutch/Shell Group	Neth./UK	2	77.1	Sweden
British Petroleum	UK	6	48.0	Indonesia
Ford Motor Corporation	USA	8	37.1	Greece
IBM	USA	11	26.2	Colombia
Unilever	Neth./UK	17	23.6	Pakistan
Petroleos de Venezuela	Venezuela	20	18.8	Israel

Source (Columns 1–4): UN Centre on Transnational Corporations, 1982.

'agribusiness' controlled by a few major concerns, tends to be concentrated on the more fertile, accessible and well-watered lands to produce for luxury goods and export. In the process, it has been argued, basic food output for the mass home population can suffer, along with the livelihood and effectiveness of traditional low-cost farmers (M. Teubal, 1980). All this offers one example out of many which show that in economic matters efficient performance depends on fitness of purpose as well as cost-effectiveness — a point ignored by conventional theory.

It is time to sum up on the whole economic dimension and what it may imply for the future of human affairs. The existing systems that hold sway among the world's peoples have come to the point where the global economy is virtually unworkable even on its own terms, seriously unstable and even counterproductive.

Essentially four different kinds of comment are in order. Firstly, let us consider the basic function of national systems in producing and satisfying consumer needs. Under both the alternative systems now in use there exists a fundamental and unresolved clash of interests between producers on the one hand and consumers on the other, a point clearly confirmed by both Raymond Aron and Ota Sik, the Czechoslovak Minister of Economy during the Dubcek experiment (O. Sik and R. Aron, 1971). This incompatibility of interests can only be reconciled today by the existence of an impartial market of equals, something that is declining in the west and minimal in the east. Further, even market systems are now highly unstable because their operations have to be harmonized in a milieu where rich independent states suffer the same internal indiscipline and seek the same remedies, with results that are cumulative on the world scene. At the same time they, and the world's financial market, may be exploited invisibly through an overgrowth of booming transnationals. At the world scale our global economic system is thus a two-tier affair of glaring disharmony that has no stable or long-term object, being run on a day-to-day basis to satisfy entrepreneurs and political manipulators.

Some idea of a rising turbulence in global economic trends can be gained from recent changes in world trade, which has normally followed a fairly sedate course. Table 33 sums up annual changes in volume of trade by region and economic group over a five-year period. The effects of some current troubles, including those of developing exporters of

TABLE 33
Changes in the Volume of World Trade, by Region, 1978–1983
(Percentage change over previous year)

Country or Group	1978	1979	1980	1981	1982	1983 (First half)
EXPORTS						
A. Developed market economies	6	7	4	2	1	−1
North America	11	8	5	−2	−6	−2
Western Europe	6	7	2	2	3	0
B. Developing market economies	4	8	−5	−6	−7	1[a]
OPEC countries	−4	3	−12	−16	−19	−4[a]
Non-oil developing countries	9	10	9	6	1	5[a]
C. European centrally planned economies	5	5	2	1	6	9
Eastern Europe	6	8	3	2	7	10
Soviet Union	3	1	2	—	6	9
TOTAL ABOVE	5	7	2	1	−1	—
IMPORTS						
A. Developed market economies	5	8	−1	−3	−1	−1
North America	7	3	−7	2	−8	0
Western Europe	3	11	1	−5	1	−1
B. Developing market economies	8	2	5	7	−1	−1[a]
OPEC countries	5	−12	15	20	5	−8[a]
Non-oil developing countries	9	10	5	3	−8	3[a]
C. European centrally planned economies	9	1	4	1	2	6
Eastern Europe	5	2	1	−5	−5	6
Soviet Union	13	1	7	8	9	7
TOTAL ABOVE	6	7	1	—	−1	—

[a]Estimates for the full year.
Source: Economic Bulletin for Europe, Vol. 35, No. 4, 1983 (UN Economic Commission for Europe, Geneva).

primary products and also those of OPEC, can be clearly seen, though not the chronic indebtedness that has beset most of the developing countries.

Two more negative points remain to be borne in mind. *First the ingraining, even conditioning, of people to the idea of competitiveness as a prime virtue, of grabbing for yourself first and all the time, has spread from the market mentality into a milieu where it has become obsolete in the face of technology's creation of sophisticated interdependence. This extra stimulus to greed, which the uncommitted seek to discount in their social life, is now a major in-built factor that throws doubt on the whole human adventure. In turn this is having a serious effect on the chances of international co-operation in conflict situations.* One can easily observe how political leaders who extol competitiveness come at once to be obsessed with confrontation, one-upmanship and scoring a win for their clique, oblivious that matters like the peace of the world may be at stake.

What then can be done to correct the more harmful mutations of market practice? In Chapter 5 some reforms were outlined that could yield important results without dislocating the system. In Chapter 9 another related idea was considered — the separating of economic government from the politics of day-to-day administration. All these proposals have been argued for in recent years, the first two actually in the United States!*

In their way, each of the above ideas exemplifies a new state of mind that has to permeate economic practice. That state of mind has to do with freedom. Without freedom, as Aldous Huxley pointed out, ". . . human beings cannot become fully human" (A. Huxley, 1957). That much is true and today much lip-service is paid to the idea of freedom, as it was two centuries ago when the liberal market was invented. But excessive freedom for self-interested business concerns, which remains a hallmark of the liberal economy, can today lead only to careless squalor, unnecessary proliferation, short-cut cheating and disregarded 'external' costs that are nobody's business. It is nobody's business, in short, to bother about anything external to money-making, so nobody does. This is the net result, nationally and worldwide, of malfunctioning sovereign economies and self-interested TNCs, quite apart from the intrinsic inefficiency of the machine itself.

All this is not inevitable. *A very few simple controls over the conduct of independent economic agents to make them responsible for their actions could revolutionize economic effectiveness in human terms. It is simply that the original reason for business freedom — to combat scarcity by releasing the dynamic drive of entrepreneurs — has long been superseded by events.*

*For some earlier contributions to solving the basic economic problem, see too *The Economics of Control*, by A. P. Lerner (Macmillan Co., New York, 1946); and Chapter 23 of *The Economics of Employment*, by the same author (McGraw-Hill, New York, 1951).

What then of the future of economic behaviour in a shrinking world? Conventional definitions of economic activity are based on the idea of scarcity. It was a view of scarcity in the face of unlimited desire that became the driving force behind the liberal market system that arose between the time of John Locke in the seventeenth century and James Mill in the nineteenth century — a principle that has remained implicit in economic thinking ever since.

Leaving aside the mechanistic psychology behind this thesis, there is a close relation between scarcity and selfishness in traditional thinking, as J. M. Keynes and V. I. Lenin have both observed. For only when scarcity has been abolished will selflessness become feasible. At present scarcity is being artificially manufactured, both by limiting production to keep up prices and by creating demand through excessive credit. This, however, cannot disguise the fact that technically the power to abolish scarcity is looming on the horizon of the more developed states some four decades earlier than Keynes himself foresaw. When it comes to be in the interests of entrepreneurs and politicians to create abundant necessities by high-productivity output, this could well be tackled with the same resolution as 'liberty ships' were mass-produced during the Second World War. The economic scene may soon be ripe for that 'quantic jump' in first principles that might, in a single stroke, create both a practical ethics and abolish much primary need.*

What, then, of the world organization of economic affairs? *Because of its global interdependence our creaking, ill-adjusted economic frame is badly in need of a standing body of the highest integrity to maintain an overseeing and early-warning role.* The UN Economic and Social Council tries to do this in its periodic sessions but it is cluttered with so many stages of reporting that it cannot function in the manner needed. *Just as the Human Rights Commission is trying, against strong opposition, to create some continuity of overview, so the time has come for a World Economic Commission to arise for a similar purpose.* This may not work smoothly at the outset since the vested interests against it will be strong. But the mere fact of creating such machinery with high authority will bring into the open and make explicit what has been implied in the world situation for many years. As much as fifty years ago, in working out a detailed scheme for a World Production Order and a World Economic Council, F. M. Wibaut was able to conclude that ". . . world economic development is incompatible with present methods of production and supply . . . As soon as such a conviction is strongly held by the inhabitants of many countries, so strongly that those who hold it can control the legislation of their

---

*For a down-to-earth outline of method, by Oskar Lange, see *On the Economic Theory of Socialism*, by O. Lange and F. M. Taylor (pp. 139–141), McGraw-Hill Paperbacks, New York, 1964.

respective states, we shall have begun to build the system on which the metamorphosis of human material standards depends". (F. M. Wibaut, 1935)

The Future of Environment

Modern concern for the environment was first concerted internationally in June 1972, at the UN Conference on the Human Environment held in Stockholm. In the decade since then the world has changed quite considerably. Between 1972 and 1982 world population increased by about 21 per cent, military expenditure by 20 per cent and total world product by some 50 per cent, the last two in real terms. Over the same period the number of states with bodies for protecting the environment rose tenfold, from around ten in 1972 to over one hundred 10 years later. The subject has now become a popular preoccupation of millions as well as a matter for attention by many governments. Indeed the second outcome, spurred on by the UN Environment Programme, is very largely a consequence of the first. For governments are obliged to respect the strength of public opinion where such exists as a real force. If that truth is once realized it can open the way not only to an upsurge of environmental care but to many other commonsense options. For this to happen two conditions have to be fulfilled. Firstly, public opinion must be capable of being openly expressed; and, secondly, the public must be receptive, unambiguously informed, and thus aware that a problem exists. Since the democratic process involves much misinformation and sophistry, these conditions can still prove onerous.

Some main features of the UN Environment Programme were outlined in Chapter 5 (including Table 15 and Figure 13), so the details need not concern us. Here it is rather difficulties in the way of implementing environmental policies, and prospects of surmounting them, that have to be addressed. These difficulties are not, as is often thought, intrinsically economic, since environmental care yields good returns — at least to the community! Rather they are familiar human failings that reduce to four in number: selfishness, ignorance, inertia and out-group hostility. That these sources of hazard act differently in different fields of environmental concern can be seen from the following rough list of some items falling within our purview (Table 34).

If ignorance and commercialism pose the most frequent problems, this is by no means the end of the story. While the second can be countered by resolute action, sheer lack of knowledge of how some complex phenomena may ramify can, by encouraging official inertia, give credence to 'business as usual'. There is in addition the vexed question of shared resources, which is where nationalism comes in.

Let us take these problems in turn. Firstly, there are several facets of

TABLE 34
Sources of Environmental Misuse

Resources	Environmental sector	Ultimate cause of misuse[a]
	ATMOSPHERE	
Atmosphere		I, S and IE
	LITHOSPHERE	
Soils		I and S
Minerals		S
	BIOSPHERE	
Forests		I and S
Other flora and fauna		I, S and IE
	HYDROSPHERE	
Surface and ground water		I, S, IE and OH
Oceans and seas		I, S and IE
	SOCIOSPHERE	
Energy activity		I, S and IE
Military activity		I and OH
Crop protection chemicals		I and S
Industrial products		S and IE
Pharmaceuticals		S and I

[a] I = Ignorance; S = Exploitative selfishness; IE = Institutional inertia; OH = Out-group hostility or nationalism.

environment where chances being taken today by the world community appear likely, or even certain, to lead to damage that is global and irreversible. Uncertainty lies mainly in the time-lag before changes already in train produce severe results. A further source of hazard is the extent to which factors of change in one component may interact elsewhere to produce effects in another. This last point explains how ignorance can so often lead to unenlightened action. These considerations can be illustrated by looking at what is happening to the world's forests, and notably tropical rain forests; to other well-defined biomes, major habitats of animal and plant communities; and to atmospheric consequences of the carbon cycle.

First of all, rich forest cover in many developing areas of the world is being rapidly and systematically destroyed for short-term non-forestry advantage and then left in an ecologically and climatically unstable state. The Brazilian rain-forest is a well-known example but what is happening in India is also typical. Here the tropical hardwood forest, which still covered 30 per cent of India's land surface as recently as 1940, is already reduced to 11 per cent and at present rates could disappear altogether in a decade if counter-measures now being taken do not succeed.

That there are several different reasons why such worldwide happenings are important can be sensed from a study of Figure 20. This shows some of the simpler interrelations between elements of the natural environment, the biotic communities and our artificially created habitat. Forest cover is

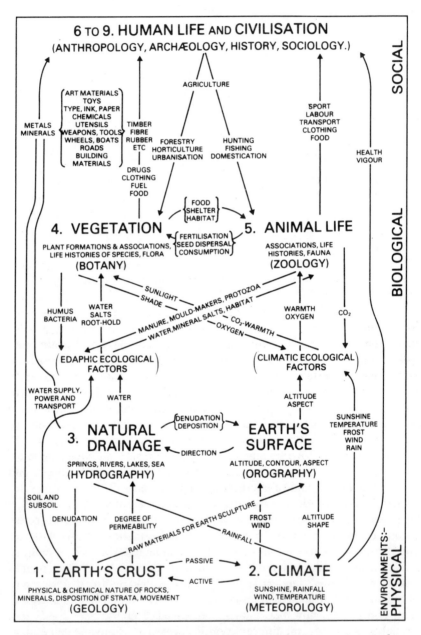

FIG. 20. Relationships between Man and his Environments (from C. C. Fagg and G. E. Hutchings, 1930).

locally linked to the hydrological cycle, to soil formation and regionally to climate. This is one reason why its brusque removal can upset a natural balance. A second reason is shown by the Indian example, where a very rich fauna previously found in wooded areas is already reduced to a large number of endangered species.

But vegetation is also bound up with the natural carbon cycle, one of the biogeochemical cycles that loom large in the working of our ecosystem. Forest clearance, as well as soil atmosphere transfers, appear to be two sources contributing to a store of carbon dioxide in the atmosphere which seems roughly comparable in amount to releases of carbon achieved by man's burning of fossil fuels. Even with some ocean storage of carbon the total atmospheric build-up caused by humans amounts to about three per cent per decade, a rate that implies major climatic changes in around 60–70 years from a 'greenhouse effect' produced by infra-red absorption. These could be supplemented in turn by independent variations in solar radius.

This carbon cycle acts intimately with energy and food systems, as well as with the oceans, atmosphere, soils, rock structure and biotic systems — a fact which brings out the many hazards that may attend thoughtless meddling with natural phenomena. The same remark is at least equally true of another involuntary but avoidable disaster in the making — a speeding-up of evolutionary change and a major loss of total species, possibly with a spurt in the rise of new and unwelcome ones, that will follow from widespread disruption of natural habitats. Not only our heedless sacking of tropical rain forests — a source of evolutionary mechanisms embracing some forty per cent of all species — but several other special habitats such as terrestrial wetlands, are bound up in a devastating and uniquely rapid process of evolutionary change caused by human beings that will lead to a disappearance of about one-tenth of all existing species and an emergence of some new ones adapted to specialized environments and new chemicals. In the view of Dr Norman Myers up to a million species could disappear over the next twenty years while adaptable ones, such as the common rat, the house fly and many 'weed' plants, may prosper alongside a much slower rise in new speciation (N. Myers, 1982). This genetic upheaval and impoverishment equals, and may exceed in its magnitude, any of those so far experienced throughout the rise of living forms within geological time. Here, then, is another instance of man's shortsightedness that has not merely grown to crisis proportions in a single generation but is now set to alter the conditions of human existence within the life-span of those now living.

The above examples refer to what are called 'global commons', or shared resources of common interest. Our final example concerns a different problem — that which arises where natural resources are shared between individual states or groups of states. When I entered the United Nations early in 1948 this question was already one of our important preoccupations so far as concerned international river basins. Since then, and despite Declarations or principles of conduct drawn up, first at the UN Conference on the Environment in 1972, then at the UN Water Conference in 1977 and again by a Group of Experts convened by the UN Environment Programme in 1978, to say nothing of prolonged studies by the International Law Commission, there has been little advance towards responsible use of the resources of shared river basins to meet hydro-electric, water supply, irrigation or multi-purpose requirements. With some exceptions, like the Indus treaty of 1960 between India and Pakistan, and others in North America, non-European agreements have been few and harmonious development minimal, with national sovereignty as the barrier on every possible occasion. That this is not a minor problem can be gauged from the fact that, in all, 214 river or lake basins (major catchment areas) are shared by two or more countries while, according to Dr A. K. Biswas, 1982) there are 44 countries where 80 per cent or more of the total area lies within international river basins. These figures show the scope for conflict, muddle or delay where a natural resource vital to sustainable development has to be exploited in an orderly way.

Within a single decade, environmental concern has become headline news for the world's people. At the technical level, too, it now ranks, after population, as an accepted global problem. Yet governments continue to hedge and haggle when they seek to transform platitudes into meaningful action. What, then, are the prospects for humans to become better adapted to their physical habitat?

As a plus it has to be remembered that just as certain individuals in a population are 'trend-setters', so are some states prominent in pursuing humane policies. Diffusion of sound practice by advocacy and example offers one source of hope for the future, but there are some others. Non-governmental professional organizations are doing and can do much to underpin all the expert researching that is mobilized through the UN Environment Programme. *Steady progress in scientific understanding in this field can now ramify freely across academic disciplines, thanks to a new awareness borne of the last decade. But how far all this can impinge on the practice of governments must depend on down-to-earth public opinion. If this force, which has already come alive in a quite new way, can maintain its early momentum, then new knowledge will not merely throw up new obligations, but new laws as well.*

Science in the Future

The world of science differs from other institutions discussed in this and the previous chapter in that while the latter deal with essential *means* to human existence science has come to concern both means and *ends*. As to *means* it is science — or rather its commercial exploitation — that fires technology and technology that decides both the *rate of change* in human activity and the *direction* that change may follow. Though both are matters of prime concern for the species, any exercise of free choice as to either the rate or the direction is so far judged to be less important than maintenance of commercial freedom.

If science as an uncontrolled means thus decides how fast we go and where, it is science as an end that orders self-conscious reason, just as a spade or a crane extend the human arm. The learning, probing, self-conscious mind, following rules of science created by human beings, has brought the species from an eolithic stage, using unworked flints, to some rough knowledge of the world, outside and in. If understanding is truly one of the ends of purposive action, it is the method of pure science which creates that end, or at least gives it meaning.

Over the last 30 years science as a source of technique has had such success in physics and biology that marketed technical gadgetry has come to pose grave new problems for social living. These problems were recognized internationally by the UN General Assembly as early as 1968 so far as concerned developments in recording devices; uses of electronics which may affect the rights of the person; a need to protect human personality in the light of advances in biology, medicine and biochemistry; and, more generally, the balance required between scientific or techno-logical progress and intellectual, cultural and moral advancement. In-quiries were pursued in these fields by the Commission on Human Rights and in September 1975 a group of six eminent international experts met in Geneva to discuss the balance referred to above — that between science/technology and other kinds of human action.

Among the conclusions reached by the Group were the following:

> Not every change or development that science and technology make feasible needs to become an actuality. Governments and societies must determine . . . whether the time is ripe for particular innovations and whether their advantages outweigh for the society the discernible disadvantages. International machinery should be entrusted with such a technological assessment for mankind as a whole.

Among questions deemed ripe for attention in this context were population planning in relation to the right to found a family; protection against hazards in the use of atomic energy; human experimentation; implications of biotechnical discoveries concerning tissue and organ transplantation, genetic manipulation of microbes or potential modifica-tions of human genome; modification of mental processes by medical means; implications of the extension of life and new attitudes to death; and social and ethical choices relative to equality in health protection and medical care. It was recommended that both the duties of the individual to the community and the rights of future generations be better defined, these questions being viewed in the context of the world population crisis and an opinion that the right of the child to be born physically and mentally sound should take precedence over the rights of parents to reproduce.

Since these early explorations of science-based threats to human rights, research and application have intensified, notably in the fields of electronics and biotechnology. As usual, developments can prove benign or potentially malignant, since demands of either sort can be promoted with equal ease. Military applications, including most space research, fall evidently into the latter category but computer and micro-chip developments, although offering real advances at the technical research level, also divert much promotional effort into ephemeral office and home 'gimmickry'. Far more sinister than any of this, and almost inevitably irresistible to governments in parliamentary democracies failing very resolute public action, is a strong threat to privacy and personal independence posed by new opportunities to exert general surveillance simply by linking up the many existing computer systems, public and private. Official aversion to such an idea will break down sooner or later under the paranoid centripetal forces of international politics. Data available from such simple sources as public utilities, employment, social security and telecommunications services, customs, banks, police, credit systems and inland revenue authorities can easily be called on by intelligence agencies, thereby negating the whole basis of democracy in government. Secrecy ensures that computer or human error, inertia in removing obsolete material or just unauthorized use of data, can all menace the individual without redress and even without his knowlege. To this can be added a whole battery of aural and visual devices available to monitor human behaviour in secret.

States, too, are not now immune to surveillance. Earth satellites may be placed in geostationary orbit 22,300 miles above the equator so as to follow the earth's rotation, or in elliptical orbit. Communications satellites used for telephone, television, etc. may be distinguished from observational types designed for weather forecasting, environmental monitoring (agriculture, hydrology, erosion, mineral assessment, fisheries, etc.) as well as intelligence-gathering. Such useful activities are extensions of competitive prestige or arms-race endeavours, but they in turn have called forth efforts through the United Nations to formulate a body of international law governing peaceful use of outer space. So far this covers a Declaration of Legal Principles Governing the Activities of States in the Exploration and Use of Outer Space (1963), a Treaty of 1966 on the same subject, and a UNESCO Declaration of 1972 on Guiding Principles covering Use of Satellite Broadcasting. But in 1983 new proposals and programmes for setting up permanent stations in outer space to pre-empt military initiative have shown no concern for legitimate international rights. The socially inbuilt competitive urge remains far too strong.

Under present conditions accelerating research and development inevitably bring to light more and more hazards, human problems or ethical considerations. The speed of this process can be illustrated by human exposure to chemical substances. In 1984 the International Labour Organization has noted that while at the end of 1965 211,934 substances were listed in the Chemical Abstracts Service Registry, five years later this figure had risen to 1.6 million and at the time of reporting had reached a total of over five million substances. Of these some 60,000 substances were in common use, but only a fraction of those known to be toxic to humans had been accorded defined occupational limits, and then in certain countries only, because of complex medical, technical or economic considerations.

Equally daunting questions are being opened up by advances in medical technique or treatment. It suffices to mention those legal and other queries raised by A.I.D., or artificial insemination by donor; by 'genetic engineering' possibilities of various kinds; or by problems in medical ethics arising in such matters as prolongation of life against the wishes of a patient, or the allocating of available facilities between costly but marginal 'headline' techniques like heart transplants as against other more mundane but widespread kinds of treatment.

Without wishing to labour these problems, it is hard to ignore a whole range of man-made nuclear hazards created by what can now be seen to have been a precipitate, irreversible post-war rush into the unknown. Risks to life and health arise from many different sources of radiation caused by humans and are often hard to quantify. In all but a few locations the supposed economic case for exploiting nuclear energy has proved illusory, but self-deception and sophistry remain to confuse the public mind on this and other aspects of the case because continually escalating armaments ensure a constant demand — actual or potential — for the plutonium that is a by-product of nuclear energy supply. All discussion of human rights implications in this field has been sidetracked, even though near-permanent accumulation of highly toxic waste from nuclear installations, including power plants, reprocessing plants and bomb manufacture, offers the clearest possible affront to future generations since no hazard-proof solution yet exists. Vitrification (enclosure in glass), with storage in salt or other deposits or in igneous rocks, has been considered for many years but never clearly perfected. Some recent studies have suggested encasing in synthetic crystalline materials or synthetic rock, but these too remain projects. This question shows up one important point: how public counterpressure can be muted where unambiguous information is hard to come by. The same can be said of another major and ever-growing ethical problem posed by burgeoning science — an inability, by humankind in general and scientists in particular, to recognize today's acquired obligation to respect the rights of non-human as well as human life in pursuing man's objectives.

At this point we should seek to counter any idea that the thesis here being probed is an anti-science one. Even a scientific frontier already mentioned — that of recombinant DNA research, or genetic engineering — now offers a chance of real advances in the future. Following the breaking of the genetic code of deoxyribonucleic acid (DNA), it has sometimes become possible to transfer genetic material from one animal or plant species or strain to another so that it is accepted by the recipient and transferred to future generations. While some human implications of this, and its extreme danger of producing unwanted strains in the absence of severe controls, tend to place a large question-mark over the whole idea, there are many areas of medicine, industry and agriculture where positive prospects can be opened up, using the skills of biochemists, microbio-logists, geneticists and chemical engineers to process materials by means of microbial agents. In medicine supplies of hormones, interferons, important vaccines and antibiotics can be improved or cheapened. Some industrial chemicals, and others required for pharmaceutical products, could be produced more easily. Agricultural uses include new high-yield plant strains and enzymes for food processing. Other applications, of particular value for the developing world, embrace a use of microbes for such purposes as nitrogen fixation, thereby reducing the need for chemical fertilizers, and for biogas production.

It is now a UNESCO objective to exploit the world's microbial gene pool for human benefit. To this end a global network of twelve Microbiological Resources Centres has been set up to manage and conserve the pool, and especially aspects like the *Rhizobium* gene–legume partnership, which, by increasing nitrogen fixation, could raise protein crop productivity in developing countries. One of these MIRCENs, located at Brisbane, forms a World Data Centre on Micro-organisms and houses the master World Directory of Collections of Cultures (C. Lewis, 1983).

How, then, in the light of all this, can one sum up the future of science as a world force? Moving on from glorious nineteenth-century traditions, when individuals made major discoveries in backyards, our present world network of science is a far more business-managed and careerist affair. Forty per cent of British scientists are now occupied in military research, spending in the process well over half the country's total research budget. But, like the world medical network, a large proportion of scientific workers remains loyal to the traditions of free inquiry in pursuit of rigorous understanding for its own sake. Despite some dilution, the closely linked-up global community of pure science is a wondrous fabric when compared to the sorry state of most human affairs, even though it could gain from having the means to reinforce its commitment to human ideals by being able to see its role more clearly.

There are two ways in which this may happen and I believe they will influence the future of science. The first is by extending the process of worldwide awareness through two-way communication. The year 1983 was designated World Communications Year, when eleven UN specialized agencies and all five regional economic commissions joined forces in action to promote the aims of Article 19 of the Universal Declaration: "Everyone has the right . . . to seek, receive and impart information and ideas through any media and regardless of frontiers."

Objective information and the greater awareness it could foster need to become part of the United Nations development process. This means a two-way interaction between world institutions and the world's peoples, a reactive interchange between world decision-making and those subjected to decisions. Scientists, too, need to become more aware of the context in which their activities are pursued, and this will surely happen.

A second way of 'humanizing' pure science, of placing it in a true human-affairs context, may develop from the fact that three worldwide networks, making for scientific understanding, awareness and human rights respectively, all rest on ideals of enlightenment that should enrich each other. To be objective and positive pure science, as a human creation, should conform to basic human rights criteria if it is to contribute to human aims. What J. D. Bernal called 'the social function of science' is to work towards a basis of objective understanding of natural phenomena as a datum against which human aims can be appraised. This means that pure science can never be inconsistent with an individual's rights to life, knowledge and self-development.

What I am here saying is that there are three forces in the modern world of change that can counter the forces of unreason and the self-motivated interests of power-seekers as they pursue the 'art of the possible'. These are the forces of objective information, of science-based understanding and of human rights. Such forces, which make for learning and conscience, are all that stand between mankind and its own involuntary distortion of the human future. This, and not a proliferation of ephemeral gadgetry, is the true measure of science's role in human affairs.

The Future of Human Rights

It has been abundantly shown here that a world code of human rights and duties — the Universal Declaration and its main supports, plus a defined right to Development — is, first of all, the minimum frame of principles that can offer individuals the way to lives of mutual fulfilment and states the means to co-operate fruitfully for a common good. But more than this, our world code offers the *only* frame of principles that can achieve this, because it is the only framework that can prevail among the world's people, given the diversity of religions, cultures, ideologies, living standards and all the manifold differences that now divide mankind. This is why, as a first step, international efforts to enlarge the scope of human rights standards and to protect and extend national human rights observance have both to be ceaselessly maintained and even intensified.

The present methods of doing this are threefold. First, new international instruments are being devised to meet gaps disclosed as new forms of discrimination against special groups come to the fore. Next, efforts are being made to set up a continuous overview of the world situation and to act on major emergencies as they occur. This could be done by appointing a UN High Commissioner for Human Rights to supplement the special missions, rapporteurs and expert groups that investigate alleged gross violations of rights as these arise throughout the world.

The third and newest mode of action is to consider some wider implications of the field of rights and duties that are opening up as the complexities of world development are realized. How, for instance, is the idea of individual rights and duties to be reconciled with and absorbed into international law which, by tradition, is thought to apply only to states?

Today the individual citizen is seen more and more to have responsibilities to respect, and rights to be protected by, the law of his state — into which any international agreements should be absorbed — but equally a responsibility to act according to conscience where he perceives a gross conflict between arbitrary state action and international humanitarian or human rights law. The Nuremberg Tribunal upheld this duty, while today more and more internal situations are coming to pose a similar problem. One example is the duty of prison officers or the military to refrain from torture or unlawful killing. Another may arise where military conscription is resisted on the grounds that the forces in question plan to use outlawed weapons of mass destruction; to occupy another country illegally; or to engage in genocide. In 1983 a study on conscientious objection to military service considered by the Human Rights Sub-Commission on Prevention of Discrimination already contains a proposal that such acts of conscience be acceptable as grounds for conscientious objection where human rights violations are expected to occur.

International law is at present in a state of transition. There seems little doubt that it will be forced to accommodate fairly soon both to the rights of the individual and to his accountability on the world scene — this despite the non-acceptance of the idea in some legal systems, including those of centrally directed states like the USSR. In the meantime it should be observed that individual citizens everywhere still fail to realize the potential power of their collective views in such areas. It is now emerging that individuals have a clear right to express themselves through collective non-violence, even in states possessing full democratic franchise, if the state in question acts in an arbitrary way against established law or announced policy.

But it is possible, and still necessary, greatly to improve the national climate of human rights observance in most countries. As a start, this can be done by setting up a National Human Rights Commission or similar body, possibly with regional or local branches, to publicize the whole idea of rights and duties and bring it far more widely and deeply into the public consciousness. Such a body must be openly accepted, so that when, for instance, a regular national report on the state of human rights is prepared — say for the Human Rights Committee of the United Nations — a copy will be furnished also to the National Commission. This kind of exercise may encourage more realistic reporting and help to create a publicly aware and concerned citizenry. Even in developing countries with a long way to go, a state of popular awareness on human rights and duties, backed up where possible by wide-ranging educational programmes, can offer a measuring-rod for judging true priorities and rates of advance. It will also draw attention to the shortcomings of officials, bureaucrats and business concerns.

What, then, is the future of human rights and duties in a total world context? Today the substance of international conventions as ratified is either written into national domestic law or, as treaties, they are deemed to take a broad precedence over existing national legislation. *It has already been shown that if the field of human rights is to include a general right to development — as it should and probably will — then the substance of all international agreements, and not simply those concerned with human rights, will in future have to be so drafted as to be openly consistent with human rights criteria.* This, in fact, will have to happen very soon if viable development worldwide is to continue. States will have to be held far more effectively accountable than now for open dereliction of human rights enactments. When most of the major international conventions on human rights have been ratified by a clear majority of all states a new situation will arise. More pressure will be exerted to achieve conformity with the accepted world code and correspondingly its status will be enhanced.

But what about effective observance by individual citizens — of each state and of the world? What of prime ministers, generals, prison officers, business men and bureaucrats? Our only real hope for a viably humane future lies in widespread acceptance of rights and duties by all. Largely this is a matter of universal education from an early age, plus the rise of a strong public opinion conditioned to see that such an acceptance is the only way to maximize everyone's true freedom. *As states develop in human terms it is more and more the public will that ultimately determines what policies are pursued.* This truth is still far too little realized, most of all in mature states. But the slow rise of more humane institutions can only assist that awareness.

11
A Final Synthesis

To bring this inquiry to a forward-looking conclusion we shall start from a simple balance sheet of the global situation as visible in 1984. From that basis, and building on any insights gained up to this point, we must presume to draw what inferences we can about the human prospect. Since our self-knowledge is mostly qualitative and partial, our insights have a low probability for predictive purposes. But prediction is not here the aim since a reasoned *projection of possibilities* is the most that should be looked for. The question at issue thus reduces to a deceptively simple form: How far can the human species contemplate a viable global future in which adaptive evolution can prevail over disruption?

Which Way to World Order?

While Figure 21 sums up the present stage of development worldwide, as reflected by 144 states, Table 35 brings together some fundamentals of the current world situation. The Table does not refer to such defects as economic inequity or political injustice which, although common enough, are symptoms, or even to overpopulation as such. Rather the stress is on facts or forces which seem to be indicators of the way the world should or should not be going if something like a tolerable global order is to lie ahead.

Table 35 shows that we live, demonstrably enough, in a single world, though not yet in a unified one. A *de facto* linking up, even a nascent unity, is suggested by seven items listed under section A of the table, but these are heavily countered by five other items from the 'negative' group. In part — as in item 2 of the table — signs of unity are simply a consequence of an explosion of communications and the printed word. In other instances they amount to an open acceptance of comprehensiveness, of an idea that the world is one and that basic needs are shared by all, as with items 3 and 9. Recognition of unity in diversity requires several constituents and one of the simpler ones is a body of world law — that is, international law extended to encompass the conditions of a world order. In the words of C. B. Purdom:

> World law should be a law for world citizens. The concept of world

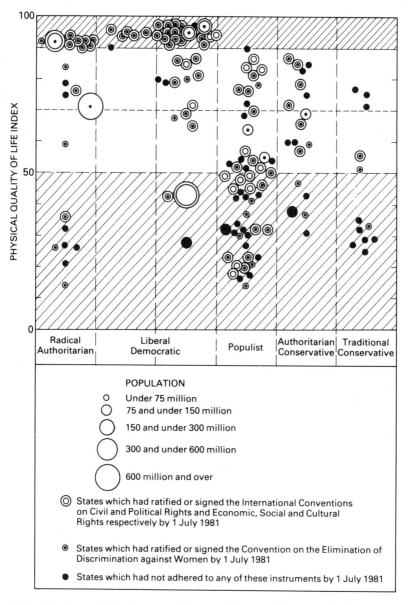

FIG. 21. State of Development, Human Rights and Systems of Government
Throughout the World.

TABLE 35

Some Main Positive and Negative Features of the World Development Climate
(1984)

(A distinction is made between items of top importance (a) and other items (b))

A. *POSITIVE ITEMS*

1. (a) PRIMARY SCARCITY. Technical power to end primary material scarcity (thereby enlarging scope for selfless co-operation), is now coming into view.

2. (a) FUNCTIONAL WORLD NETWORKS of co-operation already exist, e.g. in the pure sciences, environment, weather and communications.

3. (a) HUMAN RIGHTS. An incipient world frame is evolving for human rights promotion and monitoring.

4. (a) ROLE OF WOMEN. A major source of human betterment — women's potential contribution to world affairs — still remains to be applied.

5. (a) WORLD RESOURCES. Common administration and/or control of some major resource sectors is in prospect, e.g. Law of the Sea, supervision of the Antarctic and Outer Space.

6. (b) RIGHT TO DEVELOPMENT. This far-reaching right, for individuals and states, is now coming to be recognized.

7. (b) INTERNATIONAL LAW. Its revision is in prospect so as to recognize international rights and duties of the individual.

8. (b) SOCIO-ECONOMIC DEVELOPMENT. Regular international programmes are in operation, e.g. for health, water supply, food, human habitat and education.

9. (b) DISASTER RELIEF. A standing international agency is now co-ordinating action to deal with natural disasters as they arise.

10. (b) PURE SCIENCES. Advances in this field are concurrently opening ever-wider vistas for the exercise of human values.

B. *NEGATIVE ITEMS*

11. (a) NUCLEAR ARMS. Though the known consequences of their use renders them unusable, a self-sustaining economy/ideology conflict is making resort to nuclear arms increasingly likely.

12. (a) TOP-LEVEL WORLD REVIEW. There is still no standing machinery either to address world problems or control major conflict situations.

13. (a) THE ECONOMIC FRAME AND ITS EFFECT. Both alternative national economic systems and the world system need revision, while their model of self-seeking grossly distorts human motives.

14. (a) TECHNOLOGICAL CHANGE. There is no international monitoring of the commercial exploitation of science, which at present determines both our rate and direction of socio-economic change.

15. (a) ECOSYSTEMS. Ignorance, exploitativeness and insensibility are still sacking the earth's environments, and reducing the pool of species and resources, all to the hazard of future existence.

16. (a) TRANSNATIONAL CORPORATIONS. The uncontrolled power of these is seriously distorting national development and the world economy.

17. (a) SURVEILLANCE SYSTEMS. Proliferating monitoring systems are on course to subvert democracy and end privacy.

18. (b) ENERGY SUPPLY. Because main alternative fuel-based energy sources entail unacceptable environmental hazards for the future, the unreadiness of new renewable sources is perpetuating wrong decisions.

19. (b) WORK. A precipitate fall in conscientious performance of work is a threat to community and thus to civilization itself.

20. (b) INFORMATION AND OPINION SAMPLING. Lack of a two-way interchange of objective information and opinion measurement is cramping human potential.

21. (b) SOCIAL NIHILISM. A new ambiguity towards indiscriminate terrorism and self-assumed standards in general is diluting efforts to realize humanness worldwide.

22. (b) GLOBAL TAXATION. The lack of a comprehensive system to help correct regional imbalances delays any open acceptance of interdependence on the world scene.

---

citizenship, of rules of law running throughout the world in all continents, should underlie the conception of world order so that the feeling of 'not belonging' would disappear, and all that has hitherto been connoted by the word 'foreign' would gradually become obsolete (C. B. Purdom, 1941).

Table 35 indicates some ways, already discussed in earlier chapters, by which global rules for living are coming to be pieced together by the international community, notably in items 3, 6 and 7. This process is pushed still further by an ever-growing range of human situations fraught with ethical overtones that arise from new scientific discoveries (item 10).

But internationalism plus human rights does not add up to world order. What is still lacking is a standing, forward-looking body or bodies of the highest repute to oversee problems and problem-raising tendencies of top importance and, above all, to keep the peace. This does not imply any 'super-state', and perhaps not even a world government. But there must be at least a loose, independent, top-level standing machinery to afford a visible measure of cohesion and restraint and there has to be a World or International Authority that is in a position specifically to enforce the maintenance of peace in accord with a World Constitution. This means that national military forces should not exceed a level sufficient for internal police action, but that adequate superior force would have to be available to the Authority. As to the world's essential services, sufficient global co-ordination of matters like health, food, environment, economic affairs, population and a few more could well devolve on upgraded versions of existing UN agencies.

At the present stage something like this simple structure would suffice to knit together the community of states in a loose frame of organized co-operation. The sticking point is the rule of "great power unanimity" — otherwise known as the veto — which operates on substantive votes in the Security Council in respect of the Council's five permanent members —

China, France, United Kingdom, United States and the USSR. With the 'non-aligned movement' (which with some other states provides a progressive stance in today's UN programmes) now comprising three-quarters of all states, the Security Council's permanent members will not easily relinquish their veto — even though in 1955 the then British Minister of Defence (Mr Harold Macmillan) has spoken officially in favour of a world authority invested with enough power to supervise disarmament.

We shall return to this supreme question of the arms race later on. But in any event the general problem of international control should be approached differently, as a progressive adaptation rather than as something cut and dried. What I mean by this is that four decades ago there was no world framework, no ethical code and few binding conventions. An unseen administration in embryo, its rules and its moral backing, have all grown up in that period in parallel with, and in spite of, a rise of nuclear overkill and ideological, fear-based hatred. It therefore seems justifiable, though admittedly risky, to think about international integration in the socio-economic sphere *separately* from that of arms control.

We shall proceed on that basis. Among the main world institutions are the UN Development Programme and those dealing with Population, Environment, Health, Weather, Water, Human Habitat, Human Rights and a nascent Law of the Sea Administration. These have evolved, often with difficulty, and then been partially co-ordinated as needs have been discerned. Just as mature states have become vast structures of institutions that have grown together in the course of their evolution, so the international system too is evolving as an organic whole. Apart from a large and growing number of specific agreements, there is no compulsion on states to act in the common interest, but participation itself creates some moral pressure to do so. In only one case — that of the proposed sea-bed Administration — is there so far a body empowered to allocate and control, and this raises the main query. Wherever human obstacles obstruct desirable objectives a powerful play of vested interest proves to be the culprit, aided by inertia. In this case the autonomy of a state machine offers both power and careers to political leaders and their advisers. In the absence of some more powerful counter-attraction, even a partial surrender of sovereignty is hard to concede. Despite this, small concessions to international agreement remain frequent, so that the area of agreement slowly widens until some more radical jump is prompted by common sense.

That, at least, is the rationale that suggests itself as a first conclusion. *Security apart, the present UN international structure should grow until it offers a functional substitute for a loose world administration. This could, and should, come to comprise a standing body — a World Council of high calibre — that would mark the next tentative stage in a further evolution of the organization we call the United Nations.*

Spreading Global Values Through the Political Process

This section has to do with how moves to advance world order objectives can arise within individual states and strengthen their input to international programmes.

From 1928 onwards, well before its time had come, the writer H. G. Wells sought to outline the terms of an "Open Conspiracy":

> It seemed to me that all over the world intelligent people were waking up to the indignity and absurdity of being endangered, restrained and impoverished, by a mere uncritical adhesion to traditional governments, traditional ideas of economic life, and traditional forms of behaviour, and that these awaking intelligent people must constitute first a protest and then a creative resistance to the inertia that was stifling and threatening us. . . .
>
> This open and declared intention of establishing a world order out of the present patchwork of particularist governments, of effacing the militarist conceptions that have hitherto given governments their typical form, and of removing credit and the broad fundamental processes of economic life out of reach of private profit-seeking and industrial monopolization, which is the substance of the Open Conspiracy . . . cannot fail to arouse enormous opposition. . . . It criticizes everything in human life . . . and finds everything not good enough. It strikes at the universal human desire to feel that things are 'all right' (H. G. Wells, 1928).

This initiative was not necessarily antagonistic to existing governments and neither was it a conception of hate. Rather it was a spontaneous urge to create conditions for purposive change to match those new technical imperatives that still confront us today. How best can a vision of enlightenment be diffused within an existing worldwide political context?

Some manifest contradictions in that context have already produced an efflorescence of major hopes of change among large numbers of the world's uncommitted peoples. Mature parliamentary governments are having to take account of these waves of feeling, while those in developing states, banded together in the non-aligned movement, are moved already by a similar tension borne of their position as 'have-nots' in a world dominated by a small number of 'haves'.

There are thus two main sources in the contemporary world from which radical ideals can arise to confront an older traditional value-system extolling wealth, material possessions and corporate or national power as criteria of excellence. The new values can stem from certain strata or groups within each individual state; and from the voting power of non-aligned developing states which now comprise nearly three-quarters of the United Nations membership (Figure 22).

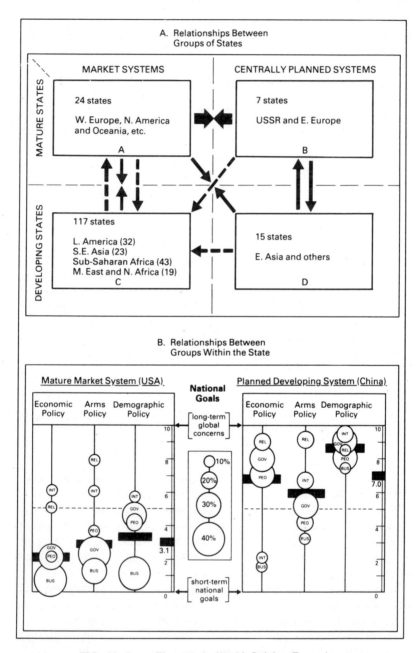

FIG. 22. Some Elements in World Opinion Formation.

Figure 22A shows how governments of the poor but internationally influential non-aligned group C, aided by members from D and thus including countries like China and Cuba as well as India and Yugoslavia, are pursuing a role in striking contrast to the economic antipathy/armed confrontation stances maintained between groups A and B plus D. In 1983, for example, it was found that C voted with group A in the UN General Assembly on only one-fifth of the issues before it. It is this affinity between C and D, aided by group B, that has created the call for a New Human Order, a New World Economic Order and a Right to Development. At the same time this idealistic component in the UN membership is reinforced by certain Western OECD states, including some, like Sweden, politically independent, and even by members of NATO like Canada under Pierre Trudeau. These latter are moved less by philosophy, be it noted, than by arms control issues and practical humanitarian assistance. Nonetheless, the wide tapestry of internationalism adds up to a powerful ideal-seeking force whose progressive stance receives little publicity but gives much added credence to United Nations programmes.

How, next, do the movements of opinion that can fire international policies come to a focus *within* individual states? In that context a state's population can be thought of as comprising seven main role-playing strata:

1. A scientific leadership.
2. A religious leadership.
3. A group of 'intellectuals' (other than 1 or 2).
4. Government (the political leadership, and its international sector).
5. The uncommitted population.
6. A privileged élite (landowners, judicial and military leaders, etc.).
7. Business decision-makers.

As sources of common aims these groups are of very unequal weight in a single country. They also vary, absolutely and relatively, from one state to another according to levels of development and ideology. In a pioneer analysis of Goals for Mankind Ervin Laszlo has looked at how five of the above groups (i.e. excluding items 1 and 6) can be ranked on a range of policy aims in different countries (E. Laszlo, 1978). Some of these extreme ranges or dimensions of policy are set out in Figure 22B, with an indication of how average national 'profiles' may be distributed along them.

How far do today's conditions favour a strongly sustained public opinion to spur on United Nations action? At present the world's press gives little coverage to the UN. But one striking feature of the 80s so far has been a spontaneous upsurge of public demand for environment and resource protection, population control and human rights observance in many countries. Governments in turn are resorting more and more to secrecy on controversial matters. Human rights debates are coming to recognize the duty of individuals, even in the public service,* to act in accord with conscience where government is devious, secretive or unlawful and conflicts of loyalty arise. Civil servants, and others with special knowledge, are responding with calls for more open government. Investigative journalists, too, are finding an expanding market for their talents.

What I may call counter-consumerism is thus being spread on a global scale by non-governmental bodies, national and international, as well as by some governments. Objective scientific and medical research groups are beginning to spell out more fully the real consequences of 'letting things slide'. A startling change, too, can be seen in the stands being taken by previously conformist religious leaders. Opinion polls have long confirmed that unprivileged citizens, when the issues before them are unambiguously stated, are now becoming highly aware and responsible overall, consistently more so than governments, not just because the public is representative of uncommitted opinion but because governments tend to hesitate until all signs are politically propitious and then go half way or less.

Against all this, two powerful opposing forces remain intact. Firstly, the élite around any government, though often highly civilized, urbane and widely informed, is by definition united, whether consciously or not, by its common interest in preserving the status quo. Secondly business management, though it has wide international expertise, is not unnaturally concentrated on preserving an untrammelled pursuit of its own special and private interests.

Even today, therefore, a Wellsian 'open conspiracy' of like-minded intelligent people will not suffice as a catalyst of essential change. Where it does not exist as an open corrective, public opinion has somehow to be created. *From the developing world there is a growing clamour for what ought to become a globally diffused system of objective information. If that demand can be publicly met, and if it can be accompanied by an objective feedback system conveying regularly sampled opinion to a world centre or to regional centres, we shall have brought into being the means that could create a new level of global awareness. Into that purposive stirring of minds some imaginative applications of the referendum could well be dropped. Like opinion sampling, which it complements, the referendum principle offers a direct road to humanly based decision-making.* As issues become graver, if not more complex, I believe there is some chance that the essence of such a scheme could be achieved, despite all the formidable hurdles that still stand in the way.

---

*The sensational acquittal in London in February 1985 of a senior civil servant in such a position, by a jury which chose to disregard legal directions, offers an example of new trends in opinion on this subject.

Raising the Sights of Social Existence

Virtually all our arrangements for living in communities are in a state of crisis. This is true both of government and the governed. Starting with the first we find that in most countries of the world the governmental machine is in disarray in the sense that it is either arbitrary, lacking a viable democratic process, or else it is hopelessly corrupt, or both. In 'mature' states the weight of complex decisions increases while the time and the means to deal with them prove insufficient, so that the machine is intrinsically creaking and ineffective in human as well as in practical terms. There is little or no attempt at overall planning.

From the ordinary citizen's standpoint the view is no better. On the latest indications (Amnesty International, 1984) some two-thirds of all governments can be regarded as using torture "as a tool of state policy", with 88 of them the subject of detailed, and often horrifying comment. According to Amnesty this practice is common to all continents, including at least five European states. Over a four-year period ending in 1983, a United Nations working group on disappeared persons has asked a large number of countries for details about 6605 suspicious disappearances, commonly without any proper explanation.

But the troubles of society are wider than this. As occupational and special-interest groups multiply in a permissive climate, they have become more and more intolerant, vying with each other to disrupt transport systems, hospitals, food supplies and the public in general, violently if necessary, in an attempt to force the state to yield to sometimes trivial demands. Parallel with this, the world has experienced a rash of indiscriminate bombing and hostage-taking, as well as kidnapping and 'hijacking', all in the same erroneous belief that a self-centred end will somehow justify an anarchic means.

We know that there is still more ground yet for social disquiet. Even in so-called affluent societies it is the norm for most people to live their lives in stunted fashion, in a milieu of ugliness, noise, dirt and too often of poverty, surrounded by advanced technical gadgetry as a substitute for the human fulfilment that is nowhere to be found. The most advanced reality that civilization has been able to offer for nine out of ten of its citizens is a reality, not of lively human aspiring, but of enveloping advertisement hoardings, dinginess, and alienation from the job. Such is the dull, stunting reality that moulds most of our budding world citizens!

One could pursue this theme, pointing on one side to the evasiveness and secrecy even of mature governments in 1984; or, on the other, to the poor quality and unreliability of work performed today as compared with fifty years ago. But it is more apt to remember the view we held at that time, that as wider education prevailed all round a more responsible society would come into view. That is one hope already proved to be the opposite of what has happened under the influence of trends at work since 1950.

But it may truly be argued that all this presents only the negative view. Against it are to be set some contrary trends that history must rate highly positive. The whole idea of common rights and duties for everyone has arisen and permeated through to all cultures since 1942. Hesitantly, but inexorably, dictators, torturers and even big business are being called to account for their actions. An ideal world code of standards now exists and people are beginning to compare those standards with their own plight. In the words of Imre Hollai of Hungary, speaking as President of the UN General Assembly on Human Rights Day 1982:

> Never before in history have so many millions of people enjoyed so wide a range of basic rights. Never before have so many been hopeful of a better life in social progress. Indeed, the most bitter and massive violations of human rights perpetrated in the world today occur in reaction to this stirring of hope and aspiration.

What conclusions can we now reach about life in communities and in the world society that lies ahead? I believe that our conclusions follow from a synthesis of what has already emerged in earlier chapters, and to this I now turn.

The Imperatives of Human Life

Humans differ remarkably little from other animals. Those differences that are crucial — speech, abstract thought, reasoning and learning, self-awareness, consciousness of past and future — can emerge only in community life. But man is not a group animal by instinct and is only partially gregarious. It seems easy for him to learn behaviour — e.g. aggressive male behaviour — that proved important at earlier stages, whereas in other animals intra-species aggressiveness is mostly a signalling device for establishing simple hierarchy. In humans that hierarchy must be organized, to maintain the community which assures protection and long nurture, cumulating learning and a material surplus. A human society is held together by the devices of government, law and custom, group-morality and personal conscience. As societies become more complex they come to comprise distinct organizations, beyond the family and its socializing role, each of which exists for a specific purpose and to perform a specific function. Such societies, as they depend more on free co-operation, must come to recognize equal rights of individuals under the law and thus a democratic process for securing acceptable government. From this aspect a fully self-governing community resembles an organic system in that its parts each perform a necessary function while the whole, in tune with its environment, fulfils its purpose insofar as it offers viable harmony in development for the full maturation of its members.

Human individuals cannot exist outside their social matrix. They develop capacities within their society, interact with and are acted upon by others. A principle of reciprocity thus arises in which help — and harm — are reciprocated. Full positive reciprocity connotes equality, so that equal reciprocity connotes ideas of justice, and inappropriately unequal reciprocity, injustice. A rising sense of personal conscience adds to the moral imperative. Human interdependence increases as society becomes more technically and juridically complex, while the Confucian maxim: "Treat each other person as you would like to be treated if you were that person", gains added weight even in unequal relationships — e.g. parent–child relations. This is the ultimate source of human rights and duties. Moreover, because the existence of separate competing societies can generate out-group hostility, these rights have now to be generalized worldwide if reciprocal justice is to prevail.

Human individuals are not totally separate. Like other animals each is a random assembly from the gene pool of the species, so that personal uniqueness lies in a configuration of potentialities produced by genetic endowment as modified through unique experience in a unique habitat and society. Individuality thus has three components. In addition to the roles of genes as modified by environment, there is the special impress of a specific culture.

This outline of fundamentals is required for two reasons: firstly, because viable human conditions, though attainable in essence, are not yet being sufficiently approached or attempted; and secondly, because a number of corollary propositions can be deduced from it which show how man's social life will change, is changing, or ought to change in the future. The following are some conclusions of this sort.

The Other Half of Humankind

Human nature embraces a gamut of traits and values which range from what Fromm has called the "patricentric" kind — power, achievement, competitiveness, individualism, authority and duty — to "matricentric" values like unconditional love, compassion, happiness and unity, peace, universality. Our world's political dichotomy, and its religious division also, alike reflect these wide extremes. The values behind today's world — the first kind — came to predominate after the Reformation and with the rise of individualist property enterprise over the last two centuries. *But our values are now facing a demand for change — a change to universalist, co-operative interdependence — as the world becomes one. The rights, and then the humane contribution, of women have now to become combined with male values.* Women's basic rights have first to be established and their contribution to the whole greatly stepped up, largely through the United Nations, as the next stage of emancipation dawns upon mankind. One big step in that direction would be an international agreement to make every Foreign Secretary a woman!

The Cultural Autonomy of States

Today, and for a variety of reasons, millions of people are being uprooted to seek life in a culture different from their own. Rural populations are flooding into the conurbations of the developing world. Many more from the Third World have migrated permanently to alien climates and alien cultures in mature states. In the past it was believed that cultural admixture, like foreign travel, was itself a good thing, and it is true enough that our contemporary world *is* graced by some eminent examples of culture change. But culture has to be recognized as a major human imprinting force. Large-scale permanent immigration of highly distinctive minorities into maturely evolved ways of life must create deep social, economic and demographic problems where none existed before, the more so if followed by demands from the immigrant to practise what may be seen as repulsive or barbaric customs. Commonly the net result might well prove a near-disaster for the immigrant, the receiving country and sometimes for the country of departure as well. The same, unfortunately, must be true of most rural populations seeking work and prosperity in the world's proliferating cities.

We must conclude that the autonomy of an indigenous culture is something to be respected. Despite the views of some activists, the notion that people en masse can demand to maintain their special cultural identity wherever they go is unrealistic and does a disservice to the cause of development. Except for indigenous communities or distinct regional minorities of long standing, the world citizen must be ready to adapt to the laws in force as he finds them. Where cultures need to change, that change should arise out of new developmental perceptions from within.

Work and Society

Essential work, such as that in the public services, is vital to any modern state and is the basis on which all citizens depend. Such essential services include those under public control, like government, public utilities and health as well as others, like banks, newspapers and public transport, that may still be in private hands.

In recent years three trends have upset this view of the importance of work. Firstly a new, permissive climate has reduced the effectiveness and reliability of much of the work performed. Secondly, a parallel fanning of unrealistic expectations has meant that more is sought from work than is being created by work. Finally, advancing technique has meant that productivity is rising faster than output from a constant work force, spelling structural change or unemployment, or both. From these trends the net result is a hazarding of public facilities like railways, utilities, airlines, health or newspapers through stepped-up confrontation organized, e.g., by self-interested activists in trade unions.

What can we conclude about the social role of work in advanced states? People are bound to their community for work, material life and intellectual existence. Without speeded-up obsolescence, inflated credit and other stimulants at least a quarter of today's work would have no meaning. Yet, a great deal of essential work remains undone. Even in prosperous areas the urban environment of millions comprises seedy streets, grubby frontages and empty lots plastered with posters, their numbering system a hollow farce. Costs are cut everywhere by dereliction, roads are crammed with noisome overloaded lorries that present a major health hazard.

Even the notion of unemployment is a *laissez faire* business concept. Every industrialized state has within its borders enough workers to meet its internal needs and it need not yet have too many. There is now a basic choice to be made: How far to accept that meaningful work remains a source of self-realization, self-respect and security; or whether slowly to reduce work overall in the interests of leisure and unpaid activity?

At present many workers are being alienated, not simply against work but against the very idea that work is intended to serve the community. *If the human component in work becomes less reliable as technology advances, this is a self-defeating contradiction. The responsible work that must still be done has to remain a vital part of life in society and not something to be endured in return for a life 'outside work'.* It is the conditions of work that have to be improved.

In turn this means that all who choose to undertake essential work in the wider public sector should now be asked to enter into a contract that ensures uninterrupted services. This change offers one important step towards gaining improved human rights for all.

Filling the New Frame of Consciousness

Human potential today needs a consciousness of self and setting that is holistic in that it rests on a view of the whole, and an open future, that is all-embracing. For ideas do not arise in a vacuum. They adjust to wider horizons as the conditions that spark them become more expansive. Ideas of world order get on the agenda as people and institutions 'raise their sights'; and that raising of sights must spring from a widening access to true facts that alone can offset the confusing double-talk of those most motivated to stay-as-we-are.

All this is part of a gigantic social process — a raising of the entire universe of discourse — that has to be engaged in first of all by concerned professionals and by the uncommitted millions who alone can *afford* to be impartial in collective judgements. That is how a new 'open conspiracy' can still arise in the world of 1984. There has to be a great awakening from the preoccupations of hate and self-interest that have rent the twentieth century. In the real world, and ultimately, all are on the same side, but they do not yet know it.

How can the convert to this holistic view apply his or her talents in daily life? In line with the principles of social existence he or she can:

— try to become less self-centred and parochial in his affiliations by looking inwards to motives, aims and goals and outwards to his society as a complex whole;
— act responsibly to secure good relationships — in family life and in community membership;
— perform his chosen work effectively for the general good, seeing solidarity with society as prior to any other special interest;
— act responsibly as a citizen in relation to world, national, regional and local affairs;
— seek to help conserve, protect and improve the natural and social environments;
— communicate with others to spread reliable information and to apply his special expertise to raise the level of enlightened action;
— remember that 'human nature' can and does change as the forms and channels of its expression become modified.

In all these endeavours it goes without saying that the Universal Declaration of Human Rights offers a standard of reference for everyone on earth.

The Task of Creating a World Economic Society

In these pages one main but unacknowledged common factor has been shown to lie behind the appalling cruelty, rapacity, intra-species aggressiveness and waste that besets modern man. It has been argued, firstly, that the essential tasks of society's economic frame — to convert natural resources into goods and services people need to sustain themselves and their social arrangements, and to distribute adequately those goods and services — have been blown up, bloated to absurd proportions; and, secondly, that *the motives called 'economic' have now become a main dehumanizing force as well as the source of our critical polarized struggle.* This group of questions deserves a book in itself, and one is in preparation. What will be said here, by way of conclusion on the subject, has not been said before. The problem of modifying the main alternative economic systems is not difficult in itself — certainly no more difficult than devising a democratic political framework. The subject has simply not been ventilated to a wider public because an effective taboo has been placed upon public discussion of good and bad points by an interested business and political élite, aided by the press and other media.

Why do we here assert so strongly that economic growth, far from being pushed up as fast as possible, has everywhere to become selective, sustainable and differentiated according to circumstances? Is it because the earth is running out of minerals and fuels? Is it because all living resources of forests, croplands, their soils and their species are being decimated towards extinction? Is it because our atmosphere and stratosphere are becoming dangerously polluted through man-made wastes? Or is it because world population is rising much too fast? All these reasons are true, and especially the last three. But to prove the case requires us to demonstrate what random economic growth entails.

In most of the developing world any gain in average income will reduce primary poverty, hunger and disease. *Provided* it is sustainable — that is, not at the expense of forest cover, soils, health and birth-rate reduction policies, which at present is often not the case — there is no question that such growth is needed. But, partly for internal reasons, and further egged on by Western marketing interests to believe that they should copy the Western life-style, developing-world leaders go far beyond this and demand a rapid catching-up with the West.

Let us now look at the respective output levels reached by the two world groups in 1980:

TABLE 36
Population and Output in Developed and Developing States — 1980

Group	Population ('000 millions)	%	Output (GNP) ('000 million $)	%	Per capita ($)
World, of which:	4.463	100.0	11,666	100.0	2619
Developed states	1.057	23.8	8,957	76.5	8477
Developing states	3.406	76.2	2,709	23.5	794

Relative to population, the first group is 10.5 times as productive as the second, so that to equalize production per head in 1980 would require a world output 3.2 times that actually achieved. Attained under present conditions, this result would have very serious consequences for world resources and environments.

But, even discounting these, how far would this catching-up expectation be a viable option? In three decades, from 1950 to 1980, the developing states increased their GDP fivefold and industrial output tenfold, in the process raising life expectancy from 45 to 58 years, literacy from 33 to 56% and reducing the birth rate from 40 to near 30 per thousand. These rates surpass those reached by the now-developed world in the nineteenth century.

Even so, these trends do not imply any *relative* advance for the developing world as a whole. To the year 2000 their *average* population growth-rate is estimated at 2.07%, while productivity in the 'developed' states advances by around 3% per year for a constant population. Unless such output is held back by some special constraint, the developing world must advance on average by 5% annually, even to retain its *relative* position. If its productive growth-rate could reach the 7% annual mean proposed by the current UN Development Programme, it would take about 110 years to attain the average level already reached by developed states in 1980!

These are mean values only, but there is nothing particularly surprising about their message. It simply confirms what anyone familiar with these matters has long known — that real overall development will always be a lengthy business. But seen in terms of political expectation the situation may well breed heightening tension and conflict over the West's trade protectionism, its access to Third World natural resources, and worldwide needs for capital.

In the developed world economic growth is no more sustainable than elsewhere. There it is justified by claiming that only a larger and larger cake can raise the standards of the disadvantaged. But just as the world economy includes some 35 states that are very, very poor, so in the mature systems up to one in eight of the population lives in a dingy poverty that persists from generation to generation, as does the squalor the process entails. Unless conservation policies are greatly stepped up everywhere, which is an urgent task, and unless output structure is re-ordered by different priorities, the carrot of indiscriminate growth is set to produce disasters for the earth *without satisfying the expressed aims for which it is pursued.*

Suppose such re-ordering *could* be done, how far can the physical layout of natural resources allow rational goals of economic life to be pursued worldwide? This is not the place to enter into detail. But there seems no reason why resources and environments still available could not suffice to permit reasonable development for some time to come. The earth's exploitable energy sources and minerals are still being increased as geological and geophysical surveys extend and recovery techniques improve. New renewable sources, and better conservation of energy, those great hopes for the future, still offer scope for better resource management. Some of the scarcer minerals, on the other hand, *are* being depleted, in part to produce armaments.

Figure 23 is an attempt to reduce the complicated situation to a simple visual form. It shows the relative distribution of conventional energy reserves and minerals of economic interest as between a threefold division of the world, distinguishing between mature market systems (right-hand corner), centrally planned systems (left-hand corner) and the market-style developing economies (top corner). At each corner the circular segments shown are proportionate to respective populations in 1980. If a resource

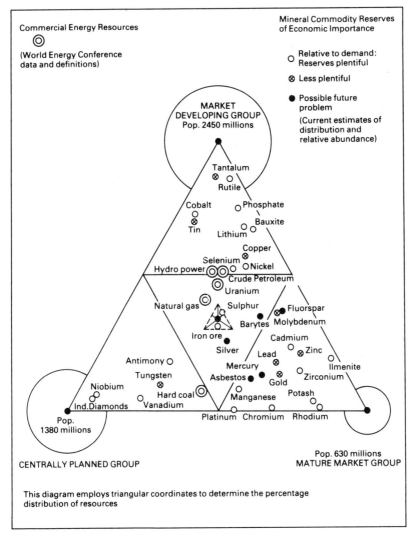

FIG. 23. Relative World Distribution of Main Economic Mineral Reserves and Energy Resources.

were located at the marked centre of the main triangle it would be equally divided between all three groups. If it is located within an outer triangle near any one corner the group in question possesses more than half the total known world reserves for that resource.

Figure 23 shows that as a whole, and within the uncertainties of present knowledge, the great diversity in spread of natural resources assures a reasonable balance between the three nominally competing groups of states, calling forth some inter-group trade but in fact more intensive imports also into deficit regions like Western Europe. Remaining untapped reserves of minerals and energy give far less cause for disquiet than does the present unchecked squandering of habitats and resources like croplands, soils and forest cover, under the scourge of short-term economic gain.

Where, then, is the barrier that prevents reform? There is, of course, no international frame yet, as there should be, for world capital investment, any more than there is to oversee the financial system in general or a global scheme of taxation. If these things did exist, the capital remittances, transfer pricing etc. which now give free rein to transnational concerns could be subjected to a measure of public order. But beyond a lack of technical overseeing of this sort there is a vital mechanism at work to prevent any government from even looking at such policies. This mechanism works as follows. The world economy comprises some 165 highly unequal but competing states, just as any one state is an assemblage of competing individuals each pursuing his own interest. Under these conditions politicians require prosperity and prosperity means a free hand for large concerns including, above all, transnational concerns. Whatever their aims or conduct, success is a key to home employment and home prosperity. If such concerns succeed the more by cutting environmental or other corners this is their business, at least until the public finds out and its ideals are outraged. Governments do now have Environment Departments, but they are 'soft' on money-making. These, very simply, are the real reasons for the freedom accorded to oligopolies and the real reason why environmental care and the public interest take second or third place, or no place at all.*

Steps to create a sustainable national economy, on which a sensible world frame could also be built, are not intrinsically difficult. They must stem from the demands of an objective public. Adjustments required both to market- and to centrally directed systems are novel, but simple and straight-forward. First the coming UN Code of Conduct for Transnational Corporations needs to be made strong and even obligatory. Within the market state some supplementary legislation will be required in respect of

---

*A different 'hidden' mechanism, equally powerful, is at work to promote city expansion even without population growth, but it will not be discussed here.

pollution, size of undertakings, information required by governments, use of natural resources and maintenance of premises, roughly in accord with ideas ventilated in Chapter 5 and later. *Without going into details discussed elsewhere, what is required is just enough control simply to ensure that commercial enterprises really operate with a 'human face' and conform to commonsense priorities. When any growth at any cost has ceased to be first priority, the urge to excessive, anti-human bigness will automatically have been ended as well.*

Is There a Future for War Control?

Everything discussed so far, including the prospect of getting agreement on a machinery to maintain a standing overview of global change, depends on whether our existing armed dichotomy, with its successive retaliatory upstepping of 'deterrence' will, as historians and persuasive projections suggest, end in an annihilation of civilized living on the earth. Even discounting more and more likely accidental error all rational signs, except one, are that the double bluff of deterrence will finally be called and an initially small, inaccurate 'first strike' will inevitably be answered by something much stronger. What then is the sign that militates against such a view? Simply that the worst 'leaders' cannot last for very long — that there can still be permutations of quality within the political spectrum.

The point of the last remark is that *by the beginning of 1984 people have come to know things about the present arms race they did not know before. When these items are suitably juxtaposed, understanding of motives, consequences and action needed can all acquire a new depth.* Let us consider what some of this new knowledge can imply.

In the first place, work done by October 1983 showed for the first time, not merely the scale of death and living death involved at different levels of nuclear strike, but exactly what must be expected to ensue in the two years or so that follow. At a Conference on Long-term Worldwide Biological Consequences of Nuclear War a high-calibre international scientific team has produced a synthesis, confirmed by other investigations, of the main physical consequences to be expected from strikes between 100 and 5000 megatons (400,000 times the Hiroshima bomb). Some 13000 megatons are already available to the two main protagonists.

An overall summing-up by 21 biologists concluded as follows:

> It is clear that the eco-system effects alone . . . could be enough to destroy the current civilization in at least the Northern hemisphere. Coupled with the direct casualties of perhaps two billion people, the combined intermediate and long-term effects of nuclear war suggest that eventually there might be no human survivors in the Northern hemisphere. In almost any realistic case . . . the possibility of the extinction of *Homo sapiens* cannot be excluded.

From this first finding certain conclusions follow. Winning a nuclear war is impossible and so is survival, in any meaningful sense, whether for the direct combatants or for any of the international community. For the sake of an ideological assumption that has no basis in fact the long evolution of life and man in geological time would be brought to nought. Because a 'nuclear winter' (darkness and −40°C in July) could ensue from a mere 100-megaton strike, 'deterrence' becomes meaningless at a level of nuclear arms long since exceeded. The lesson of this investigation is that armed and unarmed alike are now inextricably interdependent, so that in the words of the late Olaf Palme, the Swedish Prime Minister, international security has to rest on the notion of "common security", on commitment to joint survival rather than on assured mutual destruction.

How, then, is common security to be attained? Let us look first to causes. Nearly all the twelve technical innovations of the arms build-up since 1945 have come from one side only and have been reacted to by the other. Throughout, that same side has nourished and propagated an obsession that the other is bent on expansion and conquest long after such an idea has ceased to have real plausibility or basis in fact — a point now admitted by various publicists. (See, for example, Enoch Powell, 1983, and P. Worsthorne, 1983).* Inevitably, a similar myth has been reciprocated on the opposing side. To understand arms-race psychology it is useful to consider *why* the first myth is perpetuated in the absence of clear evidence, and *how* it can be sustained. As to *why*, the collective illusion is a major source of wealth and prestige (E. Powell, *op. cit.*). Politically, too, the myth is now a cohesive source of national dynamic so great that ending it would entail an unacceptable loss of face that could be attempted only after a real change of administration.

But *how* can an untenable proposition be made to flourish for 35 years? It would seem that 'intentional misunderstanding' of outsiders is a counterpart of that 'collective unconscious' discussed earlier, which can be spread and sustained within the state when opinion-makers need to 'explain' real issues by rationalizations. Humans in the group can suspend individual judgement under the influence of careful suggestion conveyed by 'authorities', including the printed word and other media, particularly if the true facts are not clearly displayed. Some examples of this have been given earlier.

Common security requires the United Nations to move towards a central organization to oversee the peace. Assuming that some time remains, the necessary climate of global opinion, as well as some conditions and even an organizational means to world control, are currently (April 1984) beginning to present themselves. One important state and one main

---

*Robert McNamara, a former Secretary of Defence and President of the World Bank, has shown a similar candour (see *The Guardian*, London, 9 August 1982).

protagonist have already declared for no first use — that they will not be the first to attack with nuclear weapons. Unless and until other nuclear powers do likewise, two deductions can be made about their conduct. Either they desire to retain the option to attack with such weapons; or they cannot bear to abandon the myth by which expanding armaments and 'deterrence' are justified; or, most likely, both.

Under the impact of growing awareness, of spreading calls for human rights and a sound environment, world opinion everywhere is coming to denounce this last stand of unreason, both within the UN General Assembly and in votes, resolutions and demonstrations worldwide. The neutrals and the non-aligned group need to be further aided by a spreading of military neutrality to further states to 'catalyse' the situation. I have in mind in particular one state that has largely cradled the modern world, founding in the process a world organization of 40 countries that itself could do much to break the mould of confrontation.*

The initial practical steps towards common security could well follow a scheme sketched out by the late Lord Russell in 1961 (Bertrand Russell, 1961). Firstly comes a Declaration by a number of concerned powers, if possible arranged under neutral auspices, acknowledging that nuclear war (and, for that matter, chemical or biological conflict) would be a final disaster and would not achieve anything that any party could desire. This would be followed by, say, a two-year moratorium, with agreement to abstain from hostile acts, propaganda, radio jamming, etc. and with a cessation of new nuclear deployment. During this period a Conciliation Committee would be organized, comprising, perhaps, four members each from East, West and neutral groups, initially with advisory powers only, which would try to reach agreement on a number of tension-reducing measures that offer no net gain to either side. The stages that would follow are already familiar since they have long been under discussion in the UN Disarmament Conference. They include suspension of nuclear tests, banning of chemical weapons, prevention of an arms race in outer space and a series of like measures. That they are not succeeding may well be because there is no central core, no prior machinery of agreement into which they can fit.

Is there any sign that these possible moves towards sanity could come to fruition? As I write (April 1984) I suggest there are three. Firstly, as the UN Conference on Disarmament was informed in February 1984, the Prime Minister of Canada, Pierre Trudeau, through a wide personal initiative supported by Commonwealth heads of government in 1983, has approached other heads of government of the Eastern and Western blocs,

*Since these words were written Group Captain Peter Johnson has in fact published just such a proposal. (See 'Neutrality: A Policy For Britain', issued by M. Temple Smith, London, 1985).

China and Sweden and has secured common interest and agreement from all sides on ten principles. These include agreement that a nuclear war cannot be won; that it must never be fought; that both sides wish to avoid risks of accidental war and surprise attack; that security should be increased at lower cost; that further nuclear proliferation should be avoided; that both sides have legitimate security interests; and that these interests cannot rest on an assumed political or economic collapse of the other side. Given sincerity here, quite independently, is clear ground for advance on the lines of Bertrand Russell's scheme.

Could a moratorium be secured? Unanimously the UN General Assembly has designated the year 1986 as an International Year of Peace. As early as 1983 international non-governmental organizations accredited to ECOSOC have been incorporated into the planning of a programme of broad objectives for the Year. Among informal proposals made by NGOs in Geneva in February 1984 was one that an agreed moratorium on armed conflict be sought and underwritten by the Security Council as well as the UN General Assembly. This would seem to be one occasion for such a step, however unlikely, provided the necessary preliminaries could be arranged in advance. Building on the Trudeau initiative, the Year would also offer an occasion to arrive at a first Declaration accepting the uselessness of war as a means of achieving great power aims.

There is another vital but unheralded opening that should be explored, preferably before the International Year begins. That is offered by the results of a UN report, issued in 1983 and drawn up through intensive work by a Group of Experts, on the Implications of Establishing an International Satellite Monitoring Agency (UN, 1983). After going deeply into technical, legal and financial aspects, the report concludes that from a technical point of view satellite observations for information gathering related to verifying ". . . compliance with treaties and for crisis monitoring is both possible and feasible". Further, there is no legal obstacle to an inter-governmental monitoring agency carrying out such activities, while the annual cost to the international community would be well under one per cent of the total annual expenditure on arms. Seeing that this body could help verify adherence to a range of existing treaties, as well as aid the adoption of several for which verification is still a main stumbling block, the proposed Agency could play an enormous part in cementing an international drive for common security. It could well become the forerunner of a real Conciliation Committee, and later perhaps of a World Authority.

Together with the two preceding ones, this chapter has arrived at some tentative conclusions about the scope and future of human potential. These conclusions need to be seen as a whole, as parts of a single evolving reality of organism-cum-environment. It remains only to end with a few general reflections.

Human behaviour as we see it flows from three or more partly distinct elements of brain structure which produce the main cognitive, emotional, social and autonomic drives that move us. Faced with a seemingly final impasse, we might well conclude that mankind's shift from organic to social evolution has been precocious and premature. Yet, in the words of H. E. Daly (1977): ". . . people are not saints, but they are not totally selfish either". Human nature, we can see, comprises two conflicting clusters of propensities, plus an ability to learn. History, on the whole, has been the story of a slow subordination of the more primitive egoistic part of human make-up to a newer, more socialized component that fosters a sense of mutuality. In the long term ignorance and selfishness have been in retreat against enlightenment and mutuality because enlightenment and mutuality are built into the strong social potential of human beings. If modern technology has brought the world's people closer together a new finality in destructive power, polarized ideology and lop-sided development have disturbed the development process and, to us, seem to have thrown it off track. Yet ideas of reciprocity and its derivative, justice, are now being marshalled as a counter-force in a global struggle for human rights and duties.

In 1983, at a United Nations Working Group on Slavery, I heard the following comment from an Indian woman representing a non-governmental organization: "There are certain human values that are true of all cultures at all times." In one sentence that remark captures a new awareness that is sweeping the globe in the face of great odds.

Yet here too lies a perennial dilemma, unforgettably stated nearly two centuries ago by Edmund Burke in his Letter to a Member of the National Assembly (1791):

> Men are qualified for civil liberty in exact proportion to their disposition to put moral chains upon their own appetites. Society cannot exist unless a controlling power on will and appetite be placed somewhere, and the less of it there is within, the more there must be without. It is ordained in the eternal constitution of things that men of intemperate minds cannot be free. Their passions forge their fetters.

To conclude this inquiry, perhaps it is worthwhile to sum up what appear to be the conditions a man-made frame of order will have to meet, whether for the nation-state or for the world, if it is to offer scope to satisfy real human potential; namely that it must be able:

— to sustain the sensitive balance of the entire human habitat;
— to absorb and survive the interplay of human motives without breakdown;

— to be effective in human terms, within a tolerable range of error, in moving towards definable objectives;

— to assure equal treatment to citizens, and to states, in respect of their basic rights, as well as public accountability for decisions reached;

— to offer reasonable means of self-fulfilment to the individual;

— to accommodate orderly change in public aims and institutions.

As to means, any steps taken to meet conditions such as these are likely to prevail to the extent that they emerge, visibly and logically, out of prior development — in other words, that they are timely, opportune, and nascent in what has gone before.

That is the way to continued evolution through learning and up to now, clumsily and at great human cost, it has worked. Yet the full adaptive process has to surpass mere learning to embrace public action — changes or reforms induced in response to visible mistakes. And insofar as mistakes are becoming irreversible, unable to be corrected, the whole human complex of learning-cum-change faces demands on wisdom and statecraft it remains ill-prepared to meet.

ANNEXES

1. The International Bill of Human Rights and its Background

2. Accessions to Human Rights International Instruments

3. The State of Multilateral Disarmament Agreements

1

The International Bill of Human Rights and its Background

What has become known as the International Bill of Human Rights comprises the Universal Declaration, adopted in 1948, and the two binding Covenants that now underpin it — those on Economic, Social and Cultural Rights and on Civil and Political Rights respectively. It is not widely known that the precursor of these international instruments was a World Declaration of the Rights of Man, originally drafted in London in 1940 by H. G. Wells and issued in 1942 in revised form, after wide public debate and refining by an eminent Committee (the Sankey Committee), as a Declaration on the Rights and Duties of the World Citizen.

This Declaration was circulated worldwide in many languages during the Second World War. In view of its continuing importance today, and for the present inquiry, the text of the 1942 version* is included in this Annex, together with that of the Universal Declaration of Human Rights and some background information on the International Bill of Human Rights.

A. The Rights of the World Citizen (H. G. Wells)

This World Declaration was the true forerunner of the Universal Declaration of Human Rights of the United Nations and of the two binding Conventions that now underpin it — the International Covenants on Economic, Social and Cultural Rights, and on Civil and Political Rights respectively — as well as of a massive continuing effort by the UN to implement a code of basic rights and duties throughout the world.

The original Wellsian idea of human rights was really part of a wider preoccupation — how to open the way to a quite new view of democracy, economic society and the political framework generally with the aim of adapting human institutions afresh to a new world habitat created by modern communications and productive technique.

The following text, which may be considered a definitive version of the World Declaration, was published as an Appendix to *Phoenix: a Summary of the Inescapable Conditions of World Reorganisation*, by H. G. Wells.

THE RIGHTS OF THE WORLD CITIZEN

Within the space of little more than a hundred years there has been a complete revolution in the material conditions of human life. Invention and discovery have so changed the pace and nature of communications round and about the earth that the distances which formerly kept the states and nations of mankind apart have now been practically abolished. At the same time there has been so gigantic an increase of mechanical power, and such a release of human energy, that men's ability either to cooperate with, or to injure and oppress one another, and to consume, develop or waste the bounty of Nature, has been exaggerated

---

*As published in *Phoenix: A Summary of the Inescapable Conditions of World Reorganisation* (Secker and Warburg, London, 1942). The Declaration is included here by permission of the Literary Executors of the Estate of H. G. Wells.

225

beyond all comparison with former times. This process of change has mounted swiftly and steadily in the past third of a century, and is now approaching a climax.

It becomes imperative to adjust man's life and institutions to the increasing dangers and opportunities of these new circumstances. He is being forced to organise cooperation among the medley of separate sovereign states which has hitherto served his political ends. At the same time he finds it necessary to rescue his economic life from devastation by the immensely enhanced growth of profit-seeking business and finance. Political, economic and social collectivisation is being forced upon him. He responds to these new conditions blindly and with a great wastage of happiness and well-being.

Governments are either becoming State collectivisms or passing under the sway of monopolist productive and financial organisations. Religious organisations, education and the press are subordinated to the will of dictatorial groups and individuals, while scientific and literary work and a multitude of social activities, which have hitherto been independent and spontaneous, fall under the influence of these modern concentrations of power. Neither Governments nor great economic and financial combinations were devised to exercise such powers; they grew up in response to the requirements of an earlier age.

Under the stress of the new conditions, insecurity, abuses and tyrannies increase; and liberty, particularly liberty of thought and speech, decays. Phase by phase these ill-adapted Governments and controls are restricting that free play of the individual mind which is the preservative of human efficiency and happiness. The temporary advantage of swift and secret action which these monopolisations of power display is gained at the price of profound and progressive social demoralisation. Bereft of liberty and sense of responsibility, the peoples are manifestly doomed to lapse, after a phase of servile discipline, into disorder and violence. Confidence and deliberation give place to hysteria, apathy and inefficiency. Everywhere war and monstrous exploitation are intensified, so that those very same increments of power and opportunity which have brought mankind within sight of an age of limitless plenty, seem likely to be lost again, and, it may be, lost for ever, in a chaotic and irremediable social collapse.

It becomes clear that a unified political, economic and social order can alone put an end to these national and private appropriations that now waste the mighty possibilities of our time.

The history of the Western peoples has a lesson for all mankind. It has been the practice of what are called the democratic or Parliamentary countries to meet every enhancement and centralisation of power in the past by a definite and vigorous reassertion of the individual rights of man. Never before has the demand to revive that precedent been so urgent as it is now. We of the Parliamentary democracies recognise the inevitability of world reconstruction upon collectivist lines, but, after our tradition, we couple with that recognition a Declaration of Rights, so that the profound changes now in progress shall produce not an attempted reconstruction of human affairs in the dark, but a rational reconstruction conceived and arrived at in the full light of day. To that time-honoured instrument of a Declaration of Rights we therefore return, but now upon a world scale.

1. *Right to Live*
By the word 'man' in this Declaration is meant every living human being without distinction of age or sex.

Every man is a *joint inheritor of all the natural resources and of the powers, inventions and possibilities accumulated by our forerunners. He is entitled, within the measure of these resources and without distinction of race, colour or professed beliefs or opinions*, to the nourishment, covering and medical care needed to realise his full possibilities of physical and mental development from birth to death. Notwithstanding the various and unequal qualities of individuals, all men shall be deemed absolutely equal in the eyes of the law, equally important in social life and equally entitled to the respect of their fellow men.

2. *Protection of Minors*
The natural and rightful guardians of those who are not of an age to protect themselves are their parents. In default of such parental protection in whole or in part, the community, having due regard to the family traditions of the child, shall accept or provide alternative guardians.

3. *Duty to the Community*
It is the duty of every man not only to respect but to uphold and to advance the rights of all other men throughout the world. Furthermore, it is his duty to contribute such service to the community as will ensure the performance of those necessary tasks for which the incentives which will operate in a free society do not provide. It is only by doing his quota of service that a man can justify his partnership in the community. No man shall be conscripted for military or other service to which he has an objection, but to perform no social duty whatsoever is to remain unenfranchised and under guardianship.

4. *Right to Knowledge*
It is the duty of the community to equip every man with sufficient education to enable him to be as useful and interested a citizen as his capacity allows. Furthermore, it is the duty of the community to render all knowledge available to him and such special education as will give him equality of opportunity for the development of his distinctive gifts in the service of mankind. He shall have easy and prompt access to all information necessary for him to form a judgment upon current events and issues.

5. *Freedom of Thought and Worship*
Every man has a right to the utmost freedom of expression, discussion, association and worship.

6. *Right to Work*
A man may engage freely in any lawful occupation, earning such pay as the contribution that his work makes to the welfare of the community may justify or that the desire of any private individual or individuals for his products, his performances or the continuation of his activities may produce for him. He is entitled to paid employment by the community and to make suggestions as to the kind of employment which he considers himself able to perform. He is entitled to profit fully by the desirableness of his products and activities. And he is entitled to payment for calling attention to a product or conveying it to consumers to whom it would otherwise be unobtainable. By doing so, he does a service for which he may legitimately profit. He is a useful agent. *But buying and holding and selling again simply in order to make a profit is not lawful.* It is speculation; it does no service; it makes profit out of want and it can be profitable only by creating or sustaining want. It tempts men directly to the interception of legitimate profits, to forestalling, appropriation, hoarding and a complex of anti-social activities, and it is equally unlawful for private individuals and public administrative bodies.

7. *Right to Personal Property*
In the enjoyment of his personal property, lawfully possessed, and subject to the limitations stated in Articles 3 and 6, a man is entitled to protection from public or private violence, deprivation, compulsion and intimidation.

8. *Freedom of Movement*
A man may move freely about the world at his own expense. His private dwelling, however, and any reasonably limited enclosure of which he is the occupant, may be entered only with his consent or by a legally qualified person empowered with a warrant as the law may direct. So long as by his movement he does not intrude upon the private domain of any other citizen, harm, or disfigure or encumber what is not his, interfere with or endanger the happiness of others, he shall have the right to come and go wherever he chooses, by land, air, or water, over any kind of country, mountain, moorland, river, lake, sea or ocean, and all the ample spaces of this, his world.

9. *Personal Liberty*
Unless a man is declared by a competent authority to be a danger to himself or others through mental abnormality, a declaration which must be confirmed within seven days and thereafter reviewed at least annually, he shall not be restrained for more than twenty-four hours without being charged with a definite offence, nor shall he be remanded for a longer period than eight days without his consent, nor imprisoned for more than three months without a trial. At a reasonable time before his trial, he shall be furnished with a copy of the evidence which it is proposed to use against him. At the end of the three months period, if he has not been tried and sentenced by due process of the law, he shall be acquitted and released. No man shall be charged more than once for the same offence.

Although he is open to the free criticism of his fellows, a man shall have adequate protection against any misrepresentation that may distress or injure him. Secret evidence is not permissible. Statements recorded in administrative dossiers shall not be used to justify the slightest infringement of personal liberty. A dossier is merely a memorandum for administrative use; it shall not be used as evidence without proper confirmation in open court.

10. *Freedom from Violence*
No man shall be subjected to any sort of mutilation except with his own deliberate consent, freely given, nor to forcible handling, except in restraint of his own violence, nor to torture, beating or any other physical ill-treatment. He shall not be subjected to mental distress, or to imprisonment in infected, verminous or otherwise insanitary quarters, or be put into the company of verminous or infected people. But if he is himself infectious or a danger to the health of others, he may be cleansed, disinfected, put in quarantine or otherwise restrained so far as may be necessary to prevent harm to his fellows. No one shall be punished vicariously by the selection, arrest or ill-treatment of hostages.

11. *Rights of Law-making*
The rights embodied in this Declaration are fundamental and inalienable. In conventional and in administrative matters, but in no others, it is an obvious practical necessity for men to limit the free play of certain of these fundamental rights. (In, for example, such conventional matters as the rule of the road or the protection of money from forgery, and in such administrative matters as town and country planning, or public hygiene.) No law, conventional or administrative, shall be binding on any man or any section of the community unless it has been made openly with the active of tacit acquiescence of every adult citizen concerned, given either by direct majority vote of the community affected or by a majority vote of his representatives publicly selected. These representatives shall be ultimately responsible for all by-laws and for detailed interpretations made in the execution of the law. In matters of convention and collective action, the will of the majority must prevail. All legislation must be subject to public discussion, revision or repeal. No treaties or contracts shall be made secretly in the name of the community. The fount of legislation in a free world is the whole people, and since life flows on constantly to new citizens, no generation can, in whole or in part, surrender or delegate this legislative power, inalienably inherent in mankind.

These are the common rights of all human beings. They are yours whoever you are. Demand that your rulers and politicians sign and observe this declaration. If they refuse, if they quibble, they can have no place in the new free world that dawns upon mankind.

B. The International Bill of Human Rights

When the Universal Declaration of Human Rights was proclaimed by the General Assembly in 1948, it was viewed as the first step in the formulation of an 'international bill of human rights' that would have legal as well as moral force. In 1976 — three decades after this comprehensive undertaking was launched by the United Nations — the 'international bill of human rights' became a reality, with the entry into force of three significant instruments:

The International Covenant on Economic, Social and Cultural Rights;
The International Covenant on Civil and Political Rights; and
The Optional Protocol to the latter covenant.

The Covenants require countries ratifying them to recognize or protect a wide range of human rights. And under the optional provisions, procedures are established allowing individuals as well as States to present complaints of rights violations.
Promotion of human rights and fundamental freedoms for all had been included in the Charter — the historic document establishing the United Nations — as one of the Organization's basic purposes. In the early days of the Organization, the Economic and Social Council and its Commission on Human Rights decided that the planned international bill of rights should consist of a declaration of general principles, having moral force, a separate

covenant legally binding on those States ratifying it, and measures of implementation. Within a relatively short time the Commission drafted the Universal Declaration of Human Rights — an historic document setting the standards for achievement of human rights.

Since its adoption by the Assembly on 10 December 1948, the Declaration has had a wide impact throughout the world, inspiring national constitutions and laws as well as conventions on various specific rights. The Declaration did not have the force of law at the time of its adoption, but since then it has had a powerful influence on the development of contemporary international law.

Having proclaimed this Universal Declaration, the United Nations turned to an even more difficult task: transforming the principles into treaty provisions which establish legal obligations on the part of each ratifying State. Eventually it was decided that two covenants rather than one were needed: one dealing with civil and political rights, the other with economic, social and cultural rights.

Agreement on the formulation of rights acceptable to all the diverse peoples, religions, cultures and ideologies in the United Nations did not come about easily. Article by article, the two covenants were drafted — first in the Human Rights Commission and then in the Assembly's Third Committee. On 16 December 1966 the Assembly adopted the International Covenants and the Optional Protocol. Another decade went by before the Covenants were ratified by a sufficient number of countries to bring them into force. Each Covenant required a minimum of thirty-five ratifications (or accessions).

When the number of ratifying countries reached thirty-five, the International Covenant on Economic, Social and Cultural Rights came into effect as of 3 January 1976. The International Covenant on Civil and Political Rights entered into force on 23 March 1976, together with its Optional Protocol (which had already received ten ratifications, the minimum needed for its entry into force).

A country ratifying the Covenant on Civil and Political Rights undertakes to protect its people by law against cruel, inhuman or degrading treatment. It recognizes the right of every human being to life, liberty, security and privacy of person. The covenant prohibits slavery, guarantees the right to a fair trial and protect persons against arbitrary arrest or detention. It recognizes freedom of opinion and expression; the right of peaceful assembly and of emigration; and freedom of association.

A country ratifying the Covenant on Economic, Social and Cultural Rights acknowledges its responsibility to promote better living conditions for its people. It recognizes everyone's right to work, to fair wages, to social security, to adequate standards of living and freedom from hunger, and to health and education. It also undertakes to ensure the right of everyone to form and join trade unions.

Generally, the Covenant provisions reflect rights set forth in the Universal Declaration of Human Rights. A major provision of both Covenants, however, had not been included in the Declaration. This was the right of all peoples to self-determination and to enjoy and utilize fully and freely their natural wealth and resources.

Implementation Measures

There are two distinct sets of implementation measures in the Covenants.

States that have ratified the Covenant on Civil and Political Rights will elect a Human Rights Committee, composed of 18 persons acting in an individual capacity. The Covenant says they should be persons of high moral character and recognized competence in the field of human rights. This Committee will consider reports submitted by the States parties and may address general comments to these States, as well as to the Economic and Social Council.

Under optional provisions of the Covenant, the Human Rights Committee may consider *communications from a State party* alleging that another State party is not fulfilling its Covenant obligations. The Committee is to act as a fact-finding body. *Ad hoc* conciliation commissions may be established, with the prior consent of the State concerned, to make available their good offices with a view to reaching friendly solutions on the basis of respect for the rights recognized in the Covenant. (These optional provisions of the Covenant itself require a minimum of 10 acceptances; as of October 1977, six States — Denmark, Finland, Federal Republic of Germany, Norway, Sweden and the United Kingdom — had indicated their acceptance.)

The Optional Protocol, which became effective in March 1976, enables the Human Rights Committee to consideration *communications from private individuals* claiming to be the victims of a violation by a State party to that Protocol of any of the rights set forth in the Covenant. (Individuals must have 'exhausted all available domestic remedies'.) Reports of the Committee are to be communicated to the States concerned. The Committee is to submit annual reports to the General Assembly.

States ratifying the Covenant on Economic, Social and Cultural Rights undertake to submit periodic reports to the Economic and Social Council on the measures adopted and the progress made towards realizing these rights. The Council may make general recommendations and may promote appropriate international action to assist the States parties in those fields.

(The above text is part of the Introduction to 'The International Bill of Human rights' *issued by the Office of Public Information, United Nations, New York, on the occasion of the 30th anniversary of the proclaiming of the Universal Declaration of Human Rights. The text of the Universal Declaration follows.)*

UNIVERSAL DECLARATION OF HUMAN RIGHTS

Preamble

Whereas recognition of the inherent dignity and of the equal and inalienable rights of all members of the human family is the foundation of freedom, justice and peace in the world,

Whereas disregard and contempt for human rights have resulted in barbarous acts which have outraged the conscience of mankind, and the advent of a world in which human beings shall enjoy freedom of speech and belief and freedom from fear and want has been proclaimed as the highest aspiration of the common people,

Whereas it is essential, if man is not to be compelled to have recourse, as a last resort, to rebellion against tyranny and oppression, that human rights should be protected by the rule of law,

Whereas it is essential to promote the development of friendly relations between nations,

Whereas the peoples of the United Nations have in the Charter reaffirmed their faith in fundamental human rights, in the dignity and worth of the human person and in the equal rights of men and women and have determined to promote social progress and better standards of life in larger freedom,

Whereas Member States have pledged themselve to achieve, in co-operation with the United Nations, the promotion of universal respect for and observance of human rights and fundamental freedoms,

Whereas a common understanding of these rights and freedoms is of the greatest importance for the full realization of this pledge,

Now, therefore, THE GENERAL ASSEMBLY *proclaims*

This Universal Declaration of Human Rights as a common standard of achievement for all peoples and all nations, to the end that every individual and every organ of society, keeping this Declaration constantly in mind, shall strive by teaching and education to promote respect for these rights and freedoms and by progressive measures, national and international, to secure their universal and effective recognition and observance, both among the peoples of Member States themselves and among the peoples of territories under their jurisdiction.

Article 1 All human beings are born free and equal in dignity and rights. They are endowed with reason and conscience and should act towards one another in a spirit of brotherhood.

Article 2 Everyone is entitled to all the rights and freedoms set forth in this Declaration, without distinction of any kind, such as race, colour, sex, language, religion, political or other opinion, national or social origin, property, birth or other status.

Furthermore, no distinction shall be made on the basis of the political, jurisdictional or international status of the country or territory to which a person belongs, whether it be independent, trust, non-self-governing or under any other limitation of sovereignty.

Article 3 Everyone has the right to life, liberty and security of person.

Article 4 No one shall be held in slavery or servitude; slavery and the slave trade shall be prohibited in all their forms.

Article 5 No one shall be subjected to torture or to cruel, inhuman or degrading treatment or punishment.

Article 6 Everyone has the right to recognition everywhere as a person before the law.

Article 7 All are equal before the law and are entitled without any discrimination to equal protection of the law. All are entitled to equal protection against any discrimination in violation of this Declaration and against any incitement to such discrimination.

Article 8 Everyone has the right to an effective remedy by the competent national tribunals for acts violating the fundamental rights granted him by the constitution or by law.

Article 9 No one shall be subjected to arbitrary arrest, detention or exile.

Article 10 Everyone is entitled in full equality to a fair and public hearing by an independent and impartial tribunal, in the determination of his rights and obligations and of any criminal charge against him.

Article 11 1. Everyone charged with a penal offence has the right to be presumed innocent until proved guilty according to law in a public trial at which he has had all the guarantees necessary for his defence.

2. No one shall be held guilty of any penal offence on account of any act or omission which did not constitute a penal offence, under national or international law, at the time when it was committed. Nor shall a heavier penalty be imposed than the one that was applicable at the time the penal offence was committed.

Article 12 No one shall be subjected to arbitrary interference with his privacy, family, home or correspondence, nor to attacks upon his honour and reputation. Everyone has the right to the protection of the law against such interference or attacks.

Article 13 1. Everyone has the right to freedom of movement and residence within the borders of each state.

2. Everyone has the right to leave any country, including his own, and to return to his country.

Article 14 1. Everyone has the right to seek and to enjoy in other countries asylum from persecution.

2. This right may not be invoked in the case of prosecutions genuinely arising from non-political crimes or from acts contrary to the purposes and principles of the United Nations.

Article 15 1. Everyone has the right to a nationality.

2. No one shall be arbitrarily deprived of his nationality nor denied the right to change his nationality.

Article 16 1. Men and women of full age, without any limitation due to race, nationality or religion, have the right to marry and to found a family. They are entitled to equal rights as to marriage, during marriage and at its dissolution.

2. Marriage shall be entered into only with the free and full consent of the intending spouses.

3. The family is the natural and fundamental group unit of society and is entitled to protection by society and the State.

Article 17 1. Everyone has the right to own property alone as well as in association with others.

2. No one shall be arbitrarily deprived of his property.

Article 18 Everyone has the right to freedom of thought, conscience and religion; this right includes freedom to change his religion or belief, and freedom, either alone or in community with others and in public or private, to manifest his religion or belief in teaching, practice, worship and observance.

Article 19 Everyone has the right to freedom of opinion and expression; this right includes freedom to hold opinions without interference and to seek, receive and impart information and ideas through any media and regardless of frontiers.

Article 20 1. Everyone has the right to freedom of peaceful assembly and association.

2. No one may be compelled to belong to an association.

Article 21 1. Everyone has the right to take part in the government of his country, directly or through freely chosen representatives.

2. Everyone has the right of equal access to public service in his country.

3. The will of the people shall be the basis of the authority of government; this will shall be expressed in periodic and genuine elections which shall be by universal and equal suffrage and shall be held by secret vote or by equivalent free voting procedures.

Article 22 Everyone, as a member of society, has the right to social security and is entitled to realization, through national effort and international co-operation and in accordance with the organization and resources of each State, of the economic, social and cultural rights indispensable for his dignity and the free development of his personality.

Article 23 1. Everyone has the right to work, to free choice of employment, to just and favourable conditions of work and to protection against unemployment.

2. Everyone, without any discrimination, has the right to equal pay for equal work.

3. Everyone who works has the right to just and favourable remuneration ensuring for himself and his family an existence worthy of human dignity, and supplemented, if necessary by other means of social protection.

4. Everyone has the right to form and to join trade unions for the protection of his interests.

Article 24 Everyone has the right to rest and leisure, including reasonable limitation of working hours and periodic holidays with pay.

Article 25 1. Everyone has the right to a standard of living adequate for the health and well-being of himself and of his family, including food, clothing, housing and medical care and necessary social services, and the right to security in the event of unemployment, sickness, disability, widowhood, old age or other lack of livelihood in circumstances beyond his control.

2. Motherhood and childhood are entitled to special care and assistance. All children, whether born in or out of wedlock, shall enjoy the same social protection.

Article 26 1. Everyone has the right to education. Education shall be free, at least in the elementary and fundamental stages. Elementary education shall be compulsory. Technical and professional education shall be made generally available and higher education shall be equally accessible to all on the basis of merit.

2. Education shall be directed to the full development of the human personality and to the strengthening of respect for human rights and fundamental freedoms. It shall promote understanding, tolerance and friendship among all nations, racial or religious groups, and shall further the activities of the United Nations for the maintenance of peace.

3. Parents have a prior right to choose the kind of education that shall be given to their children.

Article 27 1. Everyone has the right freely to participate in the cultural life of the community, to enjoy the arts and to share in scientific advancement and its benefits.

2. Everyone has the right to the protection of the moral and material interests resulting from any scientific, literary or artistic production of which he is the author.

Article 28 Everyone is entitled to a social and international order in which the rights and freedoms set forth in this Declaration can be fully realized.

Article 29 1. Everyone has duties to the community in which alone the free and full development of his personality is possible.

2. In the exercise of his rights and freedoms, everyone shall be subject only to such limitations as are determined by law solely for the purpose of securing due recognition and respect for the rights and freedoms of others and of meeting the just requirements of morality, public order and the general welfare in a democratic society.

3. These rights and freedoms may in no case be exercised contrary to the purposes and principles of the United Nations.

Article 30 Nothing in this Declaration may be interpreted as implying for any State, group or person any right to engage in any activity or to perform any act aimed at the destruction of any of the rights and freedoms set forth herein.

2

Accessions to Human Rights International Instruments

This Annex lists signatures, ratifications, accessions, etc. to the following 21 Covenants, Conventions and other Instruments as at 1 September 1983.*

	Identified in Table as No.
International Covenant on Economic, Social and Cultural Rights (1966)	1
International Covenant on Civil and Political Rights (1966)	2
Optional Protocol to the International Covenant on Civil and Political Rights (1966)	3
International Convention on the Elimination of All Forms of Racial Discrimination (1965)	4
International Convention on the Suppression and Punishment of the Crime of *Apartheid* (1973)	5
Convention on the Elimination of All Forms of Discrimination against Women (1979)	6
Convention on the Prevention and Punishment of the Crime of Genocide (1948)	7
Convention on the Non-Applicability of Statutory Limitations to War Crimes and Crimes against Humanity (1968)	8
Slavery Convention of 1926	9
1953 Protocol amending the 1926 Convention (1953)	10
Slavery Convention of 1926 as amended	11
Supplementary Convention on the Abolition of Slavery, the Slave Trade, and Practices Similar to Slavery (1956)	12
Convention for the Suppression of the Traffic in Persons and of the Exploitation of the Prostitution of Others (1949)	13
Convention relating to the Status of Refugees (1951)	14
Protocol relating to the Status of Refugees (1966)	15
Convention on the Reduction of Statelessness (1961)	16
Convention relating to the Status of Stateless Persons (1954)	17
Convention on the International Right of Correction (1952)	18
Convention on the Nationality of Married Women (1957)	19
Convention on the Political Rights of Women (1952)	20
Convention on Consent to Marriage, Minimum Age for Marriage and Registration of Marriages (1962)	21

*For further details of specific communications and objections relevant to these Instruments, see the publication *Human Rights International Instruments* (document ST/HR/4/Rev 5), United Nations, New York, 1983, which is the source of the national data contained in this Annex. A full record of States parties' declarations, reservations and objections is contained in ST/HR/4/Rev 4, issued in 1982.

Accessions to Human Rights International Instruments

States	1	2	3	4	5	6	7	8	9	10	11	12	13	14	15	16	17	18	19	20	21
Afghanistan	x	x		x		s	x	x	x	x	x	x								x	
Albania	x	s					x	x	s		x	x	x						x	x	
Algeria	s	s		x	x		x				x	x	x	x	x		x		x		
Angola					x									x	x						x
Antigua and Barbuda																					
Argentina	s	s		x		s	x		x	x		x	x	x	x		x	s	x	x	x
Australia	x	x		x	s	x	x	x	x	x	x	x	x	x	x	x	x		x	x	
Austria	x	xa	s	x		x	x		x	x	x	x		x	x	x			x	x	x
Bahamas	x			x	x	x	x		x	x	x	x							x	x	
Bahrain																					
Bangladesh				x																	
Barbados	x	x	x	x	x	x	x		x	x	x	x	x	x			x		x	x	x
Belgium	x	x		x		s	x		x		x	x			x		x	s	s	x	
Belize																					
Benin				s	x	s			x					x	x						x
Bhutan				s	x		x														
Bolivia	x	x	x	x	x	s	s				x	x	x	x	x		x		x	x	x
Botswana				x			s										x				
Brazil	x	x		x	x	s	x		x				x	x	x		s		x	x	
Bulgaria	x	x		x	x	x	x	x	x		x	x	x	x	x				x	x	x
Burma										x			s							s	
Burundi				x		s															
Byelorussian SSR	x	x		x	x	x	x	x	x	x	x	x	x	x	x				x	x	
Canada	x	xa	x	x	x	x	x	x	x	x	x	x		x	x	x			x	x	
Cape Verde				x	x	x										x					
Central African Republic	x	x	x	x	x				x			x		x	x					x	
Chad				x	x									x	x						
Chile	x	x		x		s	x							x	x			s	s	x	
China¹	x	x	x	x		x	x		s					x	x				s		s
Colombia	x	x	x	x	x	x	x							x	x		s	s	s		
Comoros						s			s										s		
Congo						x															
Costa Rica	x	x	x	xb		s	x		x			x	x	x	x	x	x		x	x	s

continued

Cuba
Cyprus
Czechoslovakia
Democratic Kampuchea
Democratic People's Republic of Korea
Democratic Yemen
Denmark
Djibouti
Dominica
Dominican Republic
Ecuador
Egypt
El Salvador
Equatorial Guinea
Ethiopia
Fiji
Finland
France
Gabon
Gambia
German Democratic Republic
Germany, Federal Republic of
Ghana
Greece
Grenada
Guatemala
Guinea
Guinea-Bissau
Guyana
Haiti

x Ratification, accession, notification of succession, acceptance or definitive signature.
s Signature not yet followed by ratification.
a Declaration recognizing the competence of the Human Rights Committee under article 41 of the International Covenant on Civil and Political Rights.
b Declaration recognizing the competence of the Committee on the Elimination of Racial Discrimination under article 14 of the International Convention on the Elimination of All Forms of Racial Discrimination.

States	1	2	3	4	5	6	7	8	9	10	11	12	13	14	15	16	17	18	19	20	21
Holy See	x			x												s	s				
Honduras	x	s	s				x	x												x	x
Hungary	x	x			x	x	x	x	x	x	x	x	s	x	x			x	x	x	x
Iceland	x	xa	x	xb	x	s	x	x	s	x	x	x	x	x				s	s	x	x
India	x	x		x	x	s	x	x	x	x	x	x	x	x				x		x	
Indonesia						s															
Iran (Islamic Republic of)	x	x		x			x		s		x	x	s	x	x						
Iraq	x	x		x			x		x	x	x	x	x	x	x	x	x	x	x	x	
Ireland	s	s		x			x		x	x	x	x	x	x	x	x	x	x	x	x	
Israel	s	s		s		s	x		x	x	x	x	x	x	x	s	x	x		x	
Italy	x	xa	x	xb	x	s	x		x	x	x	x	x	x	x		x			x	
Ivory Coast	x			x		s			x		x	x	x	x	x						
Jamaica	x	x	x	x	x	s	x				x	x	x	x	x			x	x	x	
Japan	x	x			x	s					x	x	x	x	x					x	
Jordan	x	x		x	s		x			x			x	x				x			
Kenya	x	x			s	s															
Kiribati	x	x						x						x	x						
Kuwait																					
Lao People's Democratic Republic	x			x	x	x	x			x	x	x	x							x	
Lebanon		x		x	x		x				x	x	x	x						x	
Lesotho				x		s	x			x										x	
Liberia	s	s		x	x		x		x	x	x	s	s	x	x		x	x		x	s
Libyan Arab Jamahiriya	x	x		x	x					x	x	s	x	x	x		x				
Liechtenstein																s	s				
Luxembourg	x	x	x	x		s			x	x	x	x	s	x	x		x	x		x	
Madagascar	x	x	x	x		s				x	x	x	s	x	x				x	x	
Malawi		x								x	x	x		x				x	x	x	
Malaysia											x	x									
Maldives											x	x						x	x		
Mali	x	x		x	x	x	x		x	x	x	x	x	x	x			x	x	x	x
Malta	s			x																	
Mauritania		x		s				s		x	x										
Mauritius	x	x	x	x	x		x		x	x	x							x	x	x	x
Mexico	x	x		x	x	x	x		x	x	x	x	x					x	x	x	x

continued

Monaco	x	x			x	x	x	x		x		x	x
Mongolia	x	x	x	x	x	x	x	x		x		x	x
Morocco			x	x	x	x	x	x	x	x	x	x	x
Mozambique			x	x									
Namibia			x	x									
Nauru													
Nepal	x		x	x	x	x	x	x	x	x	x	x	x
Netherlands	x	xa	x	xb	s	s	x	x	x	s	x	x	x
New Zealand	x	xa	x	x	s	x	x	x	x	x	x	x	x
Nicaragua	x	x	x	x	x	x	x	x	x	x	x		x
Niger	x		x	x	x		x	x	x	x		x	
Nigeria	x		x	x	x	x	x	x	x	x		x	x
Norway	x	xa	x	xb	x	x	x	x	x	x	x	x	x
Oman			s										
Pakistan	x		x	x	x	s	x	x	x	x	x	s	x
Panama	x		x	x	x	x	x	x	x	x			
Papua New Guinea			x	s	s				x	x	s	s	x
Paraguay	x		x	x	x		s		x	x	s	s	x
Peru	x		x	x	x	x	x	x	x	x	x	x	x
Philippines	s	s	x	x	x	x	x	x	x	s	x	x	x
Poland	x		x	x	x	x	x	x	x	x	x	x	x
Portugal	x		x	x	x	x	x	x	x	s	x	x	x
Qatar			x										
Republic of Korea	x		x	x	s	x	x	x	x	x	x	x	x
Romania	x		x	x	x	x	x	x	x	x	x	x	x
Rwanda	x		x	x	x	x	x	x	x				
Saint Lucia			x	x									
Saint Vincent and the Grenadines	x		x	x	x	x	x	x	x	x			
Samoa													x
San Marino			x		x								

---

x   Ratification, accession, notification of succession, acceptance or definitive signature.
s   Signature not yet followed by ratification.
a   Declaration recognizing the competence of the Human Rights Committee under article 41 of the International Covenant on Civil and Political Rights.
b   Declaration recognizing the competence of the Committee on the Elimination of Racial Discrimination under article 14 of the International Convention on the Elimination of All Forms of Racial Discrimination.

States	1	2	3	4	5	6	7	8	9	10	11	12	13	14	15	16	17	18	19	20	21
Sao Tome and Principe																					
Saudi Arabia					x									x	x						
Senegal	x	xa	x	xb	x	s	x		x		x	x	x	x	x					x	x
Seychelles				x	x							x	x	x	x			x		x	s
Sierra Leone				x							x	x	x	x	x			x	x	x	
Singapore												x	x								
Solomon Islands	x			x					x		x	x		x					x	x	
Somalia				x	x				x		x	x		x	x						
South Africa																					
Spain	x	x		x	x	s	x		x	x	x	x	x	x	x					x	x
Sri Lanka	x	xa		x	x	x	x		x	x	x	x	x	x	x			x	x	x	s
Sudan	x	x	x	x	x						x	x									
Suriname									x	x	x	x		x	x						
Swaziland				x								x		x	x	x					
Sweden	x	xa	x	xb	x	x	x		x	x	x	x		x	x	x	x	x	x	x	x
Switzerland									x	x	x	x	x	x	x	x	x			x	
Syrian Arab Republic	x	x		x	x	x	x		x	x	x	x									
Thailand																				x	
Togo				x			x		x			x		x	x						
Tonga				x							x										
Trinidad and Tobago	x	x	x	x	x	s	x				x	x		x	x		x	x	x	x	x
Tunisia	x	x		x	x		x	x		x	x	x	x	x	x		x	x	x	x	x
Turkey				s		s	x		x	x	x	x	x	x	x	x			x	x	
Tuvalu																					
Uganda	x	x		x	s	s	x			x	x	x		x	x		x	x	x	x	
Ukrainian SSR	x	x		x	x	x	x		x	x	x	x						x	x	x	
Union of Soviet Socialist Republics				x	x	x	x	x	x	x	x	x	x					x	x	x	
United Arab Emirates				x	x			x			x		x								
United Kingdom of Great Britain and Northern Ireland	x	xa		x		s	x	x		x	x	x		x		x	x	x	x	x	x
United Republic of Cameroon				x	x	s			x	x	x		x	x	x	x				x	x
United Republic of Tanzania	x	x		x	x	s				x	x			x	x	x		x		x	
United States of America	s	s		s	x	s	s		x	x	x	x		x	x					x	s

	C1	C2	C3	C4	C5	C6	C7	C8	C9	C10	C11	C12	C13	C14	C15	C16	C17	C18	C19	C20	C21
Upper Volta	x											x									x
Uruguay	x	x		xb								x	x	x		x				s	x
Vanuatu																x				s	
Venezuela	x			x								x				x				x	x
Viet Nam	x	x		x	x																
Yemen				x									x								
Yugoslavia	x	x		x	x				x	x		x	x	x		x				x	x
Zaire	x	x		x	s				x	x		x	x	x						x	x
Zambia				x	s							x	x	x		x				x	x
Zimbabwe												x	x								
Total number of States parties	79	76	30	121	73	51	92	25	62	45	77	96	53	92	91	10	32	11	54	91	34
Same (at 1 June 1985)	84	80	35	124	78	62	99	—	64	51	—	100	57								
Signatures not followed by ratification	8	9	6	8	6	42	4	1	6	0	0	4	6	0	0	4	8	6	8	5	8

x Ratification, accession, notification of succession, acceptance or definitive signature.

s Signature not yet followed by ratification.

a Declaration recognizing the competence of the Human Rights Committee under article 41 of the International Covenant on Civil and Political Rights.

b Declaration recognizing the competence of the Committee on the Elimination of Racial Discrimination under article 14 of the International Convention on the Elimination of All Forms of Racial Discrimination.

[1]Following on the adoption of Resolution 2758 (XXVI) of 25 October 1971 on the lawful rights of the People's Republic of China in the United Nations by the General Assembly, the Minister for Foreign Affairs of the People's Republic of China, by a note addressed to the Secretary-General, received on 29 September 1972, stated:

"1. With regard to the multilateral treaties signed, ratified or acceded to by the defunct Chinese government before the establishment of the Government of the People's Republic of China, my Government will examine their contents before making a decision in the light of the circumstances as to whether or not they should be recognized.

"2. As from 1 October 1949, the day of the founding of the People's Republic of China, the Chiang Kai-shek clique has no right at all to represent China. Its signature and ratification of, or accession to, any multilateral treaties by usurping the name of 'China' are all illegal and null and void. My Government will study these multilateral treaties before making a decision in the light of the circumstances as to whether or not they should be acceded to."

The lists therefore do not indicate that, subsequent to 1 October 1949, and prior to 25 October 1971, the Republic of China (a) ratified, acceded to or accepted the conventions listed above under the numbers 4, 9, 10, 11, 12, 19 and 20, and (b) signed, but did not ratify the conventions listed under numbers 1, 2, 3 and 21 and that the convention listed under number 7 was signed on behalf of the 'Republic of China' on 20 July 1949 and an instrument of ratification by the 'Republic of China' was deposited on 19 July 1951.

continued

[2](i) With respect to the signature by Democratic Kampuchea of the International Covenant on Economic, Social and Cultural Rights and of the International Covenant on Civil and Political Rights, the Secretary-General received, on 5 November 1980, the following communication from the Government of Mongolia:

"The Government of the Mongolian People's Republic considers that only the People's Revolutionary Council of Kampuchea as the sole authentic and lawful representative of the Kampuchean people has the right to assume international obligations on behalf of the Kampuchean people. Therefore the Government of the Mongolian People's Republic considers that the signature of the Human Rights Covenants by the representative of the so-called Democratic Kampuchea, a régime that ceased to exist as a result of the people's revolution in Kampuchea, is null and void.

"The signing of the Human Rights Covenants by an individual, whose régime during its short period of reign in Kampuchea had exterminated about 3 million people and had thus grossly violated the elementary norms of human rights, each and every provision of the Human Rights Covenants is a regrettable precedence, which discredits the noble aims and lofty principles of the United Nations Charter, the very spirit of the above-mentioned Covenants, gravely impairs the prestige of the United Nations."

Thereafter, similar communications were received from the Government of the following States on the dates indicated:

State	Date of receipt
German Democratic Republic	11 Dec. 1980
Hungary	19 Jan. 1981
Bulgaria	29 Jan. 1981
Union of Soviet Socialist Republics	13 Feb. 1981
Byelorussian SSR	18 Feb. 1981
Czechoslovakia	10 Mar. 1981

(ii) The Secretary-General received on 10 September 1981 from the Government of Viet Nam the following objection with regard to the accession of Democratic Kampuchea to the International Convention on the Suppression and Punishment of the Crime of *Apartheid*:

"The accession to the above-mentioned international Convention on behalf of the so-called 'Government of Kampuchea' by the genocidal clique of Pol Pot-Ieng Sary-Khieu Samphan, which was overthrown on 7 January 1979 by the Kampuchean people, is completely illegal and has no legal value. Only the Government of the People's Republic of Kampuchea, which is actually in power in Kampuchea, is empowered to represent the Kampuchean people and to sign and accede to international agreements and conventions.

"As a party to that Convention, the Socialist Republic of Viet Nam is of the opinion that the accession of the so-called 'Government of Democratic Kampuchea' constitutes not only a gross violation of the standards of law and international morality, but also one of the most cynical affronts to the three million Kampucheans who are the victims of the most despicable crime of contemporary history, committed by the Pol Pot régime which is spurned by the whole of mankind."

Thereafter, similar communications objecting to the accession by Democratic Kampuchea were received by the Secretary-General on 14 September 1981 from the Government of the German Democratic Republic, on 12 November 1981 from the Union of Soviet Socialist Republics, on 19 November 1981 from the Government of the Byelorussian Soviet Socialist Republic, on 3 December 1981 from the Government of Hungary, on 5 January 1982 from the Government of Bulgaria, on 13 January 1982 from the Government of Mongolia and on 17 May 1982 from the Government of Czechoslovakia.

(iii) The Secretary-General received, on 11 December 1980, an objection from the German Democratic Republic with regard to the signature of the Convention on the Elimination of All Forms of Discrimination against Women by Democratic Kampuchea. For the text of the objection and for the text of further objections to this signature by the Government of the Byelorussian Soviet Socialist Republic, the Lao People's Democratic Republic, Poland, the Ukrainian Soviet Socialist Republic and the Union of Soviet Socialist Republics, see (i) above. Similar communications objecting to the signature of the Convention by Democratic Kampuchea were received by the Secretary-General as follows:

State	Date of receipt
Hungary	19 Jan. 1981
Bulgaria	29 Jan. 1981
Union of Soviet Socialist Republics	13 Feb. 1981
Byelorussian SSR	18 Feb. 1981
Czechoslovakia	10 Mar. 1981

3

The State of Multilateral Disarmament Agreements

This Annex lists signatures and ratifications to the following Multilateral Arms Regulations and Disarmament Agreements as at 31 December 1983:*

	Entered in Force
Protocol for the Prohibition of the Use in War of Asphyxiating, Poisonos or Other Gases, and of Bacteriological Methods of Warfare	1928
The Antarctic Treaty	1959
Treaty Banning Nuclear Weapon Tests in the Atmosphere, in Outer Space and under Water	1963
Treaty on Principles Governing the Activities of states in the Exploration and Use of Outer Space, including the Moon and Other Celestial Bodies	1967
Treaty for the Prohibition of Nuclear Weapons in Latin America (Treaty of Tlatelolco) with Additional Protocols I and II	1968
Treaty on the Non-Proliferation of Nuclear Weapons	1970
Treaty on the Prohibition of the Emplacement of Nuclear Weapons and Other Weapons of Mass Destruction on the Sea-Bed an the Ocean Floor and in the Subsoil Thereof	1972
Convention on the Prohibition of the Development, Productio and Stockpiling of Bacteriological (Biological) and Toxin Weapons and on Their Destruction	1975
Convention on the Prohibition of Military or Any Other Hostile Use of Environmental Modifications Techniques	1978
Agreement Governing the Activities of of States on the Moon and Other Celestial Bodies†	1979 (adopted)
Convention on Prohibitions or Restrictions on the Use of Certain Conventional Weapons which may be deemed to be excessively injurious or to Have Indiscriminate Effects, and its Three Protocols	1980

*For details covering dates of accession, etc. see the full report on the State of Multilateral Arms Regulations and Disarmament Agreements (second edition), United Nations, New York, 1983. The summarizing data in that report have here been updated to 31 December, 1983 on the basis of information supplied by the Department of Disarmament Affairs, United Nations (Geneva Branch).

†Data refer to 1 January 1983.

Composite Table of Signatories and Parties to Multilateral Arms Regulations and Disarmament Agreements as at 31 December 1983
(s) signed; (r) ratified (including accessions and successions)

States	Geneva Protocol		Antarctic Treaty		Partial Test Ban		Outer space		Treaty of Tlatelolco		Non-proliferation		Sea-bed		BW Convention		ENMOD		Celestial bodies		Conventional weapons	
	(s)	(r)	(s)	(r)	(s)	(r)	(s)	(r)	(s)	(r)	(s)	(r)	(s)	(r)	(s)	(r)	(s)	(r)	(s)	(r)	(s)	(r)†
Afghanistan					x	x	x				x	x	x	x	x	x					x	
Albania																						x
Algeria					x																	x
Angola																						
Antigua and Barbuda									x	x												
Argentina	x	x	x	x	x		x	x	x				x	x	x	x					x	x
Australia	x	x	x	x	x	x	x	x			x	x	x	x	x	x	x	x				x
Austria	x	x			x	x	x	x			x	x	x	x	x	x				x		x
Bahamas	x					x			x	x	x	x										
Bahrain												x										
Bangladesh											x	x				x		x				
Barbados	x	x							x	x	x	x			x	x						
Belgium	x	x	x	x	x	x	x	x			x	x		x	x	x	x	x			x	
Belize																						
Benin		x			x						x		x		x	x	x					
Bhutan						x									x	x						
Bolivia					x		x		x	x	x	x	x	x	x	x	x					
Botswana						x	x				x	x		x	x	x	x					
Brazil	x	x	x	x	x	x	x	x	x	x			x	x	x	x	x	x			x	
Bulgaria	x	x			x	x	x	x	x		x	x	x	x	x	x	x	x				x
Burma					x	x	x	x							x	x						
Burundi					x		x						x		x							
Byelorussian SSR	x				x	x	x	x			x		x	x	x	x	x	x				x
Canada	x	x			x	x	x	x			x	x	x	x	x	x	x	x			x	
Cape Verde						x						x		x	x	x		x				
Central African Republic	x					x	x				x	x	x	x	x	x		x				
Chad					x						x		x		x							

† = All states ratifying the Convention so far have given notification of their acceptance of Protocols I, II and III.
* = Non-member States maintaining permanent observer missions to the United Nations.
** = Non-member and non-observer States belonging to specialized agencies.
*** = A.P. means Additional Protocol.

continued

States	Geneva Protocol (s)	(r)	Antarctic Treaty (s)	(r)	Partial Test Ban (s)	(r)	Outer space (s)	(r)	Treaty of Tlatelolco (s)	(r)	Non-proliferation (s)	(r)	Sea-bed (s)	(r)	BW Convention (s)	(r)	ENMOD (s)	(r)	Celestial bodies (s)	(r)	Conventional weapons (s)	(r)†
Chile	x	x	x	x	x	x	x		x	x					x	x			x	x		
China	x	x	x	x					x (A.P.II)***	x					x	x					x	x
Colombia					x		x		x				x		x							
Comoros																						
Congo														x	x							
Costa Rica					x	x	x		x		x	x	x		x	x						
Cuba	x						x	x			x	x	x	x	x	x		x			x	
Cyprus	x				x	x	x	x			x	x	x	x	x	x						
Czechoslovakia	x	x		x	x	x	x	x			x	x	x	x	x	x	x	x			x	x
Democratic Kampuchea											x	x										
Democratic People's Republic of Korea*											x	x	x		x							
Democratic Yemen	x				x	x	x	x			x	x	x	x	x	x	x	x			x	
Denmark	x	x	x	x	x	x	x	x			x	x	x	x	x	x	x				x	x
Djibouti																						
Dominica			x																			
Dominican Republic	x				x	x	x	x	x	x	x	x	x	x	x	x					x	x
Ecuador	x				x	x	x	x	x	x	x	x	x	x	x	x			x	x	x	x
Egypt	x				x	x	x	x	x	x	x	x	x		x	x		x				
El Salvador					x	x	x	x	x	x	x	x	x		x						x	
Equatorial Guinea											x	x	x	x	x							
Ethiopia	x				x		x				x		x	x	x	x	x	x				
Fiji	x				x	x	x	x			x		x		x	x	x					
Finland	x	x			x	x	x	x			x	x	x	x	x	x	x	x			x	x
France	x	x	x	x			(A.P.I-II)		x (A.P.II)				x	x	x		x		x		x	x
Gabon	x				x		x				x	x	x	x	x	x						
Gambia	x				x	x	x	x			x	x	x	x	x	x						
German Democratic Republic	x	x	x	x	x	x	x	x			x	x	x	x	x	x	x	x			x	
Germany, Federal Republic of	x	x	x	x	x	x	x	x			x	x	x	x	x	x	x	x			x	x
Ghana	x	x			x	x	x	x			x	x	x	x	x	x	x	x			x	x
Greece	x	x			x	x	x				x	x	x	x	x	x	x				x	
Grenada									x	x	x	x			x	x						
Guatemala	x				x				x	x	x	x	x		x	x			x		x	
Guinea	x		x	x	x		x		x	x	x	x	x		x	x					x	x

continued

Guinea-Bissau
Guyana
Haiti
Holy See*
Honduras
Hungary
Iceland
India
Indonesia
Iran (Islamic Republic of)
Iraq
Ireland
Israel
Italy
Ivory Coast
Jamaica
Japan
Jordan
Kenya
Kuwait
Lao People's Democratic Republic
Lebanon
Lesotho
Liberia
Libyan Arab Jamahiriya
Liechtenstein**
Luxembourg
Madagascar
Malawi
Malaysia
Maldives
Mali
Malta
Mauritania

† = All states ratifying the Convention so far have given notification of their acceptance of Protocols I, II and III.
* = Non-member States maintaining permanent observer missions to the United Nations.
** = Non-member and non-observer States belonging to specialized agencies.
*** = A.P. means Additional Protocol.

States	Geneva Protocol (s)	Geneva Protocol (r)	Antarctic Treaty (s)	Antarctic Treaty (r)	Partial Test Ban (s)	Partial Test Ban (r)	Outer space (s)	Outer space (r)	Treaty of Tlatelolco (s)	Treaty of Tlatelolco (r)	Non-proliferation (s)	Non-proliferation (r)	Sea-bed (s)	Sea-bed (r)	BW Convention (s)	BW Convention (r)	ENMOD (s)	ENMOD (r)	Celestial bodies (s)	Celestial bodies (r)	Conventional weapons (s)	Conventional weapons (r)†
Mauritius	x										x	x	x		x	x						
Mexico*	x	x			x	x	x	x	x	x	x	x	x	x	x	x					x	x
Monaco*	x																					x
Mongolia	x	x			x	x	x	x			x	x	x	x	x	x	x	x			x	
Morocco	x	x			x	x	x	x			x	x	x	x	x	x	x		x		x	
Mozambique																					x	
Nauru**												x										
Nepal	x	x			x	x	x	x			x	x	x	x	x	x						
Netherlands	x	x		x	x	x	x	x	x (A.P.I)	x	x	x	x	x	x	x	x	x	x		x	
New Zealand	x	x	x	x	x	x	x				x	x	x	x	x	x	x	x			x	
Nicaragua	x				x	x	x		x	x	x	x	x	x	x	x	x	x			x	
Niger					x	x	x						x		x	x						
Nigeria	x	x		x	x	x	x				x	x			x	x	x				x	
Norway	x	x	x	x	x	x	x	x			x	x	x		x	x	x	x			x	x
Oman	x																					
Pakistan	x	x			x	x	x				x	x	x		x	x					x	
Panama	x	x		x	x	x	x		x	x	x	x	x	x	x	x	x				x	
Papua New Guinea	x		x								x	x			x	x	x	x				
Paraguay	x			x			x		x	x	x	x	x	x	x	x	x					
Peru					x	x	x		x	x	x	x	x		x	x						
Philippines	x	x			x	x	x				x	x	x	x	x	x	x		x		x	
Poland	x	x		x	x	x	x	x			x	x	x	x	x	x	x	x	x		x	x
Portugal	x	x			x	x	x				x	x	x	x	x	x					x	x
Qatar	x											x										
Republic of Korea*					x	x	x				x	x	x	x	x	x	x	x			x	
Romania	x	x	x		x	x	x	x			x	x	x	x	x	x	x	x	x		x	
Rwanda	x	x			x	x	x				x	x	x		x	x						
Saint Lucia												x						x				
Saint Vincent and the Grenadines																						
Samoa					x	x	x								x	x						
San Marino**	x	x			x	x	x		x		x		x	x	x	x	x					
Sao Tome and Principe															x	x					x	
Saudi Arabia							x				x	x	x	x	x	x		x				
Senegal	x	x			x			x						x	x	x						
Seychelles	x	x						x						x	x	x						

Sierra Leone	×	×	×	×	×	×	×			
Singapore		×	×	×	×	×	×			
Solomon Islands	×			×	×	×	×		×	
Somalia		×	×	×	×	×				
South Africa	×	×								
Spain	×	×	×	×	×	×	×	×	×	
Sri Lanka	×	×	×	×	×	×	×	×	×	
Sudan	×		×	×	×	×				
Suriname	×		×	×	×	×	×			
Swaziland				×	×	×	×			
Sweden	×	×	×	×	×	×	×		×	×
Switzerland*	×	×	×	×	×	×	×		×	×
Syrian Arab Republic	×	×	×	×	×	×	×	×		
Thailand	×	×	×	×	×	×	×			
Togo	×	×	×	×	×	×	×	×		
Tonga**	×				×					
Trinidad and Tobago	×	×	×	×	×	×	×	×		
Tunisia	×	×	×	×	×	×	×	×	×	
Turkey	×	×	×	×	×	×	×			
Tuvalu**	×			×						
Uganda	×	×	×	×	×	×	×	×	×	×
Ukrainian SSR	×	×	×	×	×	×	×	×	×	×
Union of Soviet Socialist Republics	×	×	× (A.P.II)	×	×	×	×	×	×	×
United Arab Emirates				×						
United Kingdom of Great Britain and Northern Ireland	×	×	× (A.P.I & II)	×	×	×	×	×	×	×
United Republic of Cameroon	×		×	×	×	×	×	×		
United Republic of Tanzania	×	×	×	×	×	×	×	×		
United States of America	×	×	× (A.P.I & II)	×	×	×	×	×	×	×
Upper Volta	×	×	×	×						

† = All states ratifying the Convention so far have given notification of their acceptance of Protocols I, II and III.

* = Non-member States maintaining permanent observer missions to the United Nations.

** = Non-member and non-observer States belonging to specialized agencies.

*** = A.P. means Additional Protocol.

continued

States	Geneva Protocol (s)	(r)	Antarctic Treaty (s)	(r)	Partial Test Ban (s)	(r)	Outer space (s)	(r)	Treaty of Tlatelolco (s)	(r)	Non-proliferation (s)	(r)	Sea-bed (s)	(r)	BW Convention (s)	(r)	ENMOD (s)	(r)	Celestial bodies (s)	(r)	Conventional weapons (s)	(r)†
Uruguay	x	x		x	x	x	x	x	x	x	x	x	x		x				x	x		
Vanuatu																				x		
Venezuela	x	x			x	x	x	x	x	x	x	x			x	x					x	
Viet Nam		x						x				x		x	x	x					x	
Yemen		x									x	x	x	x	x	x	x	x				
Yugoslavia	x	x		x	x	x				x	x	x	x	x	x		x					
Zaire			x	x	x	x			x	x	x	x	x	x	x	x				x	x	
Zambia			x	x		x						x		x								
Zimbabwe					x																	

† = All states ratifying the Convention so far have given notification of their acceptance of Protocols I, II and III.

* = Non-member States maintaining permanent observer missions to the United Nations.

** = Non-member and non-observer States belonging to specialized agencies.

*** = A.P. means Additional Protocol.

References and Other Sources

Where two dates of publication are indicated, the second refers to that of the edition actually referred to in the text. Page references refer to words quoted in the text.

A. References

Amnesty International (1984). *Torture in the Eighties.* Amnesty International, London.
Aron, R. and Sik, O. (1971). Revolution — Or Reform? *Encounter, Vol. XXXVI No. 3,* March 1971, London.
Barbu, Z. (1971). *Society, Culture and Personality.* Basil Blackwell, Oxford.
Bernal, J. D. (1939). *The Social Function of Science.* G. Routledge and Sons, London.
Biswas, A. K. (1982). Shared Natural Resources. *Development Forum (Sept.–Oct. 1982),* Geneva.
Blondel, J. (1972). *Comparing Political Systems.* Praeger Publishers, New York.
Brandt, W., and others (1980). *North–South: A Programme for Survival.* Pan Books, London.
Brown, H. (1978). *The Human Future Revisited.* W. W. Norton, New York.
Burke, E. (1791). *Letter to a Member of the National Assembly* (contained in Vol. 6, p. 64 of the Works of Burke, 1815–1827). Rivington, London.
Calder, Lord R. (1968). On Human Rights. *The Wellsian, Vol. 11, No. 3,* H. G. Wells Society, London.
Creasey, J. (1969). *Evolution to Democracy.* Hodder and Stoughton, London.
Daes, E. I. A. (1983). *The Individual's Duties to the Community and the Limitations on Human Rights and Freedoms Under Art. 29 of the Universal Declaration.* United Nations, New York.
Daly, H. E. (1977). *Steady-State Economics.* W. H. Freeman, San Francisco.
Dilloway, A. J. (1977). *Collapse of a Myth. A Humanist Economic and Social Perspective.* British Humanist Assoc., London.
Dilloway, A. J. (1983). *Human Rights and World Order.* H. G. Wells Society, London.
Dilloway, A. J. and others (1976). *Multinational Corporations.* Int. Humanist and Ethical Union, Utrecht.
Eysenck, H. J. (1967). *The Biological Basis of Personality.* C. C. Thomas, Springfield.
Eysenck, H. J. (1972, 1977). *Psychology is About People* (p. 37). Penguin Books, Harmondsworth.
Freud, S. (1961, 1962). *Civilization and Its Discontents.* Translated and Edited by J. Strachey, W. W. Norton, New York.
Freud, S. (1928, 1962). *The Future of An Illusion* (Rev. ed.). Hogarth Press, London.
Fromm, E. (1970, 1973). *The Crisis of Psychoanalysis* (p. 94). Penguin Books, Harmondsworth.
Fromm, E. (1942). *The Fear of Freedom.* Routledge and Kegan Paul, London.
Gabor, D. (1972). *The Mature Society.* The Professional Library, London.
Goldschmidt, W. (1959). *Understanding Human Society.* Routledge and Kegan Paul, London.
Grant, J. P. (1978). *Disparity Reduction Rates in Social Indicators.* Monograph No. 11, Overseas Development Council, Washington DC.

Greentree, T. R., and Philips, R. (1979). *The PQLI and the DRR: New Tools for Measuring Development Progress.* Overseas Development Council, Washington DC.

Halliday, J. L. (1948). *Psychosocial Medicine.* W. Heinemann Medical Books, London.

Harding, A. (1966). *A Social History of English Law.* Penguin Books, Harmondsworth.

Hermann, B. (1975). *The Optimal International Division of Labour.* International Labour Office, Geneva.

Herrera, A. O. and others (1976). *Catastrophe or New Society? A Latin American World Model.* International Development Research Centre, Ottawa.

Hobhouse, L. T. (1924, 1966). *Social Development.* G. Allen and Unwin, London.

Hollis, M. (1977). *Models of Man.* Cambridge University Press, Cambridge.

Huxley, A. (1957). *Ends and Means.* Chatto and Windus, London.

Int. Union for Conservation of Nature and Natural Resources (1980). *World Conservation Strategy.* IUCN with co-operation of UNEP and World Wildlife Fund, Gland.

Keynes, J. M. (1936). *The General Theory of Employment, Interest and Money.* Macmillan, London.

Laszlo, E. (1978). *Goals in a Global Community (2 vols.).* Pergamon Press, Oxford, New York.

Lerner, A. P. (1946). *The Economics of Control.* Macmillan Co., New York.

Leontief, W. and others (1976). *The Future of the World Economy.* United Nations, New York.

Levinson, C. (1982). New Doctrines for a Changing World. *Development Forum (Vol. X, No. 9, Dec. 1982),* Geneva.

Levinson, C. (1978). *Vodka Cola.* Gordon and Cremonesi, London

Lewis, C. (1983). Taming of the Microbe. *Development Forum (Nov.–Dec. 1983),* Geneva.

Lilley, S. (1948). *Men, Machines and History.* Cobbett Press, London.

Llewellyn-Jones, D. (1975). *People Populating.* Faber and Faber, London.

Macpherson, C. B. (1977). *The Life and Times of Liberal Democracy.* Oxford University Press, Oxford.

Maslow, A. (1971). *The Farther Reaches of Human Nature.* Viking Press, New York.

McLaughlin, M. M. and ODC Staff (1979). *The United States and World Development: Agenda 1979.* Praeger Publishers, New York.

Meadows, D. H. and others (1972). *The Limits to Growth.* Universe Books, New York.

Mesarovic, M. and Pestel, E. (1974). *Mankind at the Turning Point. The Second Report to the Club of Rome.* Dutton, New York.

Mill, J. S. (1848, 1970). *Principles of Political Economy: With Some of Their Applications to Social Philosophy.* Edited by D. Winch, Penguin Books, Harmondsworth.

Morris, M. D. (1979). *Measuring the Condition of the World's Poor: The Physical Quality of Life Index.* Pergamon Press for the ODC, Oxford.

Myers, N. (1982). The Massacre That Happened in a Twinkling. *The Guardian, Jan. 14, 1982,* London.

Oulès, F. (1966). *Economic Planning and Democracy.* Transl. by R. H. Barry. Penguin Books, Harmondsworth.

Overseas Development Council (1980). *The United States and World Development: Agenda 1980.* Praeger Publishers, New York.

Pareto, V. (1935). *The Mind and Society* (4 vols., trans. A. Bongiorno and A. Livingston). Harcourt Brace, New York.

Porter, G. R. (1847). *The Progress of the Nation in its Various Social and Economic Relations, from the Beginning of the Nineteenth Century* (New Edition). John Murray, London.

Powell, E. (1983). The Ominous Misunderstanding of Soviet Intentions. *The Guardian (Oct. 10),* London.

Prebisch, R. (1983). *The Crisis of Capitalism and the Periphery.* United Nations Conference on Trade and Development, Geneva.

Purdom, C. B. (1941). *The New Order.* J. M. Dent, London.

Reader, J. (1982). *Gems (The Global Environment Monitoring System).* United Nations Environment Programme, Nairobi.

Riesman, D. (with Glazer, N. and Denney, R.) (1950). *The Lonely Crowd.* Yale University Press.

Russell, B. (1961). *Has Man a Future?,* Penguin Books, Harmondsworth.

Schoenfeld, T. M., Galtung, J. etc. (1976), in *Multinational Corporations*. Int. Humanist and Ethical Union, Utrecht.
Sewell, J. D., and ODC Staff (1980). *The United States and World Development: Agenda 1980*. Praeger Publishers, New York.
Sivard, R. L. (1982). *World Military and Social Expenditures 1982*. © World Priorities, Leesburg, Virginia, 22075 USA.
Sivard, R. L. (1983). *World Military and Social Expenditures 1983*. © World Priorities, Washington DC, 20007 USA.
Skinner, B. F. (1953). *Science and Human Behaviour*. Macmillan, New York.
Smith, A. (1776, 1970). *An Inquiry Into the Nature and Causes of the Wealth of Nations* (Books I–III), Penguin Books, Harmondsworth.
Teubal, M. (1980). The Big Six Who Control the Daily Diet of Millions. *The Guardian, 4 Feb. 1980*, London.
Tinbergen, J. (Coordinator) (1976). *RIO: Reshaping the International Order*. Dutton, New York.
UN Centre on Transnational Corporations (1982). Recent Developments Related to Transnational Corporations, in *The CTC Reporter (No. 13, Autumn 1982)*. New York.
UN Economic Commission for Europe (1983). Recent Changes in Europe's Trade. *Economic Bulletin for Europe, Vol. 35, No. 4*, Geneva.
United Nations (1978). *World Population Trends and Prospects by Country, 1950–2000*. Summary Report of 1978 Assessment. United Nations, New York.
United Nations (1979). *The World Social Situation 1978*. United Nations, New York.
United Nations (1983). *The Implications of Establishing an International Satellite Monitoring Agency*. United Nations, New York.
United Nations (1983). *The State of World Population 1983*. UN Fund for Population Activities, New York.
Weiss, T. G. (1979). The Least Developed Countries During the 1980's. *Transnational Perspectives (Vol. 5, No. 3)*.
Wells, H. G. (1905). *A Modern Utopia*. Chapman and Hall, London.
Wells, H. G. (1928). *The Open Conspiracy*. V. Gollancz, London.
Wells, H. G. (1931). *What are We to Do With Our Lives?* W. Heinemann, London.
Wells, H. G. (1942). *Phoenix: A Summary of the Inescapable Conditions of World Reorganization*. Secker and Warburg, London.
Whyte, L. L. (1948, 1950). *The Next Development in Man*. Mentor Edition, New York.
Wibaut, F. M. (1935). *A World Production Order*. Transl. by R. W. Roame. G. Allen and Unwin, London.
World Bank (1979). *World Development Report 1979*. World Bank, Washington, DC.
World Bank (1982). *World Development Report 1982*. World Bank, Washington, DC.
World Energy Conference (1974). *WEC Survey of Energy Resources*. World Energy Conference, New York and London.
Worsthorne, P. (1983). Unasked Questions About Peace. *Sunday Telegraph (13 November, 1983)*. London.
Zipf, G. K. (1949). *Human Behaviour and the Principle of Least Effort*. Addison-Wesley, Reading, Mass.

B. Other Sources of Interest

1. Selected International Sources

Food and Agriculture Organization (1983). *World Food Report 1983*. UN FAO, Rome.
Franck, T. M., Renninger, J. P. and Tikhomirov, V. B. (1982). *Diplomats' Views on the UN System: An Attitude Survey*. Policy and Efficacy Studies No. 7. UN Inst. for Training and Research, New York.
Frei, D. and Catrina, C. (1982). *Risks of Unintentional Nuclear War*. UN Inst. for Disarmament Research, Geneva.
Ganji, M. (1975). *The Realization of Economic, Social and Cultural Rights: Problems, Policies, Progress*. United Nations, New York.

252   *Is World Order Evolving?*

Tikhomirov, V. B. (1981). *Quantitative Analysis of Voting Behaviour in the General Assembly.* Policy and Efficacy Studies No. 2. UN. Inst. for Training and Research, New York.

UN Centre on Transnational Corporations (1982). The United Nations Code of Conduct on Transnational Corporations. *The CTC Reporter (No. 12, Summer 1982)*, United Nations, New York.

UN Conf. on Trade and Development (1984). *Trade and Development Report 1984 (2 vols.)* (Doc. UNCTAD/TDR/4). UNCTAD, Geneva.

United Nations Development Programme (1983). *Development: Success Stories from the UNDP* (repr. from UN Chronicle, Sept. 1983). United Nations, New York.

United Nations Environment Programme (1979). *The Environmental Impacts of Production and Use of Energy: Nuclear Energy.* UNEP, Nairobi.

United Nations Environment Programme (1982). *The State of the Environment 1972–1982.* UNEP, Nairobi.

United Nations Environment Programme (1984). *Int. Register of Potentially Toxic Chemicals Legal File (2 vols.).* UNEP, Geneva.

United Nations (1978). *Human Rights: A Compilation of International Instruments.* United Nations, New York. (New ed. 1983).

United Nations (1977). *Long-term Trends in the Economic Development of the Regions of the World*; Annex IV, Review of Recent Global Long-term Projections. United Nations, New York.

United Nations (1978). *Human Rights International Instruments.* United Nations, New York.

United Nations (1979). *The International Dimensions of the Right to Development as a Human Right* (Doc. E/CN.4/1334). United Nations, Geneva.

United Nations (1979). *The Study of Interrelationships Between Population, Resources, Environment and Development* (Doc. E/1979/75). United Nations, New York.

United Nations (1980). *Basic Facts About the United Nations.* Dept. of Public Information, UN, New York. (New ed. 1984).

United Nations (1981). *Comprehensive Study on Nuclear Weapons.* UN Centre for Disarmament. United Nations, New York.

United Nations (1981). *International Development Strategy for the Third UN Development Decade.* UN, New York.

United Nations (1981). *Interrelationships Between Population, Resources, Environment and Development* (Doc E/1981/65). United Nations, New York.

United Nations (1981). *Study of the Relationship Between Disarmament and Development* (Doc. A/36/356). United Nations, New York.

United Nations (1981). *The Regional and National Dimensions of the Right to Development as a Human Right* (Doc. E/CN.4/1488). United Nations, Geneva.

United Nations (1982). *Human Rights and Scientific and Technological Developments.* Dept. of Public Information, UN, New York.

United Nations (1983). *Economic and Social Consequences of the Arms Race and of Military Expenditures.* United Nations, New York.

United Nations (1983). *Exchange of Information on Banned Hazardous Chemical and Unsafe Pharmaceutical Products* (Doc. A/38/90, E/1983/67). United Nations, New York.

United Nations (1983). *Human Rights International Instruments (Signatures, Ratifications, etc.)* (1 Sept. 1983). United Nations, New York.

United Nations (1983). *Sources of Information on Disarmament and Related Issues.* UN Inst. for Disarmament Research, Geneva.

United Nations (1983). *Status of Multilateral Arms Regulations and Disarmament Agreements.* Second ed., 1982. United Nations, New York.

United Nations (1983). *The Law of the Sea (Official Texts).* United Nations, New York.

United Nations (1983). *Vienna International Plan of Action on Aging.* United Nations, New York.

United Nations (1983). *World Economic Survey 1983 (and Supplement).* United Nations, New York.

United Nations (1983). *World Programme of Action Concerning Disabled Persons.* United Nations, New York.

United Nations (1984). *A Quiet Revolution. The UN Convention on the Law of the Sea.* Dept. of Public Information, UN, New York.
United Nations (1984). *Review and Appraisal of the International Development Strategy for the Third UN Development Decade* (Doc. A/39/115). United Nations, New York.
World Health Organization (1981). *Development of Indicators for Monitoring Progress towards Health for All by the Year 2000.* World Health Organization, Geneva.
World Health Organization (1981). *Global Strategy for Health for All by the Year 2000.* World Health Organization, Geneva.

2. *Other Selected Sources*

Ackoff, R. L. and Emery, F. E. *On Purposeful Systems.* Aldine-Atherton, Chicago.
Bentham. J. (1789, 1820). *Introduction to the Principles of Morals and Legislation*, London.
Boulding, K. (1968). A Data-Collecting Network for the Sociosphere. *Impact of Science on Society (Vol. XVIII, No. 2).* Paris.
Carr, L. J. (1948). *Situational Analysis.* Harper and Brothers, New York and London.
Cohen, J. (1946). *Human Nature, War and Society.* Watts and Co., London.
Duncan, R. & Weston-Smith, M. (ed.) (1977, 1978). *The Encyclopaedia of Ignorance.* Pergamon Press, Oxford.
Feibleman, J. K. (1956, 1960). *The Institutions of Society.* G. Allen and Unwin, London.
Finer, S. E. (ed.) (1979). *Five Constitutions: Contrasts and Comparisons.* Penguin Books, Harmondsworth.
Fromm, E. (1956). *The Sane Society.* Routledge and Kegan Paul, London.
Gross, B. M. (1966). *The State of the Nation: Social Systems Accounting.* Tavistock Publications, London.
Hawrylyshyn, B. (1980). *Road Maps to the Future.* Pergamon Press, Oxford.
Humana, C. (1983). *World Human Rights Guide.* Hutchinson, London.
Joyce, J. A. (1980). *The War Machine.* Quartet Books, London.
Kneese, A. V. (1977). *Economics and the Environment.* Penguin Books, Harmondsworth.
Lewis, W. A. (1949, 1969). *The Principles of Economic Planning.* Unwin University Books, London.
Lewis, Sir W. A. (1979). *The Evolution of the International Economic Order.* Princeton University Press, Guildford.
Lorenz, K. (1973, 1974). *Civilized Man's Eight Deadly Sins* (Transl. M. Latzke). Methuen, London.
Macpherson, C. B. (1966, 1975). *The Real World of Democracy.* Oxford University Press, Oxford and New York.
Mead, G. H. (1934). *Mind, Self and Society.* University of Chicago Press, Chicago.
Mill, J. (1820). *Article on Government.* Fifth edition of the Encyclopaedia Britannica, London.
Osborn, R. (1959, 1970). *Humanism and Moral Theory: A Psychological and Social Enquiry.* Pemberton Books, London.
Sampson, A. (1982, 1983). *The Changing Anatomy of Britain* (Rev. ed.). Coronet Books, London.
Shotter, J. (1975). *Images of Man in Psychological Research.* Methuen, London.
Siegel, R. L. and Weinberg, L. B. (1977). *Comparing Public Policies — United States, Soviet Union and Europe.* Dorsey Press, Homewood, Ill.
Stanworth, P. & Giddens, A. (ed.) (1974). *Elites and Power in British Society.* Cambridge University Press, Cambridge.
Von Bertalanffy, L. (1950, 1969). The Theory of Open Systems in Physics and Biology, in *Systems Thinking* (ed. F. E. Emery). Penguin Books, Harmondsworth.
Wright, D. (1971). *The Psychology of Moral Behaviour.* Penguin Books, Harmondsworth.

Index

255